The Tanner Lectures on Human Values

THE TANNER LECTURES ON HUMAN VALUES

IX

1988

Laurence H. Tribe, Roger J. Bulger, Jon Elster,
Gisela Striker, F. Van Zyl Slabbert, Joseph Brodsky
Louis Blom-Cooper

Grethe B. Peterson, *Editor*

UNIVERSITY OF UTAH PRESS — Salt Lake City
CAMBRIDGE UNIVERSITY PRESS — Cambridge, London, Melbourne, Sidney

Published in North and South America
and the Philippines
by the University of Utah Press,
Salt Lake City, Utah 84112, U.S.A.,
and in Great Britain and all other countries by
The Press Syndicate of the University of Cambridge
The Edinburgh Building, Shaftesbury Road,
Cambridge CB2 2RU, and
296 Beaconsfield Parade, Middle Park, Melbourne 3206
Australia.

The paper in this book meets the standards
for permanence and durability established by
the Committee on Production Guidelines for Book Longevity
of the Council on Library Resources.

THE TANNER LECTURES ON HUMAN VALUES

The purpose of the Tanner Lectures is to advance and reflect upon scholarly and scientific learning that relates to the entire range of human values and valuation.

To receive an appointment as a Tanner lecturer is a recognition of uncommon capabilities and outstanding scholarly or leadership achievement in the field of human values. The lecturers may be drawn from philosophy, religion, the humanities and sciences, the creative arts and learned professions, or from leadership in public or private affairs. The lectureships are international and intercultural and transcend ethnic, national, religious, or ideological distinctions.

The Tanner Lecturers were formally founded on July 1, 1978, at Clare Hall, Cambridge University. They were established by the American scholar, industrialist, and philanthropist, Obert Clark Tanner. In creating the lectureships, Professor Tanner said, "I hope these lectures will contribute to the intellectual and moral life of mankind. I see them simply as a search for a better understanding of human behavior and human values. This understanding may be pursued for its own intrinsic worth, but it may also eventually have practical consequences for the quality of personal and social life."

Permanent Tanner lectureships, with lectures given annually, are established at nine institutions: Clare Hall, Cambridge University; Harvard University; Brasenose College, Oxford University; Princeton University; Stanford University; the University of California; the University of Michigan; the University of Utah; and Yale University. Each year lectureships may be granted to not more than four additional colleges or universities for one year only. The institutions are selected by the Trustees.

The sponsoring institutions have full autonomy in the appointment of their lecturers. A major purpose of the lecture program is the publication and wide distribution of the Lectures in an annual volume.

The Tanner Lectures on Human Values is a nonprofit corporation administered at the University of Utah under the direction of a self-perpetuating, international Board of Trustees. The Trustees meet annually to enact policies that will ensure the quality of the lectureships.

The entire lecture program, including the costs of administration, is fully and generously funded in perpetuity by an endowment to the University of Utah by Professor Tanner and Mrs. Grace Adams Tanner.

Obert C. Tanner was born in Farmington, Utah, in 1904. He was educated at the University of Utah, Harvard University, and Stanford University. He has served on the faculty of Stanford University and is presently Emeritus Professor of Philosophy at the University of Utah. He is the founder and chairman of the O. C. Tanner Company, manufacturing jewelers.

GRETHE B. PETERSON
University of Utah

CONTENTS

PREFACE TO VOLUME IX

The Tanner Lectures on Human Values were established at Clare Hall, Cambridge University, in 1978. Annual lectures have been delivered at the six institutions which were named permanent sponsors of the lectureships: Clare Hall, Cambridge University; Harvard University; Brasenose College, Oxford University; Stanford University; the University of Michigan; and the University of Utah.

The University of California and Yale University were added to the institutions which are designated as permanent sponsors in 1987, and Princeton University was added in 1988.

In addition, lectures have been delivered at Utah State University, the Hebrew University of Jerusalem, Australian National University, Jawaharlal Nehru University, the University of Helsinki, the University of Warsaw, the University of Buenos Aires, and the Universidad de Complutense, Madrid. A lecture will be given at the Chinese University of Hong Kong in the fall of 1988.

The Tanner Lectures on Human Values are published in an annual volume. A general index to Volumes I through V is included in Volume V.

Volume IX of the Lectures is comprised of lectures delivered during the academic year 1986–87, except for the lectures by F. Van Zyl Slabbert and Louis Blom-Cooper, which were delivered early in the year 1987–88.

In addition to the Lectures on Human Values, Professor Tanner and the Trustees of the Tanner Lectures have funded special lectureships at selected colleges and universities which are administered and published independently of the series of lectures published in the annual volumes.

On Reading the Constitution

LAURENCE H. TRIBE

The Tanner Lectures on Human Values

Delivered at
The University of Utah

November 17 and 18, 1986

LAURENCE H. TRIBE is the Ralph S. Tyler, Jr., Professor of Constitutional Law at Harvard Law School, where he has been a faculty member since 1968. Born in China of Russian Jewish parents, Tribe came to the United States at the age of five, attended public schools in San Francisco, and entered Harvard College in 1958 at the age of sixteen. He received his A.B. from Harvard summa cum laude in mathematics in 1962 and his J.D. from Harvard Law School magna cum laude in 1966. Following graduation, he served as a law clerk for Justice Mathew O. Tobriner of the California Supreme Court and then for Justice Potter Stewart of the United States Supreme Court. In 1980 he was elected a Fellow of the American Academy of Arts and Sciences.

Tribe, the recipient of four honorary doctor of laws degrees, has written or edited fifteen books and more than eighty-five articles. His major books include *American Constitutional Law*, which received the Coif Award in 1980 for the most outstanding legal writing in the nation and is widely said to be the leading modern work on the subject; a completely revised second edition of that treatise, published in 1988; *Constitutional Choices*, a book of essays published in 1985; and *God Save This Honorable Court: How the Choice of Supreme Court Justices Shapes Our History*, also published in 1985. During the past decade Tribe has been a frequent and successful litigator before the United States Supreme Court and has testified often as an expert witness before Congress on constitutional matters.

I. CHOICES AND CONSTRAINTS*

On the door to my office I have taped a cartoon that shows two people talking at a cocktail party. One of them says to the other: "No, I don't know the preamble to the Constitution of the United States of America. But I know *of* it."

That nicely captures the situation of most of us. We know *of* the Constitution, and no one fails to have plenty of opinions *about* it, but what "it" is somehow tends to elude us. The text is very brief. It can fit into a small pocket. So what is all the fuss about? Why does Justice John Paul Stevens of the United States Supreme Court say, in a speech delivered in 1984 at the University of San Diego, that "[t]he Constitution of the United States is a mysterious document"?[1] What's the mystery about?

One way to put the question is to ask: What does it mean to *read* this Constitution? What is it that we do when we *interpret* it? Why is there so much controversy over *how* it should be interpreted — and why is so much of that controversy, these days in particular, not limited to the academy or to the profession, but so public that it makes the evening news and the front pages?[2]

* This essay is a lightly edited version of the Tanner Lectures given at the University of Utah in November 1986. A measure of informality has been retained to preserve the flavor of the original lectures. Although no significant substantive points have been added, occasional references to especially relevant subsequent developments have been made in footnotes.

I wish to thank the Trustees of the Tanner Lectures for inviting me to give these lectures, and to thank the faculty and students at the University of Utah for their hospitality in making the lectures a pleasant and enriching experience. Thanks are also due to Kenneth Chesebro, J.D., Harvard Law School, 1986, for assistance in preparing the final manuscript.

[1] Stevens, "Judicial Restraint," 22 *San Diego L. Rev.* 437, 437 (1985).

[2] This question might seem self-answering after the hearings on the nomination of Judge Robert H. Bork to serve as a Supreme Court justice, held in fall of 1987, which revealed with specificity the depth of national support for vigorous protection of civil rights and civil liberties by the federal judiciary. But these lectures were delivered in November 1986.

It's no secret, of course, that the Supreme Court's school prayer
decisions in the 1960s, its abortion decision in 1973, its reaffirmation of those controversial decisions in the mid-1980s, and its
refusal to accept the Reagan administration's quite stark anti-
affirmative-action views have all given administration spokesmen — particularly Attorney General Edwin Meese and William
Bradford Reynolds, the assistant attorney general for civil rights —
and those who sympathize with them ample incentive to criticize
the Court's interpretation of the Constitution.[3] But that is hardly
new. Disagreement with the Supreme Court's laissez-faire rulings
of the early twentieth century and the Court's invalidation of key
New Deal measures into the 1930s provided ample motive for
people to attack the Court during those years.[4] Disagreement with
the desegregation and the reapportionment decision decades later
spurred loud reactions against the jurisprudence of the Warren
Court.[5] But the *level* and *tone* of the public debate has reached,
I think, something of a new pitch — one that has not been heard
at this intensity in so sustained a way since Franklin D. Roosevelt's
assault on the "Nine Old Men" in the presidential election of
1936.

In any case, it is my intention to take the dispute seriously —
not to regard it simply as a mask for disagreement with the Court's
results on particular issues, or as a mere excuse to oppose one or

---

[3] *Abington School Dist. v. Schempp*, 374 U.S. 203 (1963), and *Engel v. Vitale*,
370 U.S. 421 (1962) (school prayer); *Roe v. Wade*, 410 U.S. 113 (1973) (abortion). On the Court's reaffirmation, see *Wallace v. Jaffree*, 472 U.S. 38 (1985)
(school prayer); *Thornburgh v. American College of Obstetricians and Gynecologists*, 106 S. Ct. 2169 (1986), and *Akron v. Akron Center for Reproductive Health,
Inc.*, 462 U.S. 416 (1983) (abortion). On the Court's refusal to accept administration views, see *Johnson v. Transportation Agency*, 107 S. Ct. 1442 (1987); *United
States v. Paradise*, 107 S. Ct. 1053 (1987).

[4] See Laurence Tribe, *American Constitutional Law*, 2d ed. (Mineola, N.Y.:
Foundation Press, 1988), § 8–6, p. 580. Although that treatise was still being completed when these lectures were delivered, I refer to it from time to time in these
footnotes for those readers who might wish to examine a fuller and more current
treatment of doctrinal matters briefly addressed in text.

[5] See ibid., § 13–7, p. 1074, and § 13–8, p. 1076 (reapportionment); § 16–18,
p. 1488 (desegregation).

another judicial nominee, although to some extent it *is* simply a matter of whose ox has most recently been gored. Recognizing that such substantive disagreement plays a large role in bringing critics out into the open, in other words, does not justify inattention to the content of that disagreement. So I proceed from the premise that there is a real dispute over ways of interpreting the Constitution, and I want to try to understand what the structure of that dispute is.

If there is genuine controversy over how the Constitution should be read, certainly it cannot be because the disputants have access to different bodies of information. After all, they all have exactly the same text in front of them, and that text has exactly one history, however complex, however multifaceted. Is it that different people believe different things about how that history *bears* on the enterprise of constitutional interpretation?

Thomas Grey of Stanford, in a wonderful essay entitled "The Constitution as Scripture," builds on some earlier work by Sanford Levinson of Texas, Robert Burt of Yale, and the late Robert Cover of Yale.[6] Grey asks provocatively whether some individuals regard the history of the Constitution, both prior to its adoption and immediately thereafter, and even the history subsequent to that, as somehow a *part* of the Constitution — in much the same way that some theologians consider tradition, sacrament, and authoritative pronouncements to be part of the Bible. And he asks whether perhaps others regard the history, and certainly the post-adoption tradition and the long line of precedent, as standing entirely apart from the Constitution, shedding light on what it means, but not becoming *part* of that meaning — in much the way other theologians consider the words of the Bible to be the sole authoritative source of revelation, equally accessible to all

---

[6] Grey, "The Constitution as Scripture," 37 *Stan. L. Rev.* 1 (1984); Levinson, " 'The Constitution' in American Civil Religion," 1979 *Sup. Ct. Rev.* 123; Burt, "Constitutional Law and the Teaching of the Parables," 93 *Yale L.J.* 455 (1984); Cover, "Foreword — The Supreme Court, 1982 Term: 'Nomos' and Narrative," 97 *Harv. L. Rev.* 4 (1983).

who read it, in no need of the intervention of specialized interpreters and thus not to be mediated by any priestly class.

Perhaps the disputants agree, or at least many of them do, on what *counts* as "The Constitution" but simply approach the same body of textual and historical materials with different visions, different premises, different convictions. But that assumption raises obvious questions: How are those visions and premises and convictions relevant to how this brief text ought to be read? Is reading the text just a *pre*text for expressing the reader's vision in the august, almost holy terms of constitutional law? Is the Constitution simply a mirror in which one sees what one wants to see?

The character of contemporary debate might appear to suggest as much. Liberals characteristically accuse conservatives of reading into the Constitution their desires to preserve wealth and privilege and the prevailing distribution of both. Conservatives characteristically accuse liberals of reading into the Constitution their desires to redistribute wealth, to equalize the circumstances of the races and the sexes, to exclude religion from the public realm, and to protect personal privacy. A once largely scholarly debate conducted almost exclusively in the pages of the law journals and the journals of cognate disciplines, and occasionally in the pages of the *United States Reports*, where Supreme Court opinions appear, now erupts regularly into a flurry of charges and countercharges between persons no less august than the attorney general of the United States and a growing list of Supreme Court justices speaking outside their accustomed role as authors of formal opinions. How are we to understand such charges and countercharges?

It might help to begin at the beginning — and I really mean at the beginning. One astute observer of language and law, James White of the University of Michigan English Department and the Michigan Law School, has noticed an important difference

between the Declaration of Independence and the Constitution.[7]
The Declaration, he points out, is a proclamation by thirteen
sovereign states at a moment of crisis. It is a hopeful cry. It is an
attempt to justify revolution. It is addressed to the king of
England and even more significantly to the conscience of Europe.
It is a call for assistance and support. One can read it and understand who is speaking and who is being spoken to.

The Constitution makes a stark contrast. It is neither a justification nor a plea. It is a proclamation issued in the name of
"We the People of the United States." It has a familiar preamble
declaring its purpose: "to form a more perfect Union, establish
Justice, insure domestic Tranquility, provide for the common
defence, promote the general Welfare, and secure the Blessings
of Liberty to ourselves and our posterity." It then proceeds to
"ordain and establish this Constitution for the United States of
America" by setting forth a blueprint for the distribution of
powers and by declaring various limits on those powers.

If you think about it, that seems a supremely confident and
courageous act — to create a nation through words: words that
address no foreign prince or distant power but the very entity
called into being by the words themselves, words that address
the government that they purport to constitute, words that speak
to succeeding generations of citizens who will give life to that
government in the years to come.

The idea that words can somehow infuse a government with
structure and impose limits on that structure — that language can
directly power the ship of state and chart its course — has played
an important role in what Americans, particularly in our early
years but to some extent (although less consciously) even today,
have tended to think about the Constitution. As James Russell
Lowell wrote in 1888, "[a]fter our Constitution got fairly into

---

[7] James White, *When Words Lose Their Meaning: Constitutions and Recon-
stitutions of Language, Character, and Community* (Chicago: University of Chicago
Press, 1984), 231–47.

working order it really seemed as if we had invented *a machine
that would go of itself.*" [8]

Justice Oliver Wendell Holmes drew on a similar image, but
had no similar illusions, when he chose his words in 1920 in the
case of *Missouri v. Holland.*[9] He wrote:

> when we are dealing with words that also are a constituent act,
> like the Constitution of the United States, we must realize that
> they have called into life a being the development of which
> could not have been foreseen completely by the most gifted of
> its begetters. It was enough for them to . . . hope that they
> had created an *organism*; it has taken a century and has cost
> their successors much sweat and blood to prove that they
> created a *nation.*

"The case before us," Holmes went on, "must be considered in the
light of our whole experience and not merely in that of what was
said a hundred years ago. . . . We must consider what the country
has become in deciding" what the Constitution means.[10] Holmes
had no doubt that the very *meaning* of the thing we call "the Constitution" — even though its words, as marks on parchment carefully preserved at the National Archives, remain unaltered — was
a reality partly reconstructed (some might say "deconstructed")
by each generation of readers. And he had no doubt that that was
as the framers of the Constitution themselves originally intended.
They were, after all *framing* the Constitution, not painting its
details. (Why else call them the "framers"?)

How different an image that is from the originalist image suggested by Garry Wills in his book *Inventing America.*[11] Wills
writes that to recapture the true meaning of a text, we must forget

---

[8] Quoted in Michael Kammen, *A Machine That Would Go of Itself: The Constitution in American Culture* (New York: Knopf, 1986), 125 (emphasis added).

[9] 252 U.S. 416 (1920).

[10] Ibid., 433–34 (emphasis added).

[11] Garry Wills, *Inventing America: Jefferson's Declaration of Independence*
(New York: Doubleday, 1978), xxiv–xxvi.

what we learned, or what occurred in the interval between our time and the text's. There is every reason to see a paradox in that vision, because many of those who wrote the text of the original Constitution or voted to approve it, or wrote or voted to approve some of its amendments, supposed that the meaning, at least of the more general terms being deployed, was inherently variable. They supposed that the examples likely to occur to them at the time of the creation would not be forever fixed into the meaning of the text itself.

Dean Paul Brest of Stanford University, in an article called "The Misconceived Quest for the Original Understanding," suggests that, once we take into account the elaborate and thick evolution of constitutional doctrine and precedent, we cannot avoid seeing the original document and its history recede as a smaller and smaller object into a distant past.[12] He says it's "rather like having a remote ancestor who came over on the *Mayflower.*" [13] Of course, Brest is offering only a description of the way things are. Even if the description is accurate, some might say it's not a very good *pre*scription of the way things *ought* to be. Perhaps the Court, and commentators, should return more often to the *Mayflower* and pay somewhat less attention to all the accumulated barnacles. But as with the sailing ship, this *Mayflower* is venerated less because of the vessel it was than because of the voyage it began. Return to the source, and we find an invitation not to linger too obsessively in the past.

Consider, for example, the framers who thought that the very common practice of disqualifying the clergy from public office was consistent with the Constitution. They included at the time Thomas Jefferson, who thought that the clergy ought to be excluded from legislatures. I suspect those framers would have been surprised by any suggestion that clergy disqualification there-

[12] Brest, "The Misconceived Quest for the Original Understanding," 60 *B.U. L. Rev.* 204 (1980).

[13] Ibid., 234.

fore could *never* be declared unconstitutional. In fact, some of
the framers, including Jefferson, later concluded that clergy could
not validly be excluded. And when the Supreme Court finally
held in a case from Tennessee in the late 1970s that disqualifying
clergymen from public office is indeed unconstitutional, Justice
William J. Brennan, Jr., was entirely correct to observe in his concurring opinion that "[t]he fact that responsible statesmen of the
day, including some of the . . . Constitution's Framers, were
attracted by the concept of clergy disqualification . . . does not provide historical support for concluding that those provisions are
harmonious with the Establishment Clause." [14]

Or consider those who voted to propose the Fourteenth
Amendment to the states, or voted to ratify it. There is very little
doubt that most of them assumed that segregated public schools
were, at the time, entirely consistent with the Fourteenth Amendment. And yet I doubt that many of them would have said, if
pressed, that the Fourteenth Amendment could *never* be invoked,
as events unfolded, to reach a different conclusion about segregated public schooling. And I have no doubt that the Supreme
Court was entirely correct when in 1954 it finally held that it
could not turn the clock back to 1868, that it had to consider what
public education had *become* — to examine its status "in light of
its full development and its present place in American life" — to
decide whether segregation could still be deemed constitutional.[15]
In fact, it is not that the *meaning* of the Fourteenth Amendment
had changed; the concept was the same: subjugating an entire
race with the force of law was understood to be unconstitutional.
It took us longer than it should have to figure out that segregating
people in the public schools *amounted* to subjugating an entire
race by force of law. But the basic principle remained con-

---

[14] *McDaniel v. Paty*, 435 U.S. 618, 637 (1978). See Tribe, *American Constitutional Law*, § 14–8.

[15] *Brown v. Board of Education*, 347 U.S. 483, 492–93 (1954).

stant.[16] My conclusion is that many of the original framers and those responsible for enacting subsequent amendments, although perhaps not all, would have been aghast at the prescription of amnesia as part of the proper method of applying their words to a changing reality.

Indeed, not even the most "conservative" justices today believe that the type of amnesia which Wills described — and which Attorney General Meese has occasionally prescribed — as medication for the Constitution's supposed ills is really possible or desirable. Consider the following statement made by a Supreme Court justice in 1976: "The framers of the Constitution wisely spoke in general language and left to succeeding generations the task of applying that language to the unceasingly changing environment in which they would live. . . . Where the framers . . . used general language, they . . . [gave] latitude to those who would later interpret the instrument to make that language applicable to cases that the framers might not have forseen." [17]   The author was not Justice William J. Brennan or Justice Thurgood Marshall but then-Justice William H. Rehnquist. Or consider the statement by Justice Byron R. White, joined by Justice Rehnquist in a 1986 dissenting opinion: "As [our] prior cases clearly show, . . . this Court does not subscribe to the simplistic view that constitutional interpretation can possibly be limited to the 'plain meaning' of the Constitution's text or to the subjective intention of the Framers. The Constitution," says Justice White, "is not a deed setting forth the precise metes and bounds of its subject matter; rather, it is a document announcing fundamental principles in value-laden terms that leave ample scope for the

---

[16] Ronald Dworkin, *Law's Empire* (Cambridge, Mass.: Harvard University Press, 1986), 387–89. See also Tribe, *American Constitutional Law*, § 16–15, pp. 1477–78; § 16–21, p. 1514.

[17] Rehnquist, "The Notion of a Living Constitution," 54 *Tex. L. Rev.* 693, 694 (1976).

exercise of normative judgment by those charged with interpreting and applying it." [18]

So the "conservatives" on the Court, no less than the "liberals," talk as though reading the Constitution required something much more than passively discovering a fixed meaning planted there generations ago. Those who wrote the document, and those who voted to ratify it, were undoubtedly projecting their wishes into an indefinite future. If writing is wish-*projection*, is reading merely an exercise in wish-*fulfillment* — not fulfillment of the wishes of the *authors*, who couldn't begin to have foreseen the way things would unfold, but fulfillment of the wishes of *readers*, who perhaps use the language of the Constitution simply as a mirror to dress up their own political or moral preferences in the hallowed language of our most fundamental document? Justice Joseph Story feared that that might happen when he wrote in 1845: "How easily men satisfy themselves that the Constitution is exactly what they wish it to be." [19]

To the extent that is so, it is indefensible. The authority of the Constitution, its claim to obedience, and the force that we permit it to exercise in our law and over our lives would lose all legitimacy if it really were only a mirror for the readers' ideas and ideals. We *have* to reject as completely unsatisfactory the idea of an empty, or an infinitely malleable, Constitution. We must find principles of interpretation that can anchor the Constitution in some more secure, determinate, and external reality. But that is no small task.

One basic problem is that the text itself leaves so much room for the imagination. Simply consider the preamble, which speaks of furthering such concepts as "Justice" and the "Blessings of Liberty." It is not hard, in terms of concepts that fluid and that plastic, to make a linguistically plausible argument in support

[18] *Thornburgh v. American College of Obstetricians*, 106 S. Ct. 2169, 2193 (1986) (White, J., dissenting).

[19] Kammen, *A Machine That Would Go of Itself*, xxiii.

of more than a few surely incorrect conclusions. Perhaps a rule could be imposed that it is improper to refer to the preamble in constitutional argument on the theory that it is only an introduction, a preface, and not part of the Constitution *as enacted*. But even if one were to invent such a rule, which has no apparent grounding in the Constitution itself, it is hardly news that the remainder of the document is filled with lively language about "liberty," "due process of law," the "privileges or immunities" of citizens, and the guarantee of a "Republican Form of Government"—words that, although not *infinitely* malleable, are capable of supporting meanings at opposite ends of virtually any legal, political, or ideological spectrum.

It is therefore not surprising that readers on both the right and left of the American political center have invoked the Constitution as authority for strikingly divergent conclusions about the legitimacy of existing institutions and practices, and that neither wing has found it difficult to cite chapter and verse in support of its "reading" of our fundamental law. As is true of other areas of law, the materials of constitutional law require construction, leave room for argument over meaning, and tempt the reader to import his or her vision of the just society into the meaning of the materials being considered.

In a recent book, *Constitutional Choices*, I argued that as a result of this fluidity, judges *have* to acknowledge, as they read the Constitution, that they cannot avoid making at least *some* basic choices in giving it content.[20] For Judge Richard Posner, who reviewed my book, that was heresy. In his view, the moment I openly avow the need for choice, it follows that I argue "in effect . . . that the Constitution is exactly what we want it to be."[21] And

---

[20] Laurence Tribe, *Constitutional Choices* (Cambridge, Mass.: Harvard University Press, 1985).

[21] Posner, "Book Review," 84 *Mich. L. Rev.* 551, 551 (1986). But see Posner, "What Am I? A Potted Plant?" *New Republic*, Sept. 28, 1987, p. 23 (debunking "strict constructionist" pretensions and noting that "[t]here has never been a time," and demonstrating that, for reasons of pragmatics and policy, "nor could [there be

his particular complaint is that he suspects that I want it to be "the charter of a radically egalitarian society." [22]

What, then, is Judge Posner to make of the fact that the sort of Constitution I would want, the sort that I would probably set out to write if I had the responsibility, differs in significant respects from the Constitution that I feel bound to acknowledge is the one we have — a Constitution which I have no doubt was written in significant part to protect the propertied minority from those with less wealth? What other meaning can one possibly give to the contract and property clauses of the Constitution? And what are we to make of the fact that Judge Posner seems to read in the Constitution as it exists a sweeping ban on race-specific affirmative action, even though the text says absolutely nothing and, so far as I can determine, the history does not support, requiring government to be color-blind when it seeks to eradicate historic discrimination? [23] Are we to suppose that Judge Posner's Constitution is what *he* wants it to be?

If I were writing a Constitution for the United States — as I helped the Marshall Islands write one several years ago — I would probably favor a constitutional provision guaranteeing decent housing and employment for every person. I might even favor a constitutional provision setting a ceiling on the intergenerational transmission of wealth. But, having read and reread the document as it exists, and having thought hard about it, I have found it quite impossible to read *our* Constitution as including either of those principles. If someone made an argument to the contrary I would listen respectfully; but the fact that I *wanted* to believe it would not greatly incline me to take it more seriously. On the contrary, the fact that I wanted to believe — my sense

a time,] . . . when the courts of the United States, state or federal" could merely "find and apply" the law).

[22] Posner, "Book Review," 551.

[23] See Posner, "The DeFunis Case and the Preferential Treatment of Minorities," 1974 *Sup. Ct. Rev.* 1, 25, and Tribe, *American Constitutional Law*, § 16–22, p. 1526.

that, in the ideal society, a constitution would do well to include such provisions — might well lead me to discount the argument and any appeal it might have for me by my fear that I was in fact satisfying myself, as Justice Story would have it, that "the Constitution is exactly what [I] would wish it to be."

In this sense, although I agree with much of what Ronald Dworkin has written in his powerful new book, *Law's Empire*, I am troubled by the breadth of his notion of interpretation. In his view, to "interpret" a cultural or social practice, or a legal text, is to make of it the best thing of its kind that one believes it is capable of being. As Dworkin would have it, for example, the interpreter of a play or a poem seeks to understand it so that it becomes the best play or the best poem that it can be. And so he urges that the interpreter of a constitutional concept like "due process of law" or "equal protection of the laws" should seek to understand that concept in accord with the interpreter's larger vision of what a good constitution should be like. This approach is certainly not excluded in any a priori way by the meaning of the concept of "interpretation"; work in interpretive theory, or hermeneutics, suggests that the concept is indeed broad enough to take in what writers like Dworkin have in mind.

Yet I believe that the enterprise we are or should be about when we advance an argument in the Constitution's name must be more bounded and less grandiose than all that. The moment you adopt a perspective as open as Dworkin's, the line between what, perhaps to your dismay, you think the Constitution *says* and what you wish it *would* say, becomes so tenuous that it is extraordinarily difficult, try as you might, to maintain that line at at all. The question becomes how one can maintain the line — given the ambiguity of the Constitution's text, the plasticity of its terms, the indeterminacy of its history, and the possibility of making noises in the Constitution's language that *sound* like an argument for just about anything. What does it mean to suggest that the Constitution imposes constraints on choice — serious constraints?

How can one maintain, in other words, a stance in which reading the Constitution differs from writing one?

One thing that is plain is that there would *be* no real difference between those two enterprises if what we meant by "the Constitution" included not only the text and the history and tradition of its interpretation but also something as vague and ineffable as the essence of the American spirit — what Thomas Grey has described as the "grand and cloudy Constitution that stands in our minds for the ideal America, earth's last best hope, the city on the hill." [24] Well, *that* Constitution, which seems to me to be the one that some commentators like Michael Perry of Northwestern evoke even when they purport to be discussing something more modest, may be the stuff of bicentennial celebrations, but it is hard for me to think of it as binding law — law that unelected judges should be entrusted to expound in an enforceable way. [25] I am evidently regarded by some as an admirer of that gauzy sort of Constitution. Indeed, I figure as one of the chief villains in such derisive works as Henry Monaghan's essay, "Our Perfect Constitution." [26] Monaghan there accuses me of always seeing a silver lining even in the gray and sometimes bleak language of the document. But I want to distance myself from anything quite as mystical as all that. "Mysterious," as Justice Stevens would have it, the Constitution may be. Mysterious, but not mystical — and not even lost in the mists of the ideal.

Still, there is the haunting fact that linguistic possibility cannot be denied: the words of the Constitution are broad enough to make the loftiest claims possible. Now enter Edwin Meese and others of the "originalist" or "intentionalist" school. They say: "We have a solution. Our solution is to domesticate the words of

[24] Grey, "The Constitution as Scripture," 19.

[25] See, e.g., Michael Perry, *The Constitution, the Courts, and Human Rights: An Inquiry into the Legitimacy of Constitutional Policymaking by the Judiciary* (New Haven, Conn.: Yale University Press, 1982).

[26] Monaghan, "Our Perfect Constitution," 56 *N.Y.U. L. Rev.* 353 (1981).

the Constitution with the addition of history. History will do the trick." But notice what they do with history. *Brown v. Board of Education*, Mr. Meese says, is a wonderful example of a correct decision.[27] Notice the more than slight embarrassment: the history doesn't particularly support it; the history shows that those who wrote and ratified the Fourteenth Amendment thought, as I indicated earlier, that segregated public education was perfectly fine. So how does history solve the problem if one has a convenient bit of amnesia when history doesn't point to results that one feels in retrospect are surely right?[28] The history would also suggest that it is permissible to disqualify the clergy, to say that priests and ministers cannot serve in state legislatures or hold public office. That history, too, we would have to forget.

The fact is that history, including the history of what people expected or wished for or intended or feared — especially when it is a history of *collective* beliefs, beliefs of hundreds of members of Congress who proposed an amendment and hundreds of state legislators who voted to ratify it — is fundamentally indeterminate and can be described at a great many levels of generality and abstraction. It seems to me that, however helpful it is — and although it is indefensible to ignore it — history alone cannot serve to domesticate, discipline, and bind down text. History alone cannot eliminate in an airtight and demonstrable way the possibility of constructing out of the Constitution's phrases an argument of sorts for nearly any desired conclusion.

I say an argument "of sorts." But it would not necessarily be an argument that would deserve to be taken seriously, much less an argument that could fairly persuade. That really is the point. It may not be possible to "prove," in the way you prove a mathe-

[27] 347 U.S. 483 (1954).

[28] Some have proposed ignoring as a mere assumption, or as a clearly subordinate intent, the ratifiers' expectation that racial segregation in public schools would not be outlawed by the Fourteenth Amendment. See, e.g., Bork, "Neutral Principles and Some First Amendment Problems," 47 *Ind. L.J.* 1, 14–15 (1971).

matical conjecture to be true or false, that a particular fanciful, ingenious argument about the Constitution simply doesn't count as a plausible interpretation. But from the impossibility of that sort of proof, all that follows is that law, like literature, is not mathematics — that judicial deliberation, like all legal discussion, cannot be reduced to scientific processes of deduction and induction. And that should not be terribly surprising, although some people apparently continue to be surprised by it.

The impossibility of that kind of airtight "proof" does not, however, translate — as some seem to believe it does — into a claim of such total indeterminacy that *all* interpretations of the Constitution are equally acceptable and that the only test of which interpretation you favor should be whether it advances or retards your vision of the good society. I think it is possible to do much better than that, although not nearly as well as some might wish.

Part of the answer — the part that lies beyond the scope of these two lectures — is in no sense peculiar to *constitutional* law but relates, rather, to the deep and abiding problem of how to imagine, conceptualize, and understand the process and the practice of giving reasons — of engaging in rational persuasion — without leaning on notions of timeless, universal, and unquestionable truth. A great many people have lost faith in the idea of the timeless, the universal, and the unquestionable. And yet somehow, in their ordinary lives, they can still distinguish what sounds like a good argument from what sounds like a spurious argument. And it does not require placing judges or other interpreters of the Constitution on a phony, quasi-mathematical pedestal to conclude that, for reasons of a practical kind, it makes sense to entrust to people removed from the political fray the process of reason-giving, even in an environment where we lack the metric — the external measure — to prove conclusively that reason X is no good, that reason Y is decisive. A number of philosophers, most notably Hilary Putnam, have made extremely useful contributions to the enterprise of elaborating what reason-giving consists of in a world unbolstered by ultimate truth.[29] But the processes of constitutional interpretation and adjudication obviously cannot be called off while that enterprise is being pursued, especially if you believe, as I do, that that enterprise will go on forever.

The part of the answer that *is* peculiar to constitutional interpretation depends not on any general thesis about knowledge or interpretation but rather on features of the Constitution that we actually have. And in beginning to sort out good and bad ways of arguing about what *this* Constitution means, I think we can make considerable headway by inquiring what it is about some modes of discourse, some modes of conversation that are put forth as "constitutional argument," that makes them suspect from the start. What is it about some purported modes of constitutional analysis that makes them implausible candidates for ways of reading the Constitution we actually have?

In effect, I want to offer some *negative* observations about ways *not* to read the Constitution, before turning in the second of these lectures to the more affirmative project of *reading* the Constitution, against the backdrop of several actual cases and two hypothetical cases I will posit. Two ways *not* to read the Constitution are readily apparent. I call them reading by *dis*-integration and reading by *hyper*-integration.

When I say reading by "*dis*-integration," I mean approaching the Constitution in ways that ignore the salient fact that its parts are linked into a whole — that it is a *constitution*, and not merely an unconnected bunch of separate clauses and provisions with separate histories, that must be interpreted.

---

[29] See Hilary Putnam, *Reason, Truth and History* (Cambridge: Cambridge University Press, 1981); Michelman, "Justification (and Justifiability) of Law in a Contradictory World," in *NOMOS: Justification*, vol. 28, ed. J. R. Pennock and J. Chapman (New York: New York University Press, 1986). Cf. the discussion of nihilism in Friedrich Nietzsche, *The Will to Power*, trans. A. Ludovic (New York: Russell and Russell, 1964).

When I say reading by "*hyper*-integration," I mean approaching the Constitution in ways that ignore the no less important fact that the whole contains distinct parts — parts that were, in some instances, added at widely separated points in American history; parts that were favored and opposed by greatly disparate groups; parts that reflect quite distinct, and often radically incompatible, premises. In the beginning the Constitution as proposed by Congress in 1787 was ratified by the requisite number of states in 1787 and 1788. Twenty-six amendments were added, ten of them in 1791, the remainder from 1795 to 1971 — and so became "valid," under Article V, "to all intents and purposes, as part of this Constitution." [30] The Constitution of the United States is thus simultaneously a single entity or structure *and* a collection of enactments by the people; the whole is not a unitary, seamless proclamation. These observations may seem too obvious to be worth making. But they serve to disqualify much of what passes as constitutional argument and interpretation. Those who try to see in this complicated collage of compromise over time one single vision, and who then proceed to argue from that vision, have lost sight of the constraints imposed by our experience under a written constitution. They are not reading the Constitution we *have*, but a hyper-integrated constitution for which they yearn.

Consider more closely, then, the first fallacy — that of disintegration. Let me begin with a straightforward example, one which was a favorite of Chief Justice Warren E. Burger. The Fifth Amendment says that "no person . . . shall be deprived of life, liberty, or property, without due process of law." Chief Justice Burger used to argue, as have others, that the authors of that language obviously must have contemplated that, *with* "due process of law," a person *may* be deprived of life. Therefore, the argu-

---

[30] How to deal with the problematic nature of the Fourteenth Amendment's ratification, viewed strictly in terms of Article V, is a problem now being addressed by Bruce Ackerman, whose important work on informal amendments is still in progress. For an early phase of that work, see Ackerman, "The Storrs Lectures: Discovering the Constitution," 93 *Yale L.J.* 1013 (1984).

ment goes, capital punishment is constitutional. It's very simple; why should the Court struggle over it?

The conclusion may or may not be right; I find the question whether the death penalty is constitutional to be among the most perplexing. But the proposed method of resolving that question is profoundly disintegrated and is not really a way of interpreting *this* Constitution, because the Fifth Amendment is only part of the document. There is also the Eighth Amendment, ratified as a separate part of the Constitution. It says that "cruel and unusual punishments" shall not be imposed. Is the death penalty, then, cruel and unusual? The answer must be: it depends. Quite clearly, it was not considered cruel and unusual in 1791, when both the Fifth Amendment and the Eighth Amendment were ratified. But it might be so today.[31] That another constitutional clause evidently contemplates that death might be inflicted by government without offense to *that* part of the Constitution doesn't answer the question. Indeed, if the Fifth Amendment *did* answer it, we would be left with another dilemma, since it also seems to sanction hacking off people's limbs — by its command that no person shall be "twice put in jeopardy of life or limb." Yet no one would seriously argue today that bodily mutilation, employed on occasion as a punishment during colonial times, could withstand scrutiny under the Eighth Amendment. Again, it seems to be that what the Fifth Amendment suggests as an answer becomes only a question once the Eighth Amendment is consulted.

Consider another example. It has been urged by some, including Mark Tushnet of Georgetown University, that we ought to read the Constitution as requiring socialism — as obliterating the institution of private property. How else, he asks, can we make sense of the ideal of equality which underlies the constitutional

[31] For one argument that the death penalty today is cruel and unusual, see Brennan, "Constitutional Adjudication and the Death Penalty: A View from the Court," 100 *Harv. L. Rev.* 313, 323–31 (1986). Compare the evolution in the social meaning attributed to segregating schooling culminating in *Brown v. Board of Education*, 347 U.S. 483, 492–93 (1954), discussed in text accompanying notes 15 and 16, above.

mandate of the equal protection of the laws?[32] If all the Constitution contained was an equal protection clause, I suppose something might be said for that view. But the view becomes untenable if we also remember that, in various of its parts, the Constitution expressly affirms, sanctifies, and protects the institution of private property. It says that neither the state nor the federal government may deprive anyone of property without "due process of law," and that "private property [shall not] be taken for public use without just compensation."[33] It is a disintegrated "reading" of the Constitution to lift one provision out, hold it up to the light, see how far you can run with it, and forget that it is immersed in a larger whole.

Or consider this slightly more subtle illustration. Raoul Berger has argued that the original intent of the framers is "as good as written into the text" of the Constitution.[34] That viewpoint has become something of a manifesto, as is widely known, for the current attorney general, who speaks often of a "jurisprudence of original intent." But look at how Raoul Berger applies the theory. He looks at the Fourteenth Amendment, a text proposed to the states by Congress and voted on by thirty-seven state legislatures.[35] He purports to know that the original purpose of the Fourteenth Amendment was far less noble than some of us have come to believe; the primary intended beneficiaries of the Fourteenth Amendment, he tries to show, were racist white Republicans.[36]

[32] See Tushnet, "Book Review," 78 *Mich. L. Rev.* 694, 696–702 (1980).

[33] Amends. 5 and 14, § 1 (due process), amend. 5 (private property). Many state constitutions about the time of the revolution, perhaps reflecting a view that all property ultimately belongs to the state as custodian for the people as a whole, included no such clause. Its inclusion in the *federal* constitution marked a significant rejection of the model of "state as ultimate owner." See Tribe, *American Constitutional Law*, § 9–7, pp. 607–08.

[34] Raoul Berger, *Government by Judiciary: The Transformation of the Fourteenth Amendment* (Cambridge, Mass.: Harvard University Press, 1977), 7.

[35] See *The Constitution of the United States of America: Analysis and Interpretation*, S. Doc. 92–82, 92d Cong., 2d sess. (1972), p. 31, n. 6.

[36] Berger, *Government by Judiciary*, 10–19.

And therefore, he says, giving the Fourteenth Amendment the meaning that the modern Court has given it is ahistorical and illegitimate. Suppose that Berger's history were correct — that one really could make that confident an assertion about something as fleeting and elusive as collective intent. In fact, suppose that the *real* purpose of those who wrote the Fourteenth Amendment had been to *deny* equality to the freed slaves to whatever degree would prove politically possible. That is, suppose the Fourteenth Amendment had been a palliative designed to preserve peace but that the reason for not writing so racist a credo into the Constitution's *text* was a sense that some of the amendment's support might not withstand such candor.

Even if you assume that, and even if you *believe* in original intent, it still does not follow that it would be legitimate to read the Fourteenth Amendment to effect that purpose. Why not? Because the Fourteenth Amendment became "part of th[e] Constitution" in accord with Article V — a specific provision of the Constitution which describes the way amendments become law. They become law when they are ratified through a specified process by a certain number of states. There is nothing in Article V about ratifying the secret, hidden, and unenacted intentions, specific wishes, or concrete expectations of a group of people who may have been involved in the process of enacting a constitutional guarantee.

It does violence to the text and the history of another part of the Constitution — the part that specifies how it is that the Constitution becomes law — to look at original intent with respect to some provision in isolation, even assuming that "original intent" could be captured in the laboratory, bottled, and carefully inspected under a microscope. When the claims of specific intent surrounding any particular constitutional provision are invoked to give that provision a reading very different from what its text manifestly suggests, a disintegrated approach to the Constitution is at work—and it is an approach we should feel confident in rejecting.

Consider this final example. From time to time, the Supreme Court has invoked the Tenth Amendment as a basis for saying that some powers that are delegated to the Congress by the Constitution nonetheless violate the reserved rights of the states. Justice Brennan and a number of others on the Court have replied that this is a linguistic impossibility, because the Tenth Amendment says that all "powers *not* delegated to the United States by the Constitution, nor prohibited by it to the States, are reserved to the States respectively, or to the people." [37] It appears to follow that, if a power *is* "delegated to the United States" — delegated to Congress by Article I in the field of interstate commerce, for example — then the power in question *can't* be reserved to the states. Thus, the states have *no* reserved rights, no matter how big the federal government becomes, no matter how sweeping its powers come to be.

If the Tenth Amendment stood alone, the argument — although not logically compelled — would have considerable force. But think about the Tenth Amendment embedded in a Constitution which includes other provisions as well. What is it the framers assumed when they wrote the Tenth Amendment the way they did, expressly reserving to the states only those powers with respect to which the national legislature was *not* delegated authority by the Constitution? One of the things they assumed was a national legislature structured so as to represent, directly, the institutional interests of the states — since, at the time the Tenth Amendment was added to the Constitution, the United States Senate was composed of two senators from each state "chosen by the Legislature thereof." [38] It was not until the Seventeenth Amendment was ratified in 1913 that senators were "elected by the people" directly.

[37] See *National League of Cities v. Usery*, 426 U.S. 833, 856 (1976) (Brennan, J., joined by White and Marshall, JJ., dissenting).

[38] Art. I, § 3, cl. 1.

Thus, part of what the Tenth Amendment's structure presupposed was altered in 1913. That alteration in turn seems relevant to how the entire question of the reserved rights of the states should be considered in the latter part of the twentieth century. If the states can no longer directly represent their institutional interests in the Senate, perhaps there is room to reexamine the premises underlying the pre-1913 structure. Whether this is so raises complex questions of interpretive method that I will take up in the second lecture; to make sense of the Tenth Amendment, in addition to considering the effect of the Seventeenth Amendment, we must focus on a great deal more. The basic point, however, is that whatever our overarching theories about knowledge and interpretation might be, we can make real progress in reading the Constitution by eliminating at the start arguments that are not eligible for treatment as constitutional interpretation because they entail reading not *this* Constitution, but a desiccated, disintegrated version of it.

At the other extreme there stands the fallacy of *hyperintegration* — of treating the Constitution as a kind of seamless web, a "brooding omnipresence" that speaks to us with a single, simple, sacred voice expressing a unitary vision of an ideal political society. Of course, that would have been an impossible view to maintain early in our history: the fugitive slave clause; the Constitution's prohibition on any interference by Congress with the slave trade until the year 1808; the apportionment formula for the House of Representatives, which regarded a slave as equal to three-fifths of a person; and the other accommodations to the institution of slavery that were written into the text would have been difficult to square with many of the ideals found elsewhere in the document.[39]

---

[39] See Bell, "The Supreme Court, 1984 Term — Foreword: The Civil Rights Chronicles," 99 *Harv. L. Rev.* 4–7, 7 n.9 (1985). See generally Marshall, "Commentary: Reflections on the Bicentennial of the United States Constitution," 101 *Harv. L. Rev.* 1 (1987).

But it would be a fundamental mistake to suppose that, after ratification of the Civil War amendments, all such basic contradictions were eliminated from the Constitution, which suddenly became a coherent, consistent document. Conflicting visions — of liberal individualism on the one hand and civic republicanism on the other; of national supremacy as opposed to states' rights; of positivism as opposed to natural law — pervade the Constitution throughout its many parts. The notion that the Constitution embodies an immanent, unitary, changeless set of underlying values or principles — whether procedural or substantive or structural — seems an extraordinary intellectual conceit, one inconsistent with the character of the Constitution's various provisions as concrete political enactments that represent historically contingent, and not always wholly coherent, compromises in a document which was made in stages, incrementally, over a period of two centuries.

I do not quite share the view expressed by Bruce Ackerman of Yale, who proposed in his Storrs Lectures that we have *several* "Constitutions," some of them essentially unwritten but reflected in such national crises and readjustments as the Great Depression and the New Deal.[40] To be sure, the Constitution viewed as a historically evolving set of principles and premises has undergone crucial discontinuities at several such junctures. For me, there is nonetheless but one Constitution of the United States. Yet that Constitution cannot be confused with the unitary expression of a single idea — whether that idea be a grand Newtonian design of checks and balances or a great Darwinian vision of moral evolution or a Burkean construct for the perpetuation of tradition or a scheme for the perfection of representative democracy or any of the large number of other ideals to which commentators over the years have sought to subordinate the considerably less tidy Constitution *as it actually exists*. I would go further: the undeniably

---

[40] See Ackerman, "The Storrs Lectures."

plural and internally divided nature of the Constitution is not a sad reality; it may well be among the Constitution's greatest strengths.

It seems to have become a professional habit of constitutional commentators to superimpose their own preferred vision of what the Constitution is "really" meant to do and then to sweep aside all aspects of its text, history, and structure that do not quite fit the preferred grand design. That is not constitutional interpretation as I would wish to practice it. Perhaps I, too, have at times come close to reducing the Constitution to some central unity, the better to derive corollaries from whatever core vision I thought I saw there. In one essay published several years ago, I even went so far as to propose that, but for the manifest institutional unacceptability of its doing so, the Supreme Court might, in theory, hold a constitutional amendment incompatible with the grand design of the Constitution — the norms and premises pervading the document as a whole.[41] Although I never suggested that the Court could properly strike down a duly ratified amendment (I was careful to say the opposite), I came quite close to the view that had been advanced by Walter Murphy of Princeton — that the Constitution, correctly understood, expresses a vision sufficiently coherent that amendments radically incompatible with that vision are not law.[42]

That sort of view is a clear symptom of *not* interpreting the Constitution; little could better illustrate the hyper-integrationist fallacy. To attribute *any* unitary mission to the Constitution "as a whole" is to cross the line between *reading* the document and *writing* one of your own. My former colleague John Hart Ely, in an elegant and brilliant but I believe deeply flawed work, *Democracy and Distrust*, may have crossed that line when he

---

[41] Tribe, "A *Constitution* We Are Amending: In Defense of a Restrained Judicial Role," 97 *Harv. L. Rev.* 433, 438–43 (1983).

[42] Murphy, "An Ordering of Constitutional Values," 53 *S. Cal. L. Rev.* 703, 755–56 (1980).

proposed reading the entire document as having the central, non-substantive aim of perfecting democracy by reinforcing the effective workings of representative government.[43] From that perspective, there turn out to be some especially problematic clauses in the Constitution. There is one clause in particular that sounds awfully substantive, saying that no state "shall abridge the privileges or immunities of citizens of the United States." [44] And there is the Ninth Amendment, about which I will have much to say in the second of these lectures. Ely does *not* say that the text of these clauses, or their history, shows them to be concerned only with representative government. He says, rather, that — since the general point of the Constitution as a whole is to preserve representative government, and since judicial activism is most readily defended when it reinforces rather than undermines representation — we ought to squeeze those clauses into that vision.

But reading things *out of* the Constitution in order to bring the document into line with a theory, however noble and coherent, of what the structure as a whole is for, seems no more defensible than reading things *into* the Constitution for the same reason. To paraphrase Ely's remarks made in another context, a representation-reinforcing, democracy-perfecting form of judicial review — one which finds judges crusading *only* to make representative government work better and *never* to protect substantive human rights independent of representative government — may be "a thing of beauty and a joy forever," but, if it's not part of the Constitution, we have no business proclaiming it in the Constitution's name.[45]

Dean Jesse Choper of the University of California at Berkeley seems to me to be guilty of much the same fallacy when he powerfully develops the position that judicial review should be excluded

---

[43] John Hart Ely, *Democracy and Distrust: A Theory of Judicial Review* (Cambridge, Mass.: Harvard University Press, 1980).

[44] Amend. XIV, § 1.

[45] Ely, "The Wages of Crying Wolf: A Comment on *Roe v. Wade*," 82 *Yale L.J.* 920, 949 (1973).

altogether in matters of federalism and the separation of powers, primarily so that the federal judiciary in general, and the Supreme Court in particular, can conserve their resources for the cases that Choper believes really require active judicial involvement — cases in which the Court must protect despised minorities and unpopular claims of human rights — inasmuch as the separate branches of the national government, and the states, are capable of taking care of their own interests without such judicial help.[46] I find this sort of political analysis unpersuasive even on its own terms: I doubt that people inclined to protest the Court's protection of some downtrodden group would be much appeased if the Court were to remove itself scrupulously from disputes about the separation of powers and federal-state relations. The idea that the Court could husband its resources in that way seems rather naive.

But even if I accepted Choper's premises, I could not accept his conclusion. Constitutional protection for one branch of the federal government against another — the sort of thing we saw in the Supreme Court's legislative veto decision of 1983, and in its Gramm-Rudman decision of 1986 — or constitutional protection for state sovereignty, which I will consider in more detail in the second of these lectures, cannot properly be subtracted from the text on the instrumental ground that the Supreme Court believes, however plausibly, that its resources are better spent elsewhere.[47] Whatever else it may be, the Constitution certainly is *not* a charter for maximizing the influence of the federal judiciary in defense of liberal — or, for that matter, conservative — causes. Any mode of "interpretation" that distorts constitutional parts in support of any such goal is really not a mode of interpretation at all.

Neither the political left nor the political right has any monopoly on special-pleading versions of the constitutional enterprise.

[46] Jesse Choper, *Judicial Review and the National Political Process: A Functional Reconsideration of the Role of the Supreme Court* (Chicago: University of Chicago Press, 1980).

[47] *Immigration and Naturalization Serv. v. Chadha*, 462 U.S. 919 (1983) (veto decision), *Bowsher v. Synar*, 106 S. Ct. 3181 (1986) (Gramm-Rudman).

One of the most extraordinary examples in recent decades is found in a book called *Takings*, by Richard Epstein of the University of Chicago.[48] Epstein makes an extremely clever but stunningly reductionist argument that the whole Constitution is really designed to protect private property. Thomas Grey has aptly dubbed this "the Malthusian Constitution." [49] It is a Constitution in whose name Epstein would be prepared to strike down progressive taxes; the Social Security system; minimum wage laws; and, indeed, *all* laws that "general economic theory" condemns as tending to reduce overall wealth.[50] It is inconceivable to me that a Constitution reflecting as diverse an array of visions and aspirations as ours could be reducible to so sadly single-minded a vision as that.

But even if that vision were an elevated and lofty one, the idea that the whole Constitution could be harnessed to it seems wrong. David Richards of New York University, in a recent book entitled *Toleration and the Constitution*, works mightily to advance a constitutional vision in which the many provisions of the document expressing respect for personal dignity and individual diversity are woven into a unified fabric.[51] His ultimate ambition is to "take seriously the larger historical meaning of a written constitution as an expression of a coherent political theory." [52] But the Constitution, in my view, could not *possibly* express "a coherent political theory," however sympathetic and humane I might find its substance. It seems to me almost a contradiction in terms to suppose that one could read a Constitution composed as ours has been as though it were an expression of any unified philosophy.

[48] Richard Epstein, *Takings: Private Property and the Power of Emminent Domain* (Cambridge, Mass.: Harvard University Press, 1985).

[49] See Grey, "The Malthusian Constitution," 41 *U. Miami L. Rev.* 21, 22 (1986).

[50] Epstein, *Takings*, 200–01.

[51] David Richards, *Toleration and the Constitution* (New York: Oxford University Press, 1986).

[52] Richards, "Interpretation and Historiography," 56 *S. Cal. L. Rev.* 489, 542 (1985).

There is a suggestive analogy from the fields of algebraic topology and algebraic geometry, in which I once worked. The multidimensional curved space in which we find ourselves probably has no unified simple geometry. Locally, the space may have a Euclidian structure while globally, at large distances, its structure may be Riemannian or Lobachevskian. It may even be that the local topology is very different from the global topology. The Constitution is similarly multidimensional, and its global structure need be no more congruent with its local structure than is that of physical space. The web is not seamless. The parts do not always cohere. Anyone who says "I have here a little hologram embodying the essence of the Constitution, which can be turned round and round, revealing a seamless web," should incur your suspicion.

That insight has significance well beyond the negative. Instead of simply serving to *disqualify* otherwise attractive candidates for methods of constitutional interpretation, the insight might also provide something of an answer to those who would attack particular approaches to interpretation as subject to internal contradictions and anomalies. Many critical legal scholars, for example, have developed elaborate and often very insightful analyses designed ultimately to show that what they call "liberal constitutional scholarship" cannot meet various demands of coherence — it will have an internal contradiction here and there.[53] And it has been a commonplace in constitutional commentary for a long time to deride various approaches as insufficiently democratic or insufficiently majoritarian in character and, therefore, as contradicting some supposed need of the Constitution *as a whole* to affirm democracy.[54] But where is that "need" of the Constitution "as a whole"? When all of the supposed unities are exposed to scrutiny,

[53] See, e.g., Tushnet, "The Dilemmas of Liberal Constitutionalism," 42 *Ohio St. L.J.* 411 (1981).

[54] For a brief review of such commentary, see Brest, "The Fundamental Rights Controversy: The Essential Contradictions of Normative Constitutional Scholarship," 90 *Yale L.J.* 1063 (1981).

criticisms of that kind become considerably less impressive. Not all need be reducible to a single theme. Inconsistency — even inconsistency with democracy — is hardly earth-shattering. Listen to Walt Whitman: "Do I contradict myself? Very well then, I contradict myself." "I am large, I contain multitudes," the Constitution replies.[55]

II. TEXTS AND TACIT POSTULATES

As we celebrate the Constitution's bicentennial, it seems only natural that we ask ourselves the sorts of basic questions to which these two lectures are addressed. Those questions are, in fact, so basic and so difficult that I hope you will forgive me for the necessarily halting and tentative character of this effort to sketch my answers. More often than not, I have no answers; and those I offer, whether here or in my other writings, are almost never held with certitude, even when my tone may sound certain.

It is to be expected during this anniversary period that many people, throughout our country and around the world, will be taking an unusually close look at the sorts of answers our system has given, and continues to give, to questions of constitutional interpretation. In some countries those questions tend to be submerged because no judicially enforceable written constitution exists to be interpreted and applied. In England, for example, it is still true, as a British court put it with striking modernity more than 285 years ago, that "[a]n Act of Parliament can do no wrong, though it may do several things that look pretty odd." [56]

But an ever larger number of nations in the post–World War II period have chosen our more rebellious path rather than England's traditional one. More nations would do so, William

---

[55] Walt Whitman, "Song of Myself," *Leaves of Grass*, 9th ed. (1891–92), lines 1324–26. Cf. Emerson, "Self-Reliance," *Essays: First Series* (1841) ("A foolish consistency is the hobgoblin of little minds, adored by little statesmen and philosophers and divines").

[56] *City of London v. Wood*, 88 Eng. Rep. 1592, 1602 (1700).

Van Alstyne of Duke University has suggested, if they could somehow be assured that judges would not be too ingenious in their reading of constitutional texts.[57] The notion is that, witnessing the controversy over what our courts have done with the relatively brief text of our Constitution, others may find it best simply to say: "No thank you, we would rather avoid all of that."

But the lesson of our first two centuries under a written constitution, I believe, is really quite different from the lesson Van Alstyne suggests some people in other countries might perceive. The lesson, rather, is that judicial ingenuity, along with statesmanship of many other sorts, has probably been indispensable to our success as a constitutional democracy, and that the lines of precedent that most of us deeply regret — including decisions like the infamous *Dred Scott* opinion and others which are now almost universally castigated as disasters — followed at least as often from overly mechanical, wooden, or insensitive interpretations as from overly creative and ingenious ones.[58] The further lesson is that there exists, in any event, no formula that could eliminate altogether the need for judicial choice, although there are certainly formulas that try to *hide* that need behind proclamations of "original intent" or of the "clear meaning" of the text. And finally, the lesson is that the best way to achieve wisdom in constitutional interpretation is to subject all constitutional arguments and decisions to constant analysis and continuing critique in terms of the text, and in terms of our traditions for construing it.

For the Constitution, despite Lowell's vivid description in 1888, is *not* "a machine that would go of itself." [59] It is, rather, a text to be interpreted and reinterpreted in an unending search

[57] Van Alstyne, "Interpreting *This* Constitution: The Unhelpful Contributions of Special Theories of Judicial Review," 35 *U. Fla. L. Rev.* 209, 209–10 (1983).

[58] *Dred Scott v. Sanford*, 60 U.S. (19 How.) 393 (1857) (outrageously holding that blacks were not capable of being citizens of the United States and gratuitously announcing the unconstitutionality of the Missouri Compromise, thereby helping to provoke the Civil War).

[59] Kammen, *A Machine That Would Go of Itself*, 125.

for understanding. The fact that this search cannot be rendered perfect and infallible by any agreed-upon definition of a unitary goal, or by any single mode of proceeding, was a central theme of my argument in the first of these lectures. In that lecture, in fact, I closed by *celebrating* our Constitution's multiplicity — its character as a text containing distinct but not always consistent subtexts. I praised our Constitution's resistance to reductionist analyses designed to squeeze it into any single philosophy of state or of society.

Part of what follows from the Constitution's irreducibly plural and multiple character is that those who would demand of constitutional interpreters that they offer a perfectly coherent solution to the perennial problems of freedom and order, of individual and of community, are making a pointless request. It is one thing to say of a reader of the Constitution, including a Supreme Court justice, that she has not made a sensible, convincing argument. To say that is to level a serious critique. But to say that she has not come up with an airtight, seamless, contradiction-free argument — one that wipes away all possibility of opposition, one that demolishes every contrary view — is pointless. It's almost like criticizing Einstein for never having found a unified field theory for physical phenomena, or like criticizing a friend, to whom you go for advice on an intractable problem, for not having eliminated *all* your doubts.

It is important to see that this feature of how the text of the Constitution guides interpretation, how it *channels* choice without *eliminating* choice, is fully present even when we are applying the most seemingly specific of constitutional clauses. It is a fundamental mistake to suppose that weighty problems of interpretation arise only in the hardest cases — only where the issue is one as to which the text is unusually vague or unusually ambiguous. That's a favorite gambit of certain Supreme Court commentators. They point to a division among justices on an issue and say, "Look how they disagree, five to four. It must be that they're not really reading the Constitution, but just seeing in it a mirror of what they want to believe." But consider briefly, before turning to more involved illustrations, a couple of examples in which the text is quite clear — as clear as these things get, at any rate — and in which disagreement is nonetheless unavoidable.

Consider the prohibition in Article I of the Constitution on "Bills of Attainder." [60] Now that is a term of art, widely under-stood to mean that legislatures may not single out those whom they wish to punish. After President Nixon left office under well-known circumstances, Congress passed a statute identifying Richard Milhous Nixon *by name* and providing that, unlike *other* ex-presidents, he could not have access to his White House papers and tapes until they had been fully catalogued and reviewed by the General Services Administration. Congress was evidently unwilling to generalize its rule to cover any future president who might resign during impeachment proceedings.

A divided United States Supreme Court nonetheless concluded that this Act of Congress was no Bill of Attainder.[61] The Court reasoned that Mr. Nixon was not being punished, even though this was a somewhat humiliating restriction — one to which no past president had ever been subjected, and one which, by its terms, could apply to no future president. Besides that, the majority of the Court said, Richard Nixon is "a legitimate class of one." [62]

Several dissenters took the position that this law has all the earmarks of a forbidden Bill of Attainder: it imposes a stigma-tizing disability on someone driven from power, whether justly or not, in a way that explicitly identifies the individual or individuals to be so penalized.[63]

[60] Art. I, § 9, cl. 3: "No Bill of Attainder or ex post facto Law shall be passed."

[61] *Nixon v. Administrator of General Services*, 433 U.S. 425, 468–84 (1977).

[62] Ibid., 472.

[63] See ibid., 536–45 (Burger, C.J., dissenting).

I am inclined to think the dissent had the better of the argument. But my point is that conscientious readers of the Constitution may differ in their understanding in a case like this, involving even a fairly narrow and precise constitutional provision. It does not follow from this that the justices were simply reading their personal or political views into the text. In fact, knowing the specific justices and how they voted, I am quite confident that some justices on each side of the *Nixon* case would have preferred to read the Constitution the way the other side in fact read it. They were not voting their political preferences, or even their general ideology, but were voting on the basis of conscientiously differing readings of what the Bill of Attainder Clause reaches, and how far it goes.

Or examine another phrase that is at least relatively specific, compared with some of the grand and cloudy clauses with which we sometimes deal in constitutional law: the First Amendment's prohibition against "any law abridg[ing] the freedom of speech or of the press." Consider the following situation. A state statute of New York authorizes the closure of any building determined to be a public health nuisance, upon the finding that the building is being used as a place for "prostitution" or "lewdness." The Village Books and News Store, an adult bookstore in Kenmore, New York, owned by Cloud Books, Inc., sells sexually explicit, but not quite obscene, books and magazines. A deputy sheriff observes patrons of the store engaging in sex acts on the premises within plain view of the proprietor. Prostitutes are also seen soliciting business there. The store is found at trial to be a "public health nuisance" under the statute. Pursuant to the statute, the premises are ordered closed for a year.

As you might imagine, this scenario led to litigation. Everyone involved agreed that the books and magazines being sold on the premises were "speech," entitled to First Amendment protection. The question was whether closing the bookstore for a year under these circumstances amounted to forbidden "abridgement" of speech. Specifically, did the state have to meet the standard, which is imposed in First Amendment cases, of showing that its legitimate objectives required something as drastic as closing this store down for a whole year? In other words, did the state have to prove that a less restrictive remedy would have been inadequate to abate such nuisances? Was this a gratuitously wide-ranging suppression of speech?

The highest court of New York State said that this suppression did go too far.[64] It held the First Amendment applicable, required the state to meet a least restrictive remedy test, and found that the test was not met. In its view, the legitimate purposes of the state of New York could be served by something less drastic than closure of the bookstore for an entire year. And, in fact, the state court was able to invoke the original intent of the First Amendment's framers in partial support of its view. Original intent arguably supported the result, since a central purpose of the First Amendment, everyone agreed, was to prevent the government from imposing prior restraints on publication — and an order closing a bookstore or a movie theater obviously restrains a publishing activity in advance.

When the case reached the United States Supreme Court, three justices agreed with that view.[65] The other six justices saw the case differently. To them, it was merely incidental that this happened to be a bookstore. After all, the statute itself had nothing at all to do with speech. Its use against this business was triggered not by the *books* being sold, but by the *sex* being peddled. The case is *Arcara v. Cloud Books, Inc.*; the reason you may not have heard of it is that the opinion was handed down on the same day the Supreme Court struck down the Gramm-Rudman Balanced

[64] *People ex rel. Arcara v. Cloud Books, Inc.*, 65 N.Y.2d 324, 491 N.Y.S.2d 307, 480 N.E.2d 1089 (1985).

[65] *Arcara v. Cloud Books, Inc.*, 106 S. Ct. 3172, 3178–81 (1986) (Blackmun, J., joined by Brennan and Marshall, JJ., dissenting).

Budget Act, which tended to attract all the media attention that day.[66]

Although I am said to be a First Amendment liberal, I agree completely with Chief Justice Warren E. Burger's majority opinion in this case. If the First Amendment requires New York State to show that a one-year closure is the least restrictive alternative simply because a bookstore was involved, then consider what follows. If, for example, a TV anchorman like Tom Brokaw or Dan Rather, to avoid being late for the evening news broadcast, decides to drive at eighty miles per hour or run ten red lights in a row, and the state says "you go to jail overnight," the anchorman could say, "but you're suppressing speech! You have to prove that jail is necessary! How about just a fine?" [67] The First Amendment would become involved whenever the enforcement of otherwise valid and neutral laws happens incidentally to restrict speech. It seems to me that that is not a sound, sensible reading of the First Amendment.

Justice Sandra Day O'Connor, concurring separately in an opinion joined by Justice John Paul Stevens, was quite sensitive: she agreed that the state court had gone too far, but she quite properly left open the possibility of a First Amendment claim if a city were to use a nuisance statute like this as a *pretext* for closing down a bookstore because of the books it sold.[68] There was nothing in the record of this case suggesting that that had been done.

Three justices went the other way: Justices William J. Brennan, Thurgood Marshall, and Harry A. Blackmun dissented. They said, in effect: As far as we're concerned, whether there's a pretext or not this is unconstitutional. It goes too far; there is no showing that this much suppression of speech is necessary to achieve the

---

[66] *Bowsher v. Synar*, 106 S. Ct. 3181 (1986).

[67] This example was inspired by Justice O'Connor's concurring opinion, 106 S. Ct. at 3178.

[68] Ibid.

legitimate aims of New York. "Until today," they wrote, "this Court has never suggested that a State may suppress speech as much as it likes, without justification, so long as it does so through generally applicable regulations" unrelated to expressive conduct.[69] I think the dissenters made a respectable argument. But, with respect, I think that they and the state court were wrong.

Now, does that mean that I am more personally offended than those three justices were by the sexual activity on the premises in that case? I don't think so. Does it mean that I'm less concerned than they are about the value of free speech? That I'm more of a strict constructionist? Less concerned with original intent (after all, the state court invoked "original intent")? I doubt it. Like the case involving Richard Nixon, I think this case nicely illustrates how honest and conscientious readers of a quite specific constitutional provision, engaged in the process of genuine interpretation, can reach entirely opposite conclusions. The existence, in other words, of room for disagreement is not proof that what is going on does not deserve to be called interpretation — that there is something sinister or illegitimate going on, that we're watching some kind of shell game — any more than the existence of differences in the interpretation of any other text suggests that something is going on that doesn't deserve to be called interpretation.

It might be argued that these two cases that I happened to pick for illustration don't really test the proposition that something other than interpretation must be going on when there are differences, because in both of them the critically relevant text was relatively precise — although it did raise thorny problems of interpretation, problems in which where you end up does not necessarily depend in any obvious way on your political leanings or even your overall constitutional philosophy. But how about situations where the text itself is famously imprecise, where it may

[69] Ibid., 3179.

not even be clear which *part* of the constitutional text applies? It is situations of that kind on which I want to spend the remainder of this lecture, to ask what we can do with situations in which the constitutional nostrils flair — where there is a sense that there may be something wrong, but one flips through the document and can't quite pin down where that sense comes from.

To illustrate such a situation, one impacting on federal-state relations, consider the following hypothetical case. Assume an act of Congress, the Home-Rule Act of 1987, abolishing home rule in all the states that now have it, centralizing state and local governance in the state capitals — telling the states, in other words, that they cannot delegate a common kind of blank-check authority to their cities and counties, towns and municipalities. Analysis of such a case must examine the various reasons Congress might have for doing such a thing. But quite apart from the reasons, one must ask, in thinking about possible challenges to the validity of a federal statute which cuts this deeply into the way state and local governments decide to structure themselves, whether the statute seems to offend any relevant text in the Constitution.

Many people would gravitate toward the Tenth Amendment. It's short; it reads: "The powers not delegated to the United States by the Constitution, nor prohibited by it to the States, are reserved to the States respectively, or to the people." I suppose the very first question that a constitutional interpreter would ask is whether the Home-Rule Act of 1987 might be invalid under the Tenth Amendment on the ground that it attempts to exercise a power "not delegated to the United States by the Constitution."

To answer that question you have to ask what power Congress might be exercising here. Most likely, it is exercising the commerce power of Article I — Congress's power "[t]o regulate Commerce . . . among the several States." [70] To someone in 1920,

---

[70] Art. I, § 8, cl. 3.

that might not have seemed so obvious, but in the period from 1937 to the present the Supreme Court has seen in the Commerce Clause an extraordinarily broad authority for Congress to regulate virtually everything, however local, that might have any impact on interstate commerce.[71] And obviously, the exercise of power by localities pursuant to home rule provisions might have such an impact.

Indeed, there are some important Supreme Court decisions upholding application of the Sherman Antitrust Act to the actions of cities and towns. Boulder, Colorado, for example, acting under the Colorado home rule provisions, restricted competition among cable franchises. The Supreme Court held that, when Boulder did that, its actions were subject to the Sherman Act.[72] The actions of Colorado itself are exempt from the act; the Supreme Court in 1943 interpreted the act as not reaching action by the sovereign states.[73] But in *Boulder*, the Supreme Court held that, when municipalities exercise power pursuant to home rule provisions, they do not inherit the state's immunity from the Sherman Act. They are left out in the cold.

A sequel to *Boulder* arose in Berkeley, California, in a case in which property owners argued that Berkeley's rent control ordinance was a violation of the Sherman Act, because it too was passed pursuant to a home rule provision. Therefore, they claimed that Berkeley did not step into California's shoes — did not inherit California's immunity from the antitrust laws. In representing the city of Berkeley in the Supreme Court, I argued that the immunity issue did not have to be reached because, in fact, municipal rent control simply does not violate the antitrust laws, even though a private rent-fixing cartel would. The Court, by an 8-1 vote, upheld that view.[74]

[71] Tribe, *American Constitutional Law*, §§ 5–4 to 5–6.

[72] *Community Communications Co. v. City of Boulder*, 455 U.S. 40 (1982).

[73] *Parker v. Brown*, 317 U.S. 341 (1943).

[74] *Fisher v. City of Berkeley*, 106 S. Ct. 1045 (1986). Justice Marshall wrote for the majority. Justice Brennan dissented. Ibid., 1053.

But the Commerce Clause would certainly have *allowed* Congress to reach such municipal action had it so chosen. And, as the *Boulder* case illustrates, the Commerce Clause apparently allows Congress to regulate the way in which the states relate to their municipalities. For if the state itself had *mandated* an anti-competitive stance by Boulder, that municipal action would have been immune from all challenge under the Sherman Act. It is only because the state chose to let Boulder roll on its own, as it were, that the immunity evaporated.

But where under the Commerce Clause does Congress get the power to regulate the relationship between a state and its municipalities? How might the very *existence* of home rule have an impact on interstate commerce? Here one must perhaps be a bit imaginative, but the Court has done that to sustain all kinds of laws having less relation to commerce than this. Congress, for example, might have decided that unfettered, autonomous home rule cities are less likely to take the national economic interest into account than are cities that are kept on a short leash by the state legislature. And, being less likely to take the national interest into account — more likely therefore to act parochially — such home rule jurisdictions are more likely, cumulatively, to pose a threat to the smooth flow of interstate commerce.

As I have said, the Court has upheld, as falling within the reach of Congress's commerce power, actions founded on rationales far less tenable than that. But notice that, even though it is clear that Congress is indeed acting pursuant to power expressly delegated by the Constitution, it is still cutting deeply into the very *structure* of state government. The question you then might want to ask is this: Does the Constitution somehow reserve to the states any residual sphere of autonomy — a core of fundamental sovereignty — or must we conclude, simply because Congress is exercising a nationally delegated power, that there is no room left to make a states' rights argument? The structure of the Tenth Amendment may appear to indicate that there is no room left.

For that amendment creates a binary, either/or system: the powers *not* delegated to the United States are reserved to the states. Either a power is delegated to the United States, or it's not. If it is delegated, it cannot be reserved. End of argument.

Not quite. For one thing, the text does not say that *only* the powers not delegated are reserved. And, in any event, with another provision, sitting right next to the Tenth Amendment, the Court has not been stopped cold by the text. In construing the Eleventh Amendment, the Court has indeed *ignored* part of the text. By its terms, the Eleventh Amendment excludes from the general federal judicial power lawsuits that are brought against a state without its consent in federal court "by Citizens of another State." But the Supreme Court has had no trouble amending that language over the years to read, in effect, "by Citizens of another State *or of the same State*." [75] Indeed, the garden-variety use of the Eleventh Amendment is to prevent, for example, a citizen of Utah from suing the state of Utah in a federal district court.

That the Court has occasionally rewritten the Constitution, however, doesn't make such a practice right. Many commentators, myself included, have severely criticized the Court's recasting of the Eleventh Amendment.[76] But by comparison, a reading of the *Tenth* Amendment to bar congressional interference with home rule provisions would appear to be a far more radical judicial usurpation. After all, it is one thing to expand an amendment a little — to say that its purposes require grafting something on in order to *restrict* judicial power. It is quite another to *rewrite* it so as to change its structure and *expand* judicial power. The apparently binary structure, if not the literal text, of the Tenth Amendment would go out the window if the Court were to hold that, under that amendment, there can be powers delegated to the United States and *nonetheless* reserved to the states.

[75] See Tribe, *American Constitutional Law*, § 3–25, pp. 174–75 and n. 8.
[76] See ibid., §§ 3–25 to 3–27.

Of course you might say, as I indicated in my first lecture, that the Tenth Amendment does not sit in majestic solitude in the Constitution. Things have changed since it was written in 1791. Congress's powers have expanded radically. And the Seventeenth Amendment in 1913 stripped the states of their direct representation in the Senate, replacing legislative appointment of senators with direct election of senators. Given such changes, I suggested previously, there might be room to reexamine the meaning of the Tenth Amendment. I still believe that. But however much you reexamine the amendment, it still looks as though it creates a binary structure. Revising a specific constitutional provision *that* radically, on the ground that the surrounding circumstances have changed, really *does* expose the Court to the charge that it is not interpreting the Constitution but rewriting it.[77]

How about simply ignoring the Constitution's text? That's what the Supreme Court did in 1976 to articulate a sphere of state sovereignty protected from federal legislative incursions, in *National League of Cities v. Usury*.[78] There, the Court didn't really rely on the Tenth Amendment; the amendment was mentioned only as an illustration.[79] Instead, by a five-to-four margin, the Court relied on the general structure of the Constitution and its presupposition of state sovereignty. And it did that in order to hold that Congress, even though exercising its affirmative powers under the Commerce Clause when it extended minimum wage, maximum hour, and overtime protection to state and municipal employees, was violating state sovereignty when it did so. That was the holding of *National League of Cities*. But the doctrine lasted less than a decade.

National League of Cities was overturned in 1985 in the *Garcia* decision,[80] but not because the Court was embarrassed at

---

[77] See, e.g., Field, "Comment: *Garcia v. San Antonio Metropolitan Transit Authority*: The Demise of a Misguided Doctrine," 99 *Harv. L. Rev.* 84 (1985).

[78] 426 U.S. 833 (1976).

[79] Ibid., 842–43.

[80] *Garcia v. San Antonio Metropolitan Transit Auth.*, 469 U.S. 528 (1985).

having ignored the Tenth Amendment, or at having rewritten it. Rather, Justice Blackmun reversed his vote to form a new 5–4 majority largely for the quite pragmatic reasons that, for ten years, the Court hadn't proven capable of drawing very well the lines called for by *National League of Cities*, and that, as a political matter, states probably didn't *need* the Court's help — they could fight it out for themselves through their elected representatives. Justice Lewis F. Powell, Jr., in a powerful dissent, asked in effect: What kind of an argument is that? Would you liberals, who make that argument in this case, say that individual rights don't need this Court's protection because *individuals* are, after all, represented in the legislature? If you take rights seriously, they are rights *against* the majority. They cannot be forgotten simply because, as a practical political matter, those who hold them might also have a lot of political clout.[81]

What is to be said for *National League of Cities* itself? The decision overruling it wasn't very persuasive, as I have just suggested. But then *National League of Cities* itself was problematic. What about the idea of relying on the whole structure of the Constitution — not the Tenth Amendment considered alone but the entire structure? That idea was most powerfully advanced in Charles Black's book *Structure and Relationship in Constitutional Law*.[82] He essentially urged that meaning should be found not only in the four corners of the document but, as it were, in the angles and shapes of its corners — reading not only the lines of the text but between the lines, focusing as closely on how the pieces fit together as on their individual shapes.

One would not suppose that so-called "strict constructionists" would find that notion very appealing. But the justices who *have* found it appealing include Justice — now Chief Justice — Rehnquist, and former Chief Justice Burger. In *Nevada v. Hall*, the

[81] Ibid., 564–67 and n. 8 (Powell, J., joined by Burger, C.J., and Rehnquist and O'Connor, JJ., dissenting).

[82] Charles Black, *Structure and Relationship in Constitutional Law* (Baton Rouge: Louisiana State University Press, 1969).

Court faced the question whether states should be immune from suits brought against them by citizens of sister states suing in their own state, not federal, courts.[83] The majority of the Court found no such constitutional immunity, holding that the Constitution confers no protection against such suits in state court. Justice Rehnquist, taking the position that such protection was implicit in the very *structure* of the Constitution, argued that "[t]he tacit postulates [of the constitutional plan] are as much engrained in the fabric of the document as its express provisions." [84]

Is this reliance on the "tacit postulates" of the whole plan "strict constructionism"? In my last lecture, I described the trouble with what I called the fallacy of "hyper-integration" — of purporting to find in the "brooding omnipresence" of the Constitution one seamless system of tacit postulates, not subject to any discipline that such postulates be anchored in any particular constitutional text. I continue to regard such an undisciplined approach as fallacious. But if Chief Justice Rehnquist's technique of seeing the tacit postulates afloat in the heavens above, or seeing them swim in the melted core beneath the Constitution, is a bit too "*loose* constructionist" for you, as it is for me — and if trying to anchor the tacit postulates to the text of the Tenth Amendment won't quite do because that text must be mangled in order to achieve the goal — does it follow that we must give up? In our hypothetical case, do states possess the power to decide on home rule only at the whim of Congress?

I suggested yesterday that the Constitution is a kingdom of many mansions. There are many subtexts. To paraphrase the post-structuralist, we might therefore ask: Is there another text in the room, one that might be relevant and helpful? Perhaps there is. When Justice O'Connor dissented, for example, from part of the Supreme Court's 1982 decision in *Federal Energy Regulatory Com-*

---

[83] 440 U.S. 410 (1979).

[84] Ibid., 433 (Rehnquist, J., joined by Burger, C.J., dissenting).

mission v. Mississippi, a case in which Congress had told the public utility regulatory commissions of the states how to structure their agendas, she wrote that "federalism enhances the opportunity of all citizens to participate in representative government." [85] And she quoted Alexis de Tocqueville: " '[T]he love and the habits of republican government in the United States were engendered in the townships and in the provincial assemblies.' " She spoke of the republican spirit, meaning not "Republican" with a capital R, but civil republicanism — the public spiritedness of community.[86]

Consider Article IV, section 4, of the Constitution, an explicit text: "The United States shall guarantee to every State in this Union a Republican Form of Government." How about *that* provision as our text for protection of states' rights? There are two major obstacles. The first is that the Supreme Court held long ago that the Republican Form Clause does not create judicially enforceable rights for individuals. An individual cannot go into court and say, "The government of my state is not representative enough. I want it restructured." [87] But there are two answers to that. First, the Court has allowed individuals to go into court and make that very argument under the Equal Protection Clause of the Fourteenth Amendment in the reapportionment decisions, extended in 1986 to cases of political gerrymandering, in *Davis v. Bandemer.*[88] Second, although the Republican Form Clause may not guarantee enforceable rights to *individuals,* it does not follow that it fails to guarantee enforceable rights to *states.* After all, it says that "[t]he United States *shall guarantee to every State* in this Union a Republican Form of Government." There is a power-

---

[85] 456 U.S. 742, 789 (1982). (O'Connor, J., joined by Burger, C.J., and Rehnquist, J., concurring in the judgment in part and dissenting in part).

[86] Ibid., 789–90.

[87] See Tribe, *American Constitutional Law,* § 3–13, pp. 98–99.

[88] See ibid., §§ 13–2 to 13–8; 106 S. Ct. 2797 (1986) (*Davis*), discussed in Tribe, *American Constitutional Law,* § 13–9.

ful argument that the clause should be enforceable in an otherwise proper suit by a state against the federal government.[89]

The second obstacle to the argument is that home rule is not
itself required by the Republican Form Clause. Many states do
not have home rule; surely we cannot say that *they* have given up
representative government. My answer is that, although home
rule is not required by the Constitution's guarantee of a republican
form of government, the ability to *choose* between home rule and
centralization arguably *is* so required. The authority to decide,
consistent with the Equal Protection Clause of the Fourteenth
Amendment, how one's people will represent themselves and participate in their own governance — how their system of government will be structured — is the essence of self-government and is
protected, or should be deemed protected, by the Republican Form
Clause. Indeed, in the second edition of my treatise, I urge courts,
when they again take up arms for states' rights, to rely on the
admittedly modest limits that might be found in the Republican
Form Clause.[90] The three-part lesson I draw from this example is
that: (1) relying on an amendment written so that it doesn't seem
to apply won't quite do, and (2) relying on an overall, unstruc-
tured system of tacit postulates is too loose, but (3) searching the
Constitution for other applicable texts is always an available
option.

Now consider the second of my two hypothetical examples.
Suppose a municipality has enacted a local ordinance requiring
all families to eat at home at least once each month, with only
family members present, and to precede that meal with a "moment
of thankful silence." Is there any text in the Constitution that
might be invoked to challenge such an ordinance?

Of course one could turn to the Establishment Clause of the
First Amendment. This "moment of thankful silence" looks sus-

---

[89] See Tribe, *American Constitutional Law*, § 5–23.
[90] Ibid.

piciously like prayer; for the government to command such a moment entails government endorsement of religion. In *Wallace v. Jaffrey*, the Supreme Court struck down, as a forbidden establishment of religion, an Alabama statute which did not even require a moment of silence but simply *permitted* teachers to schedule such a moment of silence "for meditation or voluntary prayer" at the start of each public school day.[91] Nobody was required to pray, and no teacher was required to set aside the moment.

Nonetheless, the Supreme Court held that this statute violated the Establishment Clause as applied to the states through the Fourteenth Amendment. The Court's majority stressed two features of the statute absent in the imaginary family law case that I have posited. The Court stressed that, in its debate over the statute, and in the statute's text, the Alabama legislature had explicitly referred to prayer in a manner obviously designed to endorse that religious practice. The Court also stressed that the issue arose in the context of the public schools — so that the power of government, which forced students to attend, was harnessed by religion, and so that a governmental institution, the public school, *borrowed* part of its authority from sacred symbols, in a dubious mix of church and state.

In his dissent, then-Justice Rehnquist pointed out that the wall of separation between church and state is more a judicially created metaphor than anything to be found in the text of the Constitution.[92] Notice how readily the "tacit-postulate" justice becomes a strict constructionist! The early presidents, he stressed, proclaimed Thanksgiving; despite that holiday's religious significance, there was no suggestion that they were violating the Establishment Clause. And, he indicated, there is no evidence that the framers would have objected even to voluntary prayer in public

[91] 472 U.S. 38 (1985).

[92] Ibid., 91–114 (Rehnquist, J., dissenting).

schools. Yet, as he noted, this was not even *prayer* — just a moment of silence for meditation *or* prayer.

Justice O'Connor, concurring with the majority, offered a powerful rejoinder to Justice Rehnquist.[93] She argued that this history was inconclusive: public schools barely existed when the First Amendment was written; they were not a powerful presence even when the Fourteenth Amendment was written and ratified. We might recall the observation from Chief Justice Rehnquist, noted in my first lecture, that we must apply the framers' basic concepts to unforeseen circumstances.[94] If one takes that reminder seriously, then Justice O'Connor seems to have the better of the argument.

But what follows in my hypothetical? In the hypothetical, no public school is involved; there is no reference to prayer; it is only an expression of thanks that the law says must be given before the evening meal. Yet one can look at history from a somewhat different angle: Madison's Thanksgiving proclamations don't prove much since, after his presidency was over, he argued that, on reflection, even those Thanksgiving proclamations had improperly mingled government and religion.[95] And requiring Thanksgiving proclamations monthly by families could well be deemed a violation of the Establishment Clause.

But this isn't an official proclamation. The law just tells the family to give thanks in its own way, and it doesn't say they have to give thanks to anyone in particular; it simply says there should be a "moment of thankful silence." The law doesn't involve the *government* doing anything; it only tells the *family* what to do. And, in a sense, that cuts against the Establishment Clause argument. But, although government is not officially proclaiming religion through the ordinance, a different kind of argument becomes

---

[93] Ibid., 67–84 (O'Connor, J., concurring in the judgment).

[94] See Rehnquist, "The Notion of a Living Constitution," 694.

[95] See Tribe, *American Constitutional Law*, § 14–3, p. 1163, n. 40.

apparent — an argument about intrusion into the freedom of the family, perhaps its free exercise of religion.

Leaving these questions aside, I want to focus on what seems to me the most interesting aspect of this case by extracting religion from the picture altogether. Let's delete the requirement of a moment of thankful silence. Let's have a simpler law: once a month, at least, every family must sit down and have dinner together — just the family members, no friends. They don't have to say anything; they can just sit there and munch. Conversely, they don't have to be silent. But they *must* eat together as a family at least once a month. The maxim underlying such a requirement might be, I suppose, that "a family that eats together stays together."

How are we to analyze such a law? In the early 1970s the Supreme Court confronted a case not entirely unrelated to such a situation, one involving food stamps.[96] Congress had passed an amendment to the food stamp statute providing that, if a family invites nonmembers to live in, it loses its food stamps, even though the family is otherwise eligible; if there is anyone in the household who is unrelated by blood or marriage to anyone else, no food stamps are available. The Court held that Congress had violated the Due Process Clause of the Fifth Amendment. It ruled that this is an entirely irrational law — perhaps motivated by animosity to hippy communes but, in any event, irrational. The purpose of Congress in this context was to meet nutritional requirements. There is no rational relationship, said the Court, between meeting nutritional needs and insisting on a certain kind of relationship between people who happen to live together. Perhaps it occurred to the Court that if six unrelated judges lived together, they too would have been ineligible for food stamps under this provision.

But, of course, the example I have hypothesized is a bit different from that in the food stamp decision. In the food stamp

[96] *United States Department of Agriculture v. Moreno*, 413 U.S. 528 (1973).

case, Congress was essentially *starving people out* unless they conformed their living patterns to the requisite national norm. In my hypothetical case no one is being deprived of nutrition. No one is being told, "we'll kick you out of public housing," or "we won't let you eat, if you don't comply." Everyone is being told, regardless of circumstance, that their family must eat together once a month. If they don't, I suppose they are subject to a fine or might get thrown in jail. This general requirement can't be said to be quite as vicious, quite as irrational; the purpose of this even-handed law isn't nutrition: it is family togetherness as such.

But that really does bring us to the heart of the matter. What about the fact that the law invades the realm of family life? Is there anything about *that* which enables us to invoke the Constitution of the United States? True, there is not a word in the Constitution about family or family life. But there is a series of decisions under the Fourteenth Amendment, stretching back to the 1920s, recognizing a realm of autonomy for the family. Nebraska said that people couldn't have their children learn a foreign language; the Supreme Court struck that down in 1923.[97] Oregon said that parents couldn't send their children to private schools, either religious or military; the Supreme Court struck that down in 1925.[98] Oklahoma said that certain blue-collar as opposed to white-collar criminals — people repeatedly convicted of ordinary larceny instead of embezzlement — would be sterilized; the Supreme Court held that procreation, although not mentioned in the Constitution, is a fundamental right, and it struck the Oklahoma law down.[99] Connecticut said that no one can use contraceptives; in 1965, the Supreme Court in *Griswold v. Connecticut* held that that law, as applied to married couples, was an impermissible

[97] *Meyer v. Nebraska*, 262 U.S. 390 (1923).

[98] *Pierce v. Society of Sisters*, 268 U.S. 510 (1925); *Pierce v. Hill Military Academy*, 268 U.S. 510 (1925).

[99] *Skinner v. Oklahoma*, 316 U.S. 535 (1942).

invasion into the privacy of the family.[100] In 1967 the Supreme
Court held that it is unconstitutional to tell people whom they
may and may not marry, striking down Virginia's law against
interracial marriage, in a case aptly named *Loving v. Virginia*.[101]
In 1969 the Supreme Court extended the *Griswold* contraception
decision to unmarried couples in *Eisenstadt v. Baird*.[102] In 1973
the Court extended these precedents to protect a woman's right
to obtain an abortion, in *Roe v. Wade*.[103]

In 1977 a prosecutor in East Cleveland, Ohio (bless his heart
for having brought this wonderful — or perhaps more accurately,
infamous — test case) threatened to put a grandmother in jail
for living with her two grandchildren because, under the family-
law zoning code of East Cleveland, you could live with your two
grandchildren only if they were siblings, and these two happened
to be *cousins*. The mother of one of the grandsons had died when
he was one year old; he had nowhere else to live, so his grandmother took him in. The city said, in effect, "Kick him out or go
to jail!"

The Supreme Court, in *Moore v. City of East Cleveland*, struck
that law down under the Fourteenth Amendment.[104] That's the
good news. The bad news is that the decision was five to four.
And why not? The Constitution says nothing about grandmothers,
parents, children, or family — it doesn't even mention the word
"privacy." In fact, there is a mounting attack from Chief Justice
Rehnquist and others on that entire line of decisions.[105] But it

---

[100] 381 U.S. 479 (1965).

[101] 388 U.S. 1 (1967).

[102] 405 U.S. 438 (1972).

[103] 410 U.S. 113 (1973).

[104] 431 U.S. 494 (1977).

[105] It was in part because of his prominence in spearheading this attack that
Judge Robert H. Bork, nominated by President Reagan in July 1987 to fill the
Supreme Court vacancy created by the resignation of Justice Lewis F. Powell, Jr., was
rejected by the Senate, 58–42, on October 23, 1987.

would be very hard to roll them back selectively. They are all grounded on notions of family privacy, family autonomy, reproductive freedom, and marital choice that simply are not mentioned at all in the Constitution.

What, then, of the "tacit postulates" of the constitutional plan? Perhaps we can use those, citing none other than then-Justice Rehnquist, dissenting in *Nevada v. Hall*.[106] But I have argued that he went too far in abandoning the text in that case; without the Republican Form Clause, I might have concluded that there is no constitutional basis for protecting states' rights in our first hypothetical. I'm not about to fight fire with fire by adopting methods that I find unacceptable. If the *best* argument one could make from our Constitution is to say that somewhere, somehow there *must* be a tacit postulate ensuring that grandmothers don't get thrown into jail for living with the wrong grandchildren, I'd say we need a constitutional amendment to protect grandmothers. But I would not necessarily be prepared to protect them under *this* Constitution.

Fortunately, that is not the best available argument. For here we do have a text: the Due Process Clause of the Fourteenth Amendment. It says that "[n]o State shall . . . deprive any person of life, liberty, or property, without due process of law." For a long time, the Supreme Court has agreed — and all nine members of the Court as of mid-1987 agreed — that this clause entails at least *some* substantive protection as well as protection for fair procedure.[107]

And, perhaps even more helpfully, we have another portion of the Fourteenth Amendment: "No State shall make or enforce any law which shall abridge the privileges or immunities of citizens of

---

[106] *Nevada v. Hall*, 440 U.S. 410, 433 (1979) (Rehnquist, J., joined by Burger, C.J., dissenting).

[107] See *Turner v. Safley*, 107 S. Ct. 2254, 2265 (1987) (unanimously striking down a virtually total ban on marriage by prison inmates, stating that "the decision to marry is a fundamental right," even for prisoners).

the United States." It is true that, over a century ago, in the *Slaughterhouse Cases*, the Court emptied that language of nearly all its meaning.[108] The Court there held that this clause means only that, when one is exercising a right that is especially related to the federal structure, like the right to travel to Washington, D.C., to present grievances against the federal government, one is protected — a strained and strange reading indeed. The history makes quite clear that the "privileges or immunities" of United States citizenship were not meant to be limited to rights bearing peculiarly on one's relationship to the national government. They were supposed to refer to *some* set of fundamental human rights, and we still have to decide what those are.[109]

Some people have been willing to say that the privileges or immunities of United States citizenship include only those rights that are mentioned in the Bill of Rights. Such readers would construe the enumeration of certain rights in the Bill of Rights to deny or disparage others retained by the people. The framers were afraid the Bill of Rights might boomerang in exactly that way. But these statesmen were farsighted fellows. James Madison, in fact, proposed the Ninth Amendment for just that purpose — to deal with exactly that boomerang; the history shows clearly that this is why he proposed it.[110] The Ninth Amendment says: "The enumeration in the Constitution of certain rights shall not be construed to deny or disparage others retained by the people."

Now notice: the Ninth Amendment does not *create* any rights of its own force. Those who talk of "Ninth Amendment rights" are making a kind of category error. The Ninth Amendment

---

[108] 83 U.S. (16 Wall.) 36 (1873).

[109] See Tribe, *American Constitutional Law*, § 7–2, pp. 548–53.

[110] See, e.g., *Richmond Newspapers, Inc. v. Virginia*, 448 U.S. 555, 579–80 and n. 15 (1980) (plurality opinion of Burger, C.J.); Ely, *Democracy and Distrust*, 34–41; Redlich, "Are There 'Certain Rights . . . Retained by the People?'," 37 *N.Y.U. L. Rev.* 787, 810–12 (1962).

creates and confers no rights; it is a rule of interpretation. It is the *only* rule of interpretation explicitly stated in the Constitution, and it tells us that, whatever else you're going to do to explain why "liberty" does not include the grandmother's right to live with her grandchild — whatever else you're going to say to conclude that the "privileges or immunities" of national citizenship do not include the right to use contraceptives — you *cannot* advance the argument that those rights are not there just because they're not enumerated in the Bill of Rights.

Lots of people have avoided relying on the Ninth Amendment, perhaps fearing how much it might unleash. But recall my argument in the first lecture that it is illegitimate to subtract something from the Constitution just because it's out of phase with your vision of the overall plan. You may not *like* the Ninth Amendment, but it's *there*. In 1965 Justice Arthur J. Goldberg, concurring in the Connecticut birth control case, relied on the Ninth Amendment as a rule of construction.[111] And in 1980, when I argued the *Richmond Newspapers* case in the Supreme Court, on the issue of whether the First Amendment guarantees the press and the public a right of access to criminal trials, I relied primarily on the First Amendment.[112] But I thought it hard to argue that the freedom of speech is involved when people want to observe a trial and when the speakers at that trial, including the prosecutor and the accused, want it to occur in private. Freedom of speech does not include the right to hear something that a speaker doesn't want you to hear. So it was my sense that the freedom of speech argument was not conclusive in *Richmond Newspapers*, and I therefore relied in part on the Ninth Amendment. In the only other Supreme Court opinion to date relying on the Ninth Amendment, Chief Justice Burger, writing for a plurality of the Court, treated the Ninth Amendment as supporting

[111] *Griswold v. Connecticut*, 381 U.S. 479, 486–93 (1965) (Goldberg, J., joined by Warren, C.J., and Brennan, J., concurring).

[112] *Richmond Newspapers, Inc. v. Virginia*, 448 U.S. 555 (1980).

the existence of a presumed right of the press and the public to be present at criminal trials.[113]

But there has never been a Supreme Court *majority* opinion relying on the Ninth Amendment. And, despite its unique place in the Constitution as the only rule of interpretation in that entire document, quite a few people don't take it very seriously. Senator Charles E. Grassley of Iowa, for example, during the confirmation hearings on Justice Rehnquist's elevation to be chief justice, questioned the future chief about this issue and said, "do not smile when I refer to the Ninth Amendment." I was watching — Justice Rehnquist wasn't smiling at that point. But the senator assumed that the Ninth Amendment wouldn't be taken seriously.

Senator Grassley continued: "I would like to focus on . . . the protection of unenumerated rights for just a minute. No specific right is actually mentioned in that amendment as you obviously know. Exactly what specific rights do you think the framers intended to protect under [the Ninth] Amendment?" Justice Rehnquist recalled the concurrence by Justice Goldberg in the *Griswold* case. And he also recalled the case of *Bowers v. Hardwick*, the Georgia sodomy case that had been decided exactly a month earlier.[114] As to the *Hardwick* case, Justice Rehnquist said, "[I] forget whether the Ninth Amendment was directly involved, but it was the same type of case." [115] Indeed, it was much the same type of case, and the Ninth Amendment *was* very much involved. Justice Rehnquist concluded in his answer to the senator, "I just feel I can't answer as to my personal views because I have participated in some cases and they are bound to come up again." [116]

---

[113] Ibid., 579–80 (plurality opinion of Burger, C.J., joined by White and Stevens, JJ.).

[114] 106 S. Ct. 2841 (1986).

[115] Transcript of the Hearings before the Senate Judiciary Committee on the Nomination of William H. Rehnquist to be chief justice of the United States, July 30, 1986, pp. 181–83.

[116] Ibid., 183.

Of course, you don't need to look at his answer to that question in order to know where he stands on this issue. Chief Justice Rehnquist has persistently dissented from the entire line of privacy decisions and, in fact, he joined Justice White's majority opinion in the *Hardwick* case, where the Court held that the state of Georgia could criminalize consensual adult sodomy in private — at least where homosexual conduct was involved — without giving any reason beyond its moral revulsion to that act.[117]

The majority opinion for the Court in that case is worth pausing over briefly, because it could be the harbinger of an overruling of the entire line of privacy decisions going back to the 1920s. Attorney General Meese, in the cover story about him in a 1986 issue of the *New York Times Magazine*, is quoted as saying that the Reagan administration regards the Georgia sodomy decision as its major victory of the Supreme Court's 1985 term — even though it had not been a party to the case and had filed no brief.[118]

The reason the Reagan administration regards that ruling as a major victory is that the majority opinion explicitly adopts the theory that the administration has advanced for overruling *Roe v. Wade* — the theory that was accepted completely by Justice White

---

[117] The role of the Ninth Amendment in constitutional jurisprudence gained major public currency subsequent to the delivery of the lectures on which this essay is based, in the hearings before the Senate Judiciary Committee on the nomination of Robert H. Bork to be an associate justice of the Supreme Court, held in September and October of 1987. A number of senators on the committee and experts who appeared before it, including the author of this essay, criticized Judge Bork for his continued refusal to acknowledge the Constitution's protection of unenumerated rights, and his statement that the Ninth Amendment appears so uncertain in meaning that it should be regarded as a "water blot" or "inkblot" on the document. The issue of Judge Bork's attitude toward the Ninth Amendment was so central to debate over the nomination that it led to an unusually extensive dialogue between the *Wall Street Journal* editorial board and the author of this essay. See "Biden's Spite," *Wall St. J.*, Sept. 24, 1987, p. 26, col. 1 (editorial); "Reply and Rebuttal on Bork," *Wall St. J.*, Oct. 5, 1987, p. 23, col. 1 (letter of Laurence Tribe); "The Bork Disinformers," *Wall St. J.*, Oct. 5, 1987, p. 22, col. 1 (editorial); "More on the Ninth Amendment," *Wall St. J.*, Oct. 7, 1987, p. 35, col. 1 (letter of Laurence Tribe, followed by editor's note).

[118] "Mr. Power: Attorney General Edwin Meese," *New York Times*, Oct. 12, 1986, § 6, pp. 18, 92.

in dissent from the 1986 *Thornburgh* case,[119] where the Court refused to overrule *Roe v. Wade*. The theory was that such unenumerated rights as privacy really do not deserve much protection. Justice White, in dissenting from *Thornburgh* and then again in writing for the majority in *Hardwick*, said that the Court is on pretty firm ground when it protects rights spelled out in the Bill of Rights, but when it comes to these unenumerated rights, the Court really shouldn't do much, because it opens itself to the accusation that it is just imposing its values on the people of the United States.[120]

In my view, the Supreme Court must *always* try to avoid imposing its values on the people. But refusing to recognize a right so as to protect the Court's reputation against such accusations seems very much like what Dean Jesse Choper advocated in the position I criticized in the first lecture — that the Court shouldn't protect states' rights and shouldn't protect the separation of powers, because in that way it can build up a store of capital that it can use to protect unpopular personal rights. I do not think it is legitimate to read the Constitution from the perspective of maximizing the Court's political clout.

It seems to me that, if the Court refuses to protect a particular right of personal privacy on the ground that it's not quite as traditional, not quite as widely approved by the majority, as are the family rights that have been protected from the 1920s through the 1977 grandmother case, then it is effectively giving these unenumerated rights *less* protection than the provisions of the Bill of Rights get. Those provisions protect rights *from* majorities. They are protected *most* when they are least popular. To say that a right has to have a majority of the country behind it before it gets protection when it's not one of the explicitly enumerated

[119] *Thornburgh v. American College of Obstetricians and Gynecologists*, 106 S. Ct. 2169 (1986).

[120] Ibid., 2194 (White, J., joined by Rehnquist, J., dissenting); 106 S. Ct. 2844, 2846 (*Hardwick*).

rights is surely to disparage the right *because* it's not enumerated. The word "disparage" is derived from an old French verb meaning "to marry out of the peerage or beneath one's social class." To say that unenumerated rights deserve protection only when enough people think those rights ought to be protected is to relegate them to a distinctly lower and more suspect status.

In the *Hardwick* case, by a five-to-four vote the Court refused to find a right of privacy protective of the sexual activity at issue there. It turns out that Justice Powell initially voted *with* the right of privacy in *Hardwick* but then changed his vote, as he admitted in a public speech to the American Bar Association shortly after the decision was announced.[121] The Court in effect held that the state of Georgia has no obligation to say anything beyond "we find this conduct immoral." What we end up with is an unstable line between some kinds of privacy and others, not a line turning on the existence of commerce or of coercion or of demonstrable harm but a line turning on popular approval.

Obviously I'm not an unbiased observer of the *Hardwick* case; of the three cases that I have lost in the Supreme Court, that is the one I find hardest to accept — not because I thought I would win (I was too realistic for that) but because I at least hoped the Court would offer a reasoned explanation for the line that it drew. The Court ended up drawing a line between the traditional intimacies that were protected by the contraception decisions, and the less traditional intimacies — at least when homosexuals were involved — that it regarded as being at issue in the Georgia case. What of the same acts of sodomy involving heterosexuals? It is unclear what the law is in such a case, for the Court thereafter denied review in a case from Oklahoma involving the same acts by people of different sexes.[122]

---

[121] See "Powell Changed Vote in Sodomy Case," *Washington Post*, July 13, 1986, p. A1, col. 4.

[122] *Post v. State*, 715 P.2d 1105 (Okla. Cr. 1986), *reh'g denied*, 717 P.2d 1151 (1986), *cert. denied*, 107 S. Ct. 290 (1986).

What emerges is a largely arbitrary fiat. The Court will protect unenumerated, traditional, family-oriented rights, even outside of marriage — as in the case of *Eisenstadt v. Baird*.[123] It will protect such rights even among unmarried teenagers, as in a case from New York, *Carey v. Population Services International*.[124] But anatomical combinations that do not seem as traditional to the Court will not be protected. Somewhere among the "tacit postulates" of the Constitution there is apparently an anatomical catalog which the Court consults.

That seems to me the wrong way to go about developing principles of privacy. The right way, I think, would be to ask whether the Constitution's textual commitment to privacy of the home, strongly evidenced by the Third Amendment and the Fourth Amendment, and its textual commitment to freedom of assembly, which the Court has had little difficulty extending to freedom of association under the First Amendment, together create a zone of privacy for associational intimacies in the home — not a zone of total immunity from government regulation but a zone that the state cannot enter without special justification. I think that was the issue — and I don't think it should depend on which body parts are involved, or on whether the individuals are of the same sex or of different sexes.

So how about our hypothetical? The city says: "We find it immoral for a family not to have at least one meal a month as a family. We find it repellent that they can't get together for at least one meal a month." My prediction is that the Supreme Court would strike down that local ordinance. There would be several justices who would wring their hands and probably dissent, but there would be a majority to hold the law unconstitutional. As

[123] 405 U.S. 438 (1972).

[124] 431 U.S. 678 (1977) (invalidating ban on sale or distribution by any person of contraceptives to children under age sixteen, along with a ban on sale or distribution by anyone but a licensed pharmacist to persons age sixteen).

Thomas Grey wrote in a 1980 article deftly titled, "Eros, Civilization, and the Burger Court":

> [T]he Court has consistently protected traditional familial institutions, bonds and authority against the centrifugal forces of an anomic modern society. Where less traditional values have been directly protected, conspicuously in the cases involving contraception and abortion, the decisions reflect not any Millian glorification of diverse individuality, but the stability-centered concerns of moderate conservative family and population policy.[125]

The observation is a realistic one. But I regard such an approach as standing for something very different from constitutional interpretation. I do not think that the basic liberties, or the privileges and immunities of national citizenship, should be defined by a Court applying the views of the Mayo Clinic or of Planned Parenthood, whether or not one regards those views as socially enlightened. My method would be to draw on other parts of the text, coupled with history. In a landmark 1962 article about the Ninth Amendment, Dean Norman Redlich of New York University proposed looking to the *rest* of the Constitution's text to see what *sorts* of unenumerated rights the framers might have been concerned not to deny or disparage.[126] If we look at the First, Third, and Fourth Amendments, they suggest a tacit postulate with a textual root — namely, that consensual intimacies in the home are presumptively protected as a privilege of United States citizens.

In fact, the framers took for granted such "natural rights," as they would have called them, as the right to marry anyone who consents. Francis Hutcheson, father of the Scottish Enlighten-

---

[125] Grey, "Eros, Civilization, and the Burger Court," 43 *Law and Contemp. Probs.* 83, 90 (Summer 1980).

[126] See Redlich, "Are There 'Certain Rights . . . Retained by the People?'," 810–12.

ment, put it that way in a widely read eighteenth-century tract.[127] And it turns out that James Madison attended a series of lectures by John Witherspoon of Princeton, who was lecturing, based on the work of Hutcheson, about things like the right to marriage. He treated that as a special case of a right to associate if you so incline with any person you can persuade.[128] It seems to me that this historical background, when linked to the explicit textual protections for the home and for assembly, provides a plausible basis for affirming the Supreme Court's privacy decisions from the 1920s through 1977, and for concluding that those decisions are right and that *Hardwick* is probably wrong.

What, then, about the hardest case of all? For me, that remains *Roe v. Wade*, upholding a woman's right to end her pregnancy until the fetus is viable. I think it's worth asking what makes that case especially difficult. It is not the argument that the woman's side of the equation should find *no* protection in the Constitution. I think those who have said that the Court just *invented* the woman's right to bodily integrity out of whole cloth cannot have been attentive to legal developments with respect to personal privacy dating to the 1920s.[129] I would suppose that protecting your ability to control your own body would have to be on *anyone's* short list of basic liberties or privileges and immunities in our system of government. It took no great leap beyond the 1942 sterilization case and the contraception cases to say that the woman's interest in avoiding what is, after all, *involuntary* pregnancy — a pregnancy she either did not want in the first place or once wanted but no longer wants to continue — is fundamental, not to be taken lightly.[130]

[127] See Richards, *Toleration and the Constitution*, 232–33. The tract was *A System of Moral Philosophy* (1755).

[128] See Richards, *Toleration and the Constitution*, 233. See also Karst, "The Freedom of Intimate Association," 89 *Yale L.J.* 624, 667–73 (1980).

[129] See, e.g., Ely, "Wages of Crying Wolf," 927–37.

[130] *Skinner v. Oklahoma*, 316 U.S. 535 (1942) (sterilization); *Eisenstadt v. Baird*, 405 U.S. 438 (1972); *Griswold v. Connecticut*, 381 U.S. 479 (1965) (contraception).

I think what makes *Roe v. Wade* extraordinarily difficult is
the question: Why cannot the state *nonetheless* restrict this fundamental liberty in the interest of protecting the unborn? It is quite
clear, of course, that the framers of the Fourteenth Amendment
did not think of fetuses as persons, entitled to special protection.
Indeed, the amendment includes in its definition of "citizens"
"[a]ll persons *born* . . . in the United States." [131] But so what?
The state can surely take note of the fact that fetuses soon *will*
be "citizens," and that some persons *think* of them as already
entitled to the protections of personhood. So why cannot a state
act on that perception, however controversial it may be?

I think part of the answer — and I'm not sure that I have yet
found a satisfactory resolution — may lie in the *uniqueness* of the
resulting impositions on women. Senator E. J. Garn of Utah commented in 1986, when donating a kidney to his daughter, that
"[h]er mother carried her for nine months, and I am honored to
give her part of me." [132] I thought that his was a moving, feeling,
admirable remark. But notice: the law did not *compel* Senator
Garn to donate his kidney in order to keep even his own offspring
alive. And yet, if his "pro-life" views on abortion prevailed, the
law would have *compelled* his wife to remain pregnant over her
objection. It seems to me that, if the Supreme Court was justified
in protecting women from being compelled by law to remain
pregnant, the justification draws support not only from traditional
notions of liberty but also from the textual command of equal protection of the laws. Without some such equality argument, *Roe
v. Wade* would probably have been unwarranted.

Some would say that, because this equality argument is so difficult to make, and because such strong and incommensurable
values are arrayed on both sides, the correct solution is to pass
the buck to the states. Why not simply let each state decide for
itself? Fetuses would have superior rights in some states, women

---

[131] Amend. XIV, § 1 (emphasis added).
[132] *New York Times*, Sept. 10, 1986, p. A13, col. 1.

would have them in others. That could well mean that the state of Utah, if it wished, not only could have forced Senator Garn's wife to carry her pregnancy to term against her will; it also could have forced her to *terminate* the pregnancy against her will, as they do in China. If the Constitution's silence on the balance between the rights of the woman and those of the unborn means that the entire matter should be resolved by the states, that may be a knife that cuts both ways.

In this entire area, and in all of the related areas that bio-medical technology is bound to serve up as problems for the constitutional allocation of decision-making authority—whether with respect to organ transplants or surrogate parenthood or the prolongation of life or the protection of defective newborns — in all of these areas, the option of simply *extracting* constitutional argument from the picture, and passing the buck to someone else, is nonexistent. Even deciding that the matter should be left for the states to decide is nonetheless a decision. Deciding that the fate of fetuses or of women or of organ donors should be left to the local majority in each state is a fateful and an important decision. It might be justified, but it's not a nondecision.

And *if* such a decision is made, then it just postpones the question which every state legislator who takes an oath to uphold the Constitution must ask himself or herself: What does the Constitution permit or compel me to do in this area? Does it permit me to override this or that freedom of choice? Does it permit me to decree the death of this or that person or future person?

These are profoundly troubling questions. The fact that there is disagreement about them, as I have suggested earlier, doesn't mean that, in talking about them, we are somehow getting beyond the outer limits of interpretation. For there is disagreement even at the very core of constitutional provisions. What the difficulty of these issues *does* tell us is that courts would do well to proceed with caution and humility — to avoid the rush to sweeping, global, across-the-board solutions.

It is in this respect that I think the Supreme Court in hindsight may be criticized for its performance in *Roe v. Wade*. The Court's sweeping, quite legislative, trimesterized solution — going vastly beyond the facts of the case before it — subjected it to severe criticism. After all, the record in the case, although one wouldn't know it from reading the Court's opinion, indicated that the woman involved had apparently been the victim of a gang rape (a claim she retracted in 1987), and yet the state of Texas had required even her to carry her pregnancy to term. Surely the Court could have said that, in those circumstances, it violated her rights to be forced to remain pregnant; the Court could have left for another day the difficult problems of line-drawing among degrees and sources of involuntariness.

Apart from the advice of going slow — of proceeding by a common-law-like method of case-by-case formulation and re-formulation — is there anything more that can be said about these tragic choices, these truly difficult puzzles? I think there is. I think we can urge one another, along with the judges who bear a special responsibility in constitutional matters, to engage in rea-soned conversation with as open a set of minds as we can possibly muster. I do not think we should lament the close divisions within the Court over the most difficult issues. I think we should instead welcome the opportunity that such divisions create for a dialogue within the Court that is visible outside its walls. I think a great opportunity is wasted when the justices talk past one another rather than grappling seriously with the divergent premises and perspectives that the nine of them bring to the interpretive mis-sion. As I indicated in the first lecture, the Constitution *itself* embodies a multitude of irreconcilable differences.

Thus I believe that we should welcome forthright clashes within the Court and should resist anything that would tend to homogenize its membership or tilt the entire tribunal too uni-formly in any one direction. Of course, it's sometimes nice to have a clear majority opinion, and many lawyers and lower-court judges are sometimes confused by the multiplicity of voices. Sometimes, as in *Brown v. Board of Education*, it is crucial that the Court speak with unanimity. And in some contexts like the military, it may be important for there to be less dissent than elsewhere.

But there are higher values than that of clear signals from the top. And one of those higher values is the open ventilation of conflicting views on the meaning of the Constitution, both as a way of engaging the nation in debate and as a way of modeling what such a debate at its best can be. To have a chance to add one's voice to that process — as a teacher and scholar commenting on constitutional issues, and as an advocate arguing constitutional cases — seems to me to be among life's greatest honors.

*On Hippocrates, Thomas Jefferson
and Max Weber:
The Bureaucratic, Technologic Imperatives
and the Future of the Healing Tradition
in a Voluntary Society*

ROGER J. BULGER

THE TANNER LECTURES ON HUMAN VALUES

Delivered at
Clare Hall, Cambridge University

March 9 and 10, 1987

ROGER J. BULGER, M.D., has been president and chief executive officer of the Association of Academic Health Centers in Washington, D.C., since February 1, 1988. For the nearly ten years prior to that, he was president of The University of Texas Health Science Center at Houston.

A native of New York City, Dr. Bulger earned his M.D. degree at Harvard Medical School in 1960.

A year after his appointment to the faculty at the University of Washington in Seattle in 1966, Dr. Bulger was appointed assistant dean for clinical affairs at the medical school and medical director of the University of Washington Hospital.

In 1970 Dr. Bulger joined the Duke University Medical Center as associate dean for medical education and chief of the Division of Allied Health Professions.

In 1972 Dr. Bulger began a four-year association with the Institute of Medicine of the National Academy of Sciences, serving as its executive officer and as acting president for extended periods of time between presidents. During the same time, he was professor of medicine at the George Washington University School of Medicine in Washington, D.C.

From 1976–78, Dr. Bulger was chancellor, dean of the medical school, and professor of medicine and of family and community medicine at the University of Massachusetts in Worcester.

During the past fifteen years, he has written widely on and been active in various health policy initiatives. He has authored many articles and two books, the most recent of which is *In Search of the Modern Hippocrates* (1987).

It is of course a marvelous honor and challenge to be asked to deliver the Tanner Lectures, to follow in the footsteps of such distinguished predecessors and to, in fact, participate for even such a brief period in the spectacular intellectual life of this great university. The intent of the Tanner series is to examine important issues from the perspective of human values, which in turn requires the examiner to reach beyond his discipline or specialty; it is for this stimulation that I am most appreciative of this opportunity.

It is my purpose to reflect upon the current status of health care and health policy in the United States, exploring some essential human values considerations with an eye toward the future and the possibility of attaining the highest quality humanistic health care. In this attempt to ascertain where we Americans have been in health care delivery, where we are, and where we might be going, there will be ample opportunity for me to make comparisons with the situation here in Great Britain. However, I shall not yield to those temptations, trusting that my colleagues in their commentaries will take on the challenge of comparative examinations of the British system. Many Americans have what I call the Alexis de Tocqueville Syndrome, which is founded in deep envy of that wonderful Frenchman who came to America in the mid-nineteenth century and described it peerlessly. The patient suffering from the de Tocqueville Syndrome is characterized by an extraordinary certainty that he or she fully understands another culture or another nation after having been there for a few weeks or months or even a few years. The most severely afflicted believe they know how to solve all of the major problems in the other country and are annoyingly outspoken in their efforts to enunciate those solutions for all to hear. During my years at Emmanuel College in 1955, I received a permanent immunization to the de Tocqueville Syndrome. Thus, I trust you will understand why I shall limit myself to occasional observations about differences in health care between England and the United States and shall leave the value judgments and things I don't know about to others.

This lecture is an attempt at an interpretive analyis of the current and future American health care delivery system with all its problems and challenges. Inevitably, there will be comparisons made with the British system, but it is important to note at the onset that the inevitable cross-cultural thinking I have had to do in preparation has led me to a deeper appreciation of differences between the two countries.

I seek not to preach a kind of societal moral relativism; rather, I seek only to observe that in contrast to the British, Americans currently give more weight to individual choice than to fairness of distribution of health services. In 1981, Kingman Brewster defined "the Voluntary Society" (which included the United Kingdom and the United States) as one which permitted the lives of its citizens to be as voluntary as possible.[1] For Brewster, as probably for most of us, freedom of the individual is the cornerstone of both our nations. But for Americans, newly arrived in a rough and inhospitable world, the Declaration of Independence held out something more — "certain unalienable rights . . . life, liberty and the pursuit of happiness."

There are two other basic values worth remembering about the foundations of the values of America: the first is that people didn't come to America because they were rich, satisfied with their lot, and happy; and the second is that people didn't come to America because they were in love with governments. Thus, no matter how bad the ghetto into which the American immigrant arrived, there was never a doubt that he or she or the children would be able to get out — hope for a better tomorrow seems

[1] Kingman Brewster, "The Voluntary Society," in *The Tanner Lectures on Human Values*, vol. 4 (Salt Lake City: University of Utah Press, 1983).

encoded in our genes. Also, the early Americans hated governments; in 1987, the distrust of centralized power is almost as strongly felt by many Americans toward Washington, D.C., as it was by those Americans of two hundred years ago toward England.

As our restless people dealt with frustration, loneliness, failure, or unhappiness by pushing ever westward to new frontiers, there grew over generations the belief that one could *always do* something to improve one's lot, that life would get better and better for each generation, that the technological genius of each generation would increase humankind's capacity to control nature. As the frontiers closed, the American quest for a better future turned toward science and technology; our new frontier led to the land of "things," most recently high-technology "things." To our dismay, our land of things has not brought happiness, even when individual liberty is preserved and even when individual choice is emphasized; cultural boredom, anomie, personal meaninglessness, and narcissism seem to be gaining on us. Countering these forces are the advocates for personal development, for the creation of a competent citizenry instead of a cloying consumerism — and again self-determination for the individual is a value on the rise in America.

It is at least partly in this context that a revolution in health care delivery is upon us. In my view, any health care enterprise of the future must be in tune with these basic American values. That is, twenty-first-century health care in the American version of the Voluntary Society must begin with the idea of allowing the individual to fulfill his or her potential as a person, of providing freedom of choice wherever possible, of keeping alive the hope of a new beginning, of repair or reconstruction if disease should strike. It should not be under the total control of the central government. The inefficiencies which might come from a system which emphasizes diversity should also allow some room for the development of new technologies, which offer hope even though they might not be cost-effective on other grounds.

Having thus established the principal societal values which should be held inviolable in the development of health policies, let us now turn to the great ideas shaping the modern health enterprise in Western democracies. I have chosen to group these ideas within one or the other of two major themes to be considered: (1) the theme of the healer, which can be referred to as the Hippocratic theme; and (2) the theme of the organizing and financing of the delivery of health services, which will be referred to as the bureaucratic theme. It is my view that the values inherent in the Hippocratic theme are coming increasingly into conflict with the values inherent in the bureaucratic theme. I shall discuss each of the themes separately in an effort better to understand and to articulate the thematic values essential to each. It should then be easier to understand the nature and to anticipate the seriousness of conflicts arising out of value clashes emanating from these two roots.

Central to the action at the interface between these two themes over the next decade will be an ongoing debate over how to ration or allocate scarce resources. For me, Guido Calabresi and Philip Bobbitt, in their book *Tragic Choices*, have elucidated the most fruitful conceptualization of this range of issues.[2] In order to illustrate the intertwining and interrelatedness of these various threads in the fabric of our unfolding future, I sometimes imagine an ongoing quadrilateral discussion involving Thomas Jefferson (representing the values of the Voluntary Society), Hippocrates (representing the modern, scientific healer), Max Weber (representing the necessary bureaucratization of modern society), and Guido Calabresi and Philip Bobbitt (representing the inherently tragic nature of making choices).

---

[2] Guido Calabresi and Philip Bobbitt, *Tragic Choices* (New York: Norton, 1978).

THE HIPPOCRATIC THEME

The oath of Hippocrates means more to the American public and the average American patient than many physicians realize. This ancient oath, containing so many particulars which most young, modern physicians do not believe, remains the bedrock of the commitment made each year by thousands of graduating medical students. Most thoughtful physicians who have reflected on its meaning conclude that the ancient oath remains popular late in the twentieth century precisely because it proclaims a commitment to the best interests of the patient and to high professional competence. Now we think that Hippocrates did not write the oath and probably wouldn't have subscribed to a lot of it. Healing up to Hippocrates' time involved talking, praying, and blatant shamanism; and Hippocrates was vehemently against all that. Occasionally, doctors would be hired to end a life, with or without the patient's consent; but Hippocrates based his healing on a natural philosophy that placed humankind in harmony with nature rather than in control of it; he based his interventions on observation, practicality, proof, and the constant self-warning not to do harm to the patient. His science was dedicated firmly to the patient's welfare. The physician sought honor through doing right by the sick person. No longer could the physician be hired to poison someone or to become a purposeful agent of death. He eschewed words as therapeutic, calling medicine the silent art. His written descriptions of some of his cases are masterpieces in clinical observation and deduction. He was thus the father of scientific medicine.

Pedro Lain Entralgo, the well-known Spanish psychiatrist, traced the history of the spoken word in therapy during the past three millennia.[3] Of course, the blossoming of the therapy of the word came with Freud. Lain Entralgo points out, in fact, that

[3] Pedro Lain Entralgo, *The Therapy of the Word in Classical Antiquity* (New Haven: Yale University Press, 1970).

Aristotle understood the essentials of psychiatry's roots and even advocated the therapeutic value of the audiences' emotional catharsis through attending the tragedies of the theater. He attributes the greater than two-thousand-year wait for the Freudian insights to the severe proscriptions of Hippocrates and his followers against the use of the word shamanism and cheering speech in the medical model. This is not the place to attempt a history of psychiatry since Freud, but it is fair to say that psychoanalysis and psychotherapy by and large have traveled a separate road from mainstream medical practice, with psychosomatic medicine serving for many years as a somewhat insecure bridge between the more biochemically oriented mainstream and the softer sciences of Freudian psychiatry.

In the past two decades, however, the revolutionary advances in the neurosciences have brought mind and body, emotion and molecule together in ways that tend to give words a new therapeutic currency. Instead of the handful of neurochemicals known in the 1960s to function in the brain, it is now clear that our brain is an extraordinary pharmacy, able to modulate a situation with great precision in response to a wide variety of stimuli. It is now clear that doctoring is more than deciding which medicine to use to help a patient; the best doctors will work to create an environment in which the patient can allow his or her own therapeutic capacities to work.

Possibly, the well-known placebo effect is the best example of this; fully 30 percent of patients in certain situations will report significant improvement when given something they believe is curative but which in effect is physiologically inert. One well-known cardiologist claims that, if he can meet at the hospital emergency room one of his patients suffering from an acute heart attack and tell him or her that everything is under control and will be all right, then he can dispense with the usual dose of morphine, presumably because the patient's own endorphins have taken over.

The reverse is also true; words can have adverse effects. Words and actions that distress, anger, or upset a seriously ill person can be a negative force on the healing process. Doctors who used to belong to the most mechanistically inclined groups now can envision in molecular terms why one can get better results by establishing and maintaining a trust relationship with one's patients, or why a destroyed and distrustful relationship can contribute to a less than optimal result in addition to a malpractice suit. Scholars like Erik Erikson, who analyze the nature of the therapeutic relation now have more heed paid to them; body language, non-verbal and verbal communication skills, and interviewing techniques are getting more and more attention from a profession which for too long has been restricted by an unnecessarily narrow biochemical vision and a scientific gestalt that kept it from fully utilizing approaches the results of which couldn't be adequately explained in molecular terms. Even now, the laying on of hands inherent in the manipulations of osteopaths and chiropractors are in my view sadly undervalued by traditional medicine, both for the direct benefits of muscle relaxation and neuromuscular relief and for the indirect benefits of direct contact with the caring hands of a concerned and competent professional. A tension headache is better cured by muscles relaxed by a healer's hands than by Valium.

America is a less authoritarian place than most other countries. Still, in years past, one did what the doctor ordered, and one did it just because the doctor said to. The therapeutic relationship rested on a trust built upon a perception of the doctor's competence and an acceptance that the doctor knew best. Many forces in our society have worked against this aspect of the doctor-patient relationship. Malpractice suits have become more and more prominent, underscoring the fallibility of the doctor; public education and sophistication about things medical have led patients to have more doubts and ask more questions; health and medical affairs have become important media items such that currently most newspapers across the United States print in featured articles the gist of the most important articles published that day in the leading medical journals, sometimes two or three days before the doctor even receives the journal in the mail.

Two major forces of the bureaucratic theme are working against the therapeutic relationship, so central to the Hippocratic theme. They are the adversarial relationship so characteristic of the legal profession in the United States and the growing bureaucratic perception that the doctor should be the rationer of health care. How can you be the patient's friend and trusted advocate while being a potential adversary and rationer at the same time?

In the early 1960s the doctrine of informed consent swept into American medicine through the clinical research window but has had since then a far-reaching effect on the day-to-day practice of medicine, where patients are required to sign documents that indicate that they have had explained to them all the details of side effects and costs and benefits of a proposed intervention before such is undertaken.

The American courts have reached into the medical record, exposing every detail to public scrutiny in nasty malpractice cases; increasingly over the past decade there have emerged serious proponents of giving the patients their own medical records, an approach which certainly requires a tactful write-up, but an honest one, by the doctor. Influential physicians began to advocate telling the cold truth to all patients about their condition, albeit they might advocate telling them in a humane and warmly sensitive way. Advocates of this approach point to the growing literature from dying patients, a literature which describes the isolation and degradation of the terminal patient, made all the worse by the doctor's denial of the truth. There are many examples of dramatic alterations in patient behavior after having someone tell them the truth; the American patient dying of cancer will generally prefer a doctor who will tell him or her the truth and will stick with him or her through thick or thin until the end over a doctor who adopts a falsely cheerful attitude, never speaking about the disease or the likely outcome and distancing him or herself emotionally from the real situation of the patient. The belief has grown in American medicine that this candor about death, once so seldom practiced here, has allowed death with dignity to become more standard.

Candor and truthfulness have spilled over into all elements of the doctor-patient relationship to the extent that Sissela Bok believes that giving placebos is dishonest, deceitful, and ultimately destructive to the patient and to medicine.[4] Although not everyone fully accepts Bok's rather purist approach to these points, most people now believe that candor, honesty, full disclosure, and openness on the part of the physician form the basis of that special trust which is central to the formation of the desired therapeutic relationship.

With unquestioned physician authority essentially a thing of the past, clearly and continually demonstrated integrity is required. The authoritarian nature of the doctor-patient relationship has so diminished as an operative mode in America that a popular newswriter recently referred to her new doctor as George Smith, J.P., where the J.P. stands for junior partner. Her doctor presents her with options, information, decision trees, statistical probabilities, side effects of proposed medications, both relatively benign and downright terrifying. Her J.P. also teaches her how to live "healthfully."

Although there is obviously great overlapping of values shared by the American and British medical professions, this matter of informed consent may be a key difference between them. In America, largely as a result of the informed-consent movement and court opinions, the pendulum has swung from the doctor to the patient as the decision maker. Repeatedly, the courts have punished doctors in malpractice decisions for not recognizing that the

---

[4] Sissela Bok, *Lying and Moral Choice* (New York: Vintage Books-Random House, 1979).

patient is in charge and in fact needs to know all the known, salient details about his case. The argument for "informed consent" in America rests on the "liberty interests" of the individual as defined only twenty-five years ago by our judiciary, making it a complex matter to reverse this new American tilt toward the patient as captain of the ship.[5] The Supreme Court has decided that in fact the medical record belongs to the patient. In Britain, on the other hand, the Sidaway case in December 1984 produced a decision that left the doctor essentially in charge of the information flow to the patient; in England the doctor is still firmly in charge, required to tell the patient no more than is customary.

A further ramification of the informed-consent movement in the United States was indicated by Charles Begley, an American health economist, who concluded in a recent essay, "A prospective payment system that asked physicians to allocate limited resources may not be able to tolerate the patient-oriented doctrine of informed consent." [6] Certainly, the National Health Service (NHS) is essentially a prospective payment system; if Begley is correct, one might expect that, should an American-sized informed-consent movement strike England, there will emerge increasing conflict in the system.

Although it may be stretching the point, the informed-consent movement seems connected to the move to recapture citizen competence, to reassert the individual's responsibility for his or her own health and welfare, and to emphasize that the next great advances in the improvement of the health status of the American people would be made through education and behavior modification. Although these efforts at health promotion and disease prevention are society-wide, it is clear that the family or primary physician is a very important player. More and more doctors,

---

[5] Jay Katz, *The Silent World of Doctor and Patient* (New York: Free Press, 1984).

[6] Charles E. Begley, "Prospective Payment and Medical Ethics," *Journal of Medicine and Philosophy* 12 (1987): 107–22.

previously disease and treatment oriented, appreciate these days that some of their most effective contributions come in the prevention areas.

The whole nation takes pride in our improving statistics in lung cancer, cardiac disease, stroke, and hypertension. We know that, with the exception of lung cancer, the reasons for the advances are not clear. We believe in general, however, that the movement to individual responsibility for one's own health is important. In my view, this movement is not unconnected with the informed-consent movement and the general effort to demythologize the physician and to reduce his or her power and influence. Although this outcome of or association with the informed-consent movement must be recognized as highly positive, it is also true that, viewed strictly from the perspective of the Hippocratic healing tradition, the informed-consent movement may not prove to have been universally positive.

THE BUREAUCRATIC THEME

Policy-making in America can be characterized in Professor Don Price's famous phrase, "creeping incrementalism," meaning two steps forward, one step backward, perhaps three sideways, and then another forward. Calabresi and Bobbitt's concept of "tragic choices" overlaps "creeping incrementalism" and seems to explain many of our societal choices.

In brief, it is Calabresi and Bobbitt's view that every societal choice leaves someone out, even consigning them to death; in time, since society cannot tolerate this, a shift in values must occur to favor in some way those who suffered under the previous policy. The tragedy in a way is spread around without our ever having to admit publicly that we commit some to death. A good example is the military draft guidelines which tend to exempt from service certain people. In biology, the argument used to be whether form followed function or whether structure determined function; it seems to me that the physical characteristics of America, its size and diversity, are an important influence on the "creeping incrementalism" of our national policy development. A democracy, particularly a large and diverse one, expresses many values through its national policies; in national policies choices are made that favor some people and their values and detract from others — hence, Calabresi and Bobbitt's term "tragic choices" and their view that fairness in the democratic society requires a periodic shifting to address the interests of those whose lives and values have not been emphasized under current policies; so the pendulum swings, destined only to move again in yet another direction so as to allow the entire nation to persist in the myth that it is not sacrificing some people with each decision. For America then, "tragic choices" and "creeping incrementalism" are all of a piece and are likely to be characteristic of our policy-making as long as we survive as a democratic state. But that doesn't mean that a coherent story cannot unfold. Let us turn to the health policy story of the United States over the past four decades.

Looked at from a policy perspective, national health policy in the post–World War II period has been an unqualified success. Although the times and climate favored the fullest flowering of the great American problem-solving technique (that is, once the problem has been carefully identified, throw large amounts of money at it and eventually it will be solved), there is much of which our nation can be proud. What was evolving during the fifties and early sixties was the concept of all citizens' right to health care of the highest order. The federal government was on a roll; Uncle Sam would deal with all important matters.

It was determined that our hospitals were old and dilapidated and contained too few beds. A law was passed, money was identified, and within a decade or so we had lots of modern hospital beds.

We needed more science and technology for the benefit of the public. Therefore, disease by disease, we attacked the research and specialty care needs of our nation; James Shannon, the director of the National Institutes of Health (NIH); Senator Lister Hill of Alabama; and Congressman John Fogarty of Rhode Island led a small group of influential leaders in the successful fight to increase the nation's spending on biomedical research. We trained specialists and researchers, thus enlarging our medical school faculties by sixfold over the past fifteen or twenty years.

We perceived a severe doctor shortage. Congress passed a law, and the number of medical school graduates increased from 7,000 in 1967 to 16,000 in 1985. We perceived a need for more specialists. We passed a law to support specialty training. We perceived a need for more primary care doctors, so the Congress appropriated the requisite dollars to stimulate the growth of family practice residencies.

We perceived a need for broader accessibility to health care for all sectors of our society. We developed Medicare and Medicaid, gave tax credits to employers who provided health insurance for their workers, and elevated the proportion of our population with health insurance to greater than 85 percent. Over the past ten years, minorities and the poor have clearly improved their access to health care, with blacks visiting the doctor as often as the average white client and, in many states, achieving equal access to all hospitals. In other words, great strides were made toward the achievement of a single class of care for all.

In all of these changes, the profession of medicine through its primary organization, the American Medical Association (AMA), fought to preserve what it perceived to be the best interests of the doctor. In the late 1940s, and early 1950s, the AMA successfully fought off the U.S. government in all major health initiatives. As pointed out by Wilbur Cohen, the passage in 1965 of the Social Security legislation establishing Medicare demonstrated for the first time that the power of the AMA could be broken; and it has been diminishing more or less ever since.

The one area in which the AMA has retained its success rate in the policy arena has been in the maintenance of the fee-for-service system of payment for physicians. As the financing system evolved in both the public and the private sectors, the physician always received "reasonable and customary" fees. Until the widespread advent of health insurance, both public and private, there was a proud and important tradition among physicians, wherein they freely devoted their services to people who couldn't pay and equally generously gave their time to educate medical students and residents. The so-called Robin Hood syndrome occurred, in which the well-to-do supported the physician and those efforts he or she was able and willing to give away.

Within a decade, that tradition of contributing free care and free teaching dissolved. Payment was received through "third party" insurers (including Medicare and Medicaid), who paid for whatever the physician did according to "usual and customary" standards. Now, therefore, the third-party payers were paying physicians at rates that previously allowed them to carry on like Robin Hood, except that the Medicare and Medicaid programs provided reimbursement for the elderly and poor, assisting the trend to some dramatic income increases for many physicians. Increasingly, teaching physicians learned how to bill for their services while teaching, again especially for the poor. A significant characteristic of much of medical practices was disappearing too; and that was the direct payment of the physician by the patient for personal services rendered. Though the loss of this way of transacting business was fought by the profession, and very sincerely so, the rapid expansion of physician incomes and the obvious enhancement of accessibility to health care for those previously unable to pay rendered this opposition ultimately insignificant. This same trend toward cross-subsidization of care for the poor and for teaching costs occurred with hospitals; and, almost imperceptibly, these two major efforts were loaded onto the cart being pulled by the private insurers on behalf of employers.

In the 1930s, at the Rip Van Winkle Clinic in New York State, a successful prepaid program was established wherein for

a flat fee all necessary health care would be provided to participants. This was the first Health Maintenance Organization
(HMO). During World War II Henry J. Kaiser provided a system
of total health care for his workers which evolved in the postwar
era to include a growing number of subscribers, largely in Hawaii
and the West Coast of the United States. Other similar institutions sprang up here and there and flourished in modest ways
through the 1960s and 1970s; the HMO effort was a crusade for
some and was strongly advocated by many experts, but it experienced great difficulty in getting widespread national acceptance.
Far less than 10 percent of the population was ever enrolled in
these health care plans prior to the past few years. Most doctors
preferred the solo practice of medicine or group practices, which
generally allowed for more independence, were more profes-
sionally satisfying, and were usually more lucrative than employment in an HMO. Organized medicine and other elements of
society actively opposed the flourishing of HMOs. It was not
uncommon for people to be HMO members until they got really
sick and then they would go outside the HMO to get the level of
expertise they wanted or thought they needed.

Health care benefits became an important item in labor relations as contracts which provided health care as an increasingly
major fringe benefit for large numbers of workers were negotiated
by labor unions and management. Complete health insurance is
a wonderful fringe benefit, because it is of potentially great financial value should serious illness strike the individual. It was very
appealing for both labor and management to negotiate; therefore
there was a rapid expansion of private insurance programs available to the working population and to their families. For reasons
that have always been obscure to me, but must obviously have
related to financial performance, the insurance carriers persisted
in covering in-hospital care more rapidly than out-of-hospital care.
They also paid more for procedures or laboratory tests than they
did for the doctor's time. Thus, the patient would typically have

to pay from his or her own pocket for a diagnostic evaluation done in the out-patient clinic, whereas, if hospitalized, the insurance company would cover all expenses. Further, the doctor would frequently find that his or her patient or the patient's family would prefer to have the patient stay in the hospital for continuing therapies or rehabilitative services which could have been provided on an out-patient basis. Such a course of extended hospitalization seemed to hurt no one and often on the surface seemed to help everyone, impacting only on the insurance premium which was, of course, spread across a large, impersonal, and unaware group.

This approach to paying hospitals and doctors obviously encouraged the provision of more services, more procedures, and more tests, because, in general, they seemed to be "free" to the patient. There were other results from this kind of approach. For example, as malpractice suits began to increase, doctors found it easier to practice "defensive" medicine, ordering tests that were largely unnecessary for diagnosis but might come in handy in case they were sued. Another example is the incentive this reimbursement mechanism provided to family physicians to become adept at certain procedures which were reimbursable in the ambulatory setting to make up for income not forthcoming for the time that the doctor might spend talking with the patient.

As one might have guessed, in addition to increased accessibility to effective health care for our citizenry, the net result of all these policies has been a steady annual growth in health care costs and expenditures. Along with these signs of success, there naturally came the detractors or the advocates of the "other side of the coin." For the detractors, the costs were too high; the hospitals were over-bedded and therefore must not be running efficiently; doctors' incomes were growing more rapidly than others' and their conspicuous consumption was annoying; pharmaceutical companies were seen to be controlling our lives, encouraging us through advertising to becoming a pill-taking society and thereby profiting from our weaknesses; new technologies and drugs were being utilized on patients too soon and without adequate testing. As the proportion of the health care dollar that was paid by the government increased, the federal dollars available to other significant constituents diminished, and pretty soon the health care dollar became a worthy target for competing constituencies.

As a result, the federal attempts to regulate and control health care costs grew, and each of these governmental efforts was seen as an intrusion by the basically politically conservative profession of medicine, which therefore resisted them. The forces for centralized governmental approaches gathered strength and we saw a wide variety of regulatory and planning efforts flow from the administrations of Lyndon Johnson, Richard Nixon, and Jimmy Carter. In some states, hospital charges were strictly regulated by state agencies. Highly intrusive innovations labeled as "quality assurance" mechanisms were widely implemented, even though these massive governmentally sponsored efforts were really aimed at cost control rather than quality enhancement. In spite of this, there was little demonstrable effect upon the ever-escalating costs of health care.

I remember clearly an informal meeting in 1973 in Washington, D.C., at which a distinguished British physician listened to a description of the new Professional Services Review Organizations that the U.S. government was putting in place. His response was one of amazement, because, he said, the National Health Service would never agree to intrude on the independent authority of the physician to practice medicine to such an incredible extent.

Important societal voices (in addition to those of the detractors discussed above) began to be raised in opposition to these increasing costs, to the domination of high technology in health care, and to the seemingly unlimited authority of the physician. Critics aimed to demythologize the physician and the so-called medical model through which, it was claimed, the profession had for years maintained its stranglehold on health policy and health care. Such critics pointed out that relatively large proportions of patients entering a hospital acquired other, sometimes lethal, diseases while there. Epidemiologists poked holes in long-established treatment modalities, showing in one famous situation that a sham operation produced results at least as positive as did the venue then in vogue.

Archie Cochrane, the well-known British epidemiologist, was for a time in the mid-1970s an extremely influential force in policy circles in Washington, D.C. He frequently referred to a published British study, which showed that those people who received treatment at home for an acute myocardial infarction did better than those who went into the coronary care unit in the hospital. This came at a time when U.S. hospitals had just gone into competition with each other to put in place, at great expense, the highly expensive coronary care unit. The British study, as well as Dr. Cochrane's appealing personal presentation of the data, did much at that time to cast doubt in the federal bureaucracy about the unqualified success of high technology and underscored the growing belief that cost control was too big an issue to be left solely to the judgment of the physician, who directly or indirectly controlled 70 percent of the total health care bill. That Dr. Cochrane's results could not fairly be transposed to the United States (partly because most American males did not have a wife at home willing or able to nurse him through a heart attack) made no matter to the impact on federal policymakers.

At this point, my history must be interrupted for a discussion of a movement in the American polity, which at first seemed completely unrelated to health care but which was gaining strength and momentum. When the windmills, at which this movement aimed, actually were toppled, it became clear that analogous efforts might succeed in health care. I refer to the process of deregulation of a series of American industries, thought of since the 1930s as quasi-public utilities requiring oversight by especially created, specific federal agencies to protect the public interest. Martha Derthick and Paul Quirk, in their recent book *The Politics of Deregulation*, have made a convincing argument that, contrary

to popular belief, the successful deregulation of the trucking, air-
line, and telecommunications industries represented a victory of
rational analysis by expert economists acting in concert with the
regulatory agencies and the Congress to overcome the powerful
special-interest coalitions, represented by the corporations and
unions, which profited for so long through the regulatory arrangements.[7] The steps taken in each of these three instances of dramatic executions of the sacred cows of government regulation
are matters of public record in the 1970s and early 1980s. The
outcomes from the public's perspective, and even to some extent
from the business community's, have been laudatory, more positive perhaps than most people expected. The changes were accomplished quite rapidly, are working to people's benefit, and seem
irreversible for the foreseeable future. In each instance, competition in the marketplace was encouraged, government control
and influence were minimized, the power of the unions were
diminished, and new wage schedules were established to meet
price competition. Pro-competition economists and lawyers like
Alain Enthoven and Clark Havighurst argued that the same thing
could and should be done for health care, a service industry which
should be placed in the marketplace like everything else.

By 1980, when Ronald Reagan swept into power, the scene
was set for dramatic change in the health care arena. The profession of medicine generally supported the business-oriented, deregulation approach espoused by Reagan and his commitment to
the reduction of government power and its capacity to interfere
with market forces. He was, by and large, the doctors' cup of tea.
The airlines, trucking, and telecommunications industries had been
deregulated or were close to that condition; but, piece by piece,
under Reagan and the Congress, so has the health care industry
been deregulated. In the process, organized medicine appears to
have lost forever its ability to preserve the fee-for-service system.

[7] Martha Derthick and Paul Quirk, *The Politics of Deregulation* (Washington, D.C.: Brookings Institute, 1985).

In successfully holding off Big Brother in the form of Uncle Sam as the major employer of physicians, America seems ready to substitute corporations as major employers of physicians as part of total health care delivery packages for large segments of the population. Joining forces with the Reagan government in its approach to cost control was a powerful new ally in the form of the business associations of corporations seeking to improve the market success and sophistication of the aggregate purchaser of health care and committed to reducing the costs of providing health care for their employees. Unions were losing their credibility and their clout; the president's trouncing of the Air Controller's union early in his first term proved that point. The fact that over $500 in health care costs went into every new car meant that health care got partially blamed for the U.S. loss to the Japanese of world preeminence in automobile sales. For the first time, businesses decided to become prudent aggregate buyers of health care, and a variety of new initiatives to cut costs came into being.

The most striking personifications of these changes are represented by Lee Iacocca, Donald Fraser, and Joseph Califano.[8] In the fifties and sixties, they represented industry, labor unions, and government, respectively, in seeking to increase access to health care, advocating the individual's basic right to health care, and promoting centralized planning and regulatory apparatus to control costs of health care. Now, they all serve on the Chrysler Corporation Board, linked in their effort to reduce the company's costs, attempting to eliminate cross-subsidization so that no Chrysler health care dollars go either to care for the poor or for the education of future doctors.

For-profit hospital chains attracted attention and have had such a meteoric rise into the national consciousness that the Institute of Medicine (IOM) of the National Academy of Sciences conducted a major study of the impact of the for-profit chains on

---

[8] Joseph A. Califano, *America's Health Care Revolution* (New York: Random House, 1986).

American health care.[9] Completed in 1986, this study showed that for-profit chains were neither more efficient nor less effective in delivering care than their not-for-profit counterparts and that they often provided their stockholders with profits to an amount equal to an excess of charges over those levied by their not-for-profit counterparts. Further, the IOM study showed that the rise in the number of hospitals and beds owned by for-profit chains came largely as a result of their acquisition of so-called proprietary hospitals (that is, hospitals which were previously owned by individuals on a for-profit basis) ; the acquisitions usually resulted in an upgrading of the facility and an increase in quality over that produced by the often local (frequently physician) ownership.

Finally, the enormous success enjoyed over a relatively brief period on the stock market by the more successful of these companies disappeared when it became evident that these profits came only because of their companies' adroit manipulation of the old system of reimbursement, which had been standard through 1983.

When the government changed in 1984 to payment of hospitals according to a diagnosis-related pre-set formula, the incentives changed to favor care provided with a minimum of laboratory tests, procedures, and consultations. Thus, if a hospital could take care of a patient for X dollars less than the formula designated for that disease, then the hospital could realize X dollars of profit. Under these new conditions, the for-profit chains lost their edge. They had failed to appreciate the need to switch to out-of-hospital care to make a profit in the new order and they were left holding the bag; the doctors stood to profit just as handsomely from caring for people out-of-hospital. Suddenly, the incentives were reversed and behavior was changed; the ill-prepared for-profit chains have been suffering, and it seems highly unlikely that they will dominate the industry.

[9] The Institute for Medicine, *For-profit Enterprise in Health Care* (Washington, D.C.: National Academy Press, 1980).

The average length of stay in a hospital has dropped by as much as four days per stay, and out-patient surgeries have emerged; and one can foresee the day when the hospital will be essentially a large intensive-care unit.

The HMOs are ideally placed to take advantage of this new situation. In Minneapolis/St. Paul, where HMOs now have greater than 50 percent of the market, much of interest is being learned. For example, subscribers will change HMO's for a fifteen-dollar-a-month differential; they will change for more convenient or for more courteous service; and they assume that there is high-quality medical professional care in each situation until they become convinced otherwise.

HMOs deliver a full range of health care to a population by reversing the trend in America from increasing numbers of specialists to a distribution of physicians more heavily laden with family or general physicians. They also employ the primary physician in a gatekeeper role much as occurs in the NHS, except that HMOs tend to be large group practices wherein primary care doctors share offices and resources with specialists; and therefore, these gatekeepers tend to concur with specialists about the proper time for referral.

The large aggregate purchaser of health care has become highly sophisticated and is generally seeking a contractual arrangement that will guarantee a lower cost but preserve quality. To provide these elements requires health facilities — both in-hospital and out — financial support, and good doctors. In the past, it was the doctor who was in short supply; but now, thanks to the so-called surplus of well-educated young physicians, there are plenty of talented people willing to work for a salary in order to be able to practice at all. The revolution in health care delivery is thus being fueled by the increased size of the physician pool; and it is this fact that explains the ambiguity in health policy circles about the need or value of reducing medical school class sizes.

While some people are seeking a return to past conditions, other health care experts, like Paul Ellwood, predict a sweeping change, with the great majority of health care in the United States by the year 2000 being delivered by health care corporations of various sorts. Ellwood thinks there may be ten or twenty mega corporations providing health care nationally, backed up by a larger number of regionally based and smaller companies. While his predictions may be extreme, the trend is still going in his direction. Whether for-profit or not-for-profit, the vertically integrated corporations' domination of health care in the United States is a distinct possibility. How these changes will get implemented and how they will affect the Hippocratic tradition is unknown.

Organized medicine appears deeply disappointed. After fighting so valiantly against the forces advocating increasing government control, which remained in the ascendancy throughout the sixties and seventies, it helped to elect the anti-big-government forces of the Reagan administration. At last, no more health planning or regulation; no more giveaway programs providing all patients the potential to receive care anywhere; no more professional service review organizations (PSROs), health planning agencies, or National Health Service Corps; no chance of Uncle Sam becoming the doctors' employer!

Alas, it is now dawning on the AMA that it has been hoisted on its own petard. Health care got deregulated all right. The enterprise got treated as a business. The Federal Trade Commission refused to allow any discussion of proper fees and banned the ban on physician advertising. The government reversed financial incentives so as to discourage hospital care; it took steps to open hospital staffs to more physicians and other personnel; it struck down barriers to HMO development; and it has done nothing significant to stem the tide of foreign medical graduates swelling physician ranks and has thus not implemented a policy favoring a diminished output of new physicians. Financial incentives and budget cuts have made for a fiercely competitive business environment as doctors' groups, hospitals, and other companies fight over the population for market share, sometimes with advertisements that would make an automobile salesman blush. There is even a for-profit clinical research company in Tennessee.

Gradually, it is dawning on medicine's leaders that doctors are in danger not of employment by Uncle Sam but of employment by any one of a number of health care companies. The companies can be expected to pay as little as possible to attract the necessary talent and might discharge those doctors who make trouble, who do not see patients rapidly enough or who are too noisy in their patient advocacy. What previous presidents couldn't do in twenty years of believing that health care was a right — that is, control expenditures — this president has accomplished in six years, even though it is now clear that health care is no longer considered a "right."

Health care has become a business and it has become a melange of big businesses; the solo or small businessman is out. Thus, the rules of big business will govern the enterprise increasingly. The manager will become more powerful than the doctor; market-sensitive practices will guide the behavior of the group; price and profits will become major considerations; wholesale deals and cut rates will become commonplace as negotiated contracts increasingly govern daily practices; advertising, loss-leaders, market-share, and interest in consortia or related businesses will become commonplace and will dominate the rhetoric and context of the business. A characteristic model might be that a for-profit hospital chain would buy an insurance company to provide know-how and financing for large-population health care; then the new conglomerate would hire doctors and build medical office buildings, acquire nursing homes, psychiatric hospitals, pharmacies, and hospital supply companies. This is called vertical integration and will occur just as readily with not-for-profit chains. The conglomerate is so big, it might as well be the government from the perspective of the individual physician.

Whether we should cap our nation's health expenditures at 12 percent of the gross national product or 15 percent or 18 percent, there is no doubt that demand already outstrips what we are happy to spend on health care. Therefore difficult choices must be made and priorities set, often based upon institutional or governmental policies. These sorts of choices in a democratic society, where adherence to values is never the result of a top-down mandate, must inevitably entail a constant shifting to emphasize values apparently neglected by previous policies. The winners and the losers are subject to change, so that the fact may be disguised from public view that societal choices in fact consign some people to the loser category.

Shall we ration and how shall we ration are key questions facing us in the years ahead. As a first-year medical student in 1956, after observing a dramatic and life-saving repair of a tiny baby's congenital heart defects using the then-dramatic technique of extracorporeal heart-lung bypass, I overheard two visiting Russian doctors say, in congratulating the American surgeon, that in Russia they would have simply had a new baby. So far apart in 1956, I'm not so sure of the distance today between that Russian view and ours.

As our life-styles and technologies increase our life expectancies, our mortality rates decrease, but our incidence of morbidity or years of life associated with some disability increase. Thus, the choices of the present and future will not always be between this or that life-saving intervention and its attendant costs but increasingly will be tied to the years gained of quality life per dollars expended based on cost-benefit analyses. Careful and quantitative analytic studies will be able to determine with ever-increasing accuracy the number of years of acceptable quality of life that can be purchased by a set number of health care dollars; the temptation will become strong and the pressure compelling always to go with the most good for the dollars available. Such an approach may have much to recommend it, but it could lead one to replace all the hips that need fixing in the country before transplanting any more hearts or livers, because the hip transplant produces such dramatic improvements, usually for over ten years.

Most frequently, when thinking about rationing health care dollars, the focus is on controlling access to technology; seldom is physician or nurse time considered. In this regard, two true stories are relevant. The first involves the 1970 studies involving graduating Princeton divinity students who, in what they thought was a real-life situation, one at a time passed a groaning suffering man lying beside the path.[10] In reality, the modern-day sufferer was a trained psychological observer who scored each person on their reactions to his plight. Each of the students had been placed in different situations: some were in a great hurry, others less so, others not at all; some had just read the Parable of the Good Samaritan, some had not. When the results of the experiment were analyzed, the only factor which correlated positively with whether the students stopped to offer assistance was how much time the individual had to spare.

Allow me to juxtapose that study with the plight of a recently graduated obstetrician. This lady, a single parent with two relatively young children, was precluded from entering private practice in the city where she lived because she was already $65,000 in debt and couldn't afford the $60,000 required for malpractice insurance. Therefore, she joined a group practice providing prepaid care to a large population of subscribers and was promptly informed by the nonphysician clinic manager that her "quota" was to see five patients per hour. She felt it was impossible to give good care or to educate adequately either pre- or post-partum patients under these circumstances, but she had no alternatives other than quitting. To quit was economic suicide for her and her children, and yet she was prevented from rendering to her patients

---

[10] John M. Darley and C. Daniel Batson, "From Jerusalem to Jericho: A Study of Situational and Dispositional Variables in Helping Behavior," *Journal of Personality and Social Psychiatry* 27 (1973): 100–108.

what she regarded as reasonable care. She turned to a senior colleague (and friend of mine) for moral counseling; I wonder what he told her, for this represents the quintessential conflict of the decade before us as the Hippocratic theme meets the bureaucratic theme on the playing field of "rationing."

In this case, the commodity being rationed is not a technology but the time necessary to establish and develop the therapeutic relationship between doctor and patient, and the rationer is the manager and not the doctor. Where will it all lead? To the unionization of doctors, to protect not only their economic interests but their role as advocates for their patients and the final arbiters of their own time management as it relates to contact with individual patients?

In the United Kingdom, the political process makes the macro-decision as to how much money is to be spent but has maneuvered the doctors into the position of rationer (a position which it seems to me will ultimately have devastating effects on the trust between patient and doctor so essential to a healthy transaction). In the United States, the political process has been unable (and I believe will always be unable) to make the rationing decisions necessary to keep the lid on costs; politicians and bureaucrats frequently berate the doctors for not carrying out this function of deciding not to give treatment to some patients. However, the malpractice courts await those U.S. physicians who deviate from the normal standard. Thus, there is little chance that doctors will be placed in the system as the "rationers"; nor, in my opinion, should they be so placed, with the exception of that situation surrounding the attempt to have a dignified death. In that situation the doctor may withhold an available therapy, not because it is to be saved for someone else, but because such restraint is actually the best treatment for the patient.

And now it is time for me to admit defeat, to admit that I too have contracted the Alexis de Tocqueville Syndrome (at least a modified form of it) and to pass along my current analysis of

what has been for me one of the more perplexing differences
between the American and the British practices of medicine. More
than a common language separates us. The issue to which I refer
was identified in 1963 by the American Nobelist in Economics,
Kenneth Arrow, when he noted the intrinsic conflict between the
doctor as the supplier of services and the doctor as advocate for
the patient. Intellectually I understood that statement, but in practice I thought it presented no real problem; therefore I took it as
a rather arcane insight, although somehow I have continued to
remember it from time to time. More recently, the American
authors Henry J. Aaron and William B. Schwartz in their book
The Painful Prescription make no bones about their observation
that British physicians, both general practitioners and specialists,
are making the rationing decisions in certain key instances.[11] The
most striking example for an American reader is that of turning
down patients for dialysis because of age. I know Bill Schwartz
and he is a thoughtful and careful person. I also know several
British physicians quite well, and they all claimed that they did
not make rationing decisions; they made medical decisions. One
physician with many years of practice in London to her credit said
she had never had a patient turned down by a specialist. I found
it hard to bring these two perceptions of the same phenomena into
some sensible alignment until I understood more clearly the significant differences in the doctrines of informed consent in our
two countries. The informed-consent decisions of the American
judiciary essentially make the patient the decision maker, not the
doctor. It is expected that the doctor presents all the reasonable
options to the patient and family, that the authority has become
so decentralized that it in effect rests within each patient and, by
implication, that the trust of the patient in the doctor rests upon
the latter's demonstrated competence and the honesty and integrity
with which he or she deals with the patient.

[11] Henry J. Aaron and William B. Schwartz, *The Painful Prescription* (Washington, D.C.: Brookings Institute, 1984).

In the United Kingdom in 1985, the House of Lords, by split vote to be sure, decided the Sidaway case by explicitly denying the informed-consent doctrine extant in America and declaring that the patient had a right to hear only what was customary and necessary from the doctor's point of view. Further conversations convince me that most British doctors and patients agree with the implications of the lords' decision. When it is common sense to the doctor that an expensive, extraordinary intervention is unnecessary, it is consistent with the gatekeeper policy for him or her simply to make that decision for the patient by not recommending referral. In fact, these decisions to the British doctors are medical decisions, whereas to American doctors, the very same decision is a rationing decision and not a medical decision. For example, even if an American doctor was personally unenthusiastic about putting an elderly patient on chronic dialysis, he would undoubtedly feel that the option must be presented to the patient and that, if the patient chose dialysis, he the doctor would be obliged to carry it out. The British patient would be confused by the American physician, and the American patient would feel badly shortchanged by the information and choices offered by a British doctor.

This is the intellectual context out of which the American economist Charles Begley, from Kenneth Arrow's view of the conflict between physicians as suppliers and advocates, adopts the position that the role of gatekeeper (as in the NHS and in American HMOs) is fundamentally incompatible with the American doctrine of informed consent. I believe the lawyers and the doctors and the policymakers have a lot of hard thinking and negotiating to do on these matters. It is gratifying to me finally to understand how the British doctors and patients have maintained the integrity of their relationship in the face of these tough decisions, but I fear the turbulence which may emerge if the American view of informed consent is adopted in England.

Thus, the American politicians have turned to the marketplace to do their job for them — and who's to say whether this approach might not have great benefits. This decentralization has had some interesting if unexpected fall-out. For example, I have a friend with a complex neurological disorder who is a subscriber to a prepaid comprehensive care plan; when it became clear that he would benefit by having an expensive, new high-tech intervention to speed his convalescence, he was interviewed by a special group of people not including his doctor to determine whether the plan would purchase it for him or not. This of course is similar to the much-maligned process used in Seattle, Washington, to determine which few patients would get into the chronic dialysis program; the doctors advocated their patients and a board of anonymous lay members made the decisions. The intellectual world scoffed, saying logic and justice required random selection or universal availability.

Under the deregulated, decentralized systems approach to health care evolving in the United States, the main problem will be how to guarantee a requisite level of care for the poor and underinsured. How we answer that problem will be the true measure of our values, of our national character, and of the quality of our beliefs. If we deal successfully with the issue of the poor and underserved, we may well have achieved an approach to providing adequate health care for all in a context fully supportive of the American values of voluntarism and freedom of choice that apparently is, for us, better than the more centralized approach we were following toward a single, NHS-like establishment.

A period of confusion, rapid change, and great debate over value-laden issues (such as is now being experienced in the United States regarding health care) cries out for the emergence of philosophers who can clarify issues, define central questions, and help the society toward a rational resolution of the policy crises with which it is dealing. I'm pleased to say that bonafide card-carrying philosophers have entered this fray, and one of them has recently published what is, in my view, a comprehensive and illuminating analysis which has the potential to help shape and clarify our nation's thinking on some of the crucial health-related questions. I refer to Norman Daniels's treatise published in 1985 by Cambridge University Press, *Just Health Care*.[12] Professor Daniels attempts to extend John Rawls's principle of distributive justice to health care and courageously attacks the most pressing and difficult issues.

In brief, he argues that health care is of a different order from other commodities or services and that the principle governing health policy should be what he calls "the fair equality of opportunity account," implying that society has the obligation, based upon the Rawlsian theory of justice as fairness, to see to it that each person has access to the health care required to allow him or her equal opportunity as a citizen within the constraints of his or her own innate talents and skills. Daniels further concludes that the arrangements necessary to provide this care would not violate any basic provider liberties and should not necessarily do economic injustice to doctors. In his view, the restrictions on autonomy in treatment decisions derived from just resource allocation policies will not harm the rights of either patients or doctors or the essence of the doctor-patient relationship as long as the society understands its obligation to exclude the rationing decisions from the physician's portfolio of responsibilities.

Although I lay no claim to being a professional philosopher, I commend Professor Daniels's work to you and find in it the best set of arguments I have yet come across yielding some principles for policy development. Whether his views can gain enough exposure to impact the body politic in a timely fashion is problematic.

While we seek greater justice for our people in the more appropriate dispersal of services and strive to control the costs of health care, we must take care not to discourage our best potential

[12] Norman Daniels, *Just Health Care* (Cambridge: Cambridge University Press, 1985).

scientific healers from entering the profession. There is strong evidence that this may be happening. The so-called malpractice crisis is driving doctors out of practice and is a strong factor in redirecting promising students into non-health care fields.

In a recent newspaper article, Dr. Thomas B. Ducker, a Baltimore neurosurgeon, clearly places the blame on malpractice suits for the loss of trust between doctor and patient and between doctor and doctor.[13] He states that he no longer is forthcoming about his own mistakes at morbidity and mortality conferences — consequently he learns less from his mistakes and others learn nothing from them. Dr. Ducker concludes his essay as follows: "Somehow, some way, we must begin to restore the relationship of trust that once existed between doctor and patient, and between doctor and doctor. Otherwise, today's troubles will pale against the grief that awaits medicine in the future." These are words that accurately describe the feelings of many excellent American physicians now in practice.

Clearly our primary societal values (such as freedom for the individual, hope, distrust of government) and our major bureaucratic values are in conflict with the best expression of our Hippocratic values. Our desire for high technology is, in some ways, self-defeating; the more we yield to the technologic imperative, the more alienated patients seem to feel. Doctors sometimes are at the eye of the storm, receiving blame from bureaucrats, politicians, and the public. Some doctors seem to blame their woes on the so-called medical-industrial complex if not the malpractice lawyers.

I believe it will not be easy to sustain and nurture the Hippocratic tradition and its twenty-first-century offspring, the scientific healer. To succeed, doctors must retreat to a definition, articulation, and defense of the core of physicianhood, the core that rests in the Hippocratic tradition, and they should leave unto Caesar

---

[13] Thomas B. Ducker, "We Need a Cure for the Lack of Medical Trust," *Houston Chronicle*, February 2, 1987, op-ed page.

those things that are Caesar's. The profession of medicine is not doing a good job protecting Hippocrates' turf. We have forgotten that death is not an option but a certainty; that the doctor's job is to minimize suffering and pain just as much as it is to cure. Pain is, after all, not a single gene, single protein, single defect lesion. It is a symptom which is the sine qua non of suffering, the very stuff physicians are here to minimize. It can be treated sometimes with surgery; sometimes with medicine; sometimes with placebos, massage, or physical therapy; sometimes with words; and sometimes by techniques without known scientific basis. Often, pain can't be overcome, and the doctor must help the sufferer to endure.

I believe this means that, just as our biomedical sciences continue to produce new curative technological interventions, just as our social and behavioral sciences develop new strategies to encourage life-style changes in healthful directions, so the medical profession should extend its intellectual boundaries to include the fuller exploration and understanding of the therapeutic relationship or, if you will, healing. Anthropology and psychology can, in my view, forge a constructive, productive linkage with the neurosciences (including neuropharmacology) to extend our knowledge in this important area. Along the way, we must continue to ask the question, How can the physician be the patient's friend and trusted advocate while being a potential adversary and rationer at the same time?

Thoughtful physicians must rally more intensely around the vision of their Hippocratic tradition; they should encourage their leaders to worry less about the governmental threat, less about the threat of the business coalitions, less about the threat of the for-profit chains, less about the corporatization of medical practice, and to worry more about preserving the essentials of the profession of scientific healing, begun by Hippocrates and threatened as never before by our incredible scientific, technologic, and financial successes and by our own ignorance, inattention, and misunderstanding of the very essence of physicianhood.

In sum, I believe an accommodation can be reached between the values of the Hippocratic theme and those of the bureaucratic theme; a stronger Hippocratic theme will lend a necessary balance to the societal and bureaucratic values such that the United States can have a humane, fair, and effective health care delivery system built around the therapeutic relationship between patients and health professionals dedicated to their service. In our fanciful ongoing discussions including Thomas Jefferson, Max Weber, and Guido Calabresi and Philip Bobbitt, surely that is what Hippocrates would be arguing for.

Taming Chance:
Randomization in Individual and Social Decisions

JON ELSTER

THE TANNER LECTURES ON HUMAN VALUES

Delivered at
Brasenose College, Oxford University

May 6 and 7, 1987

JON ELSTER, born in 1940, divides his life between Norway, France, and the United States. He is currently Professor of Political Science and Philosophy at the University of Chicago and Research Director at the Institute for Social Research, Oslo. He has also taught at the University of Paris and the University of Oslo. He has been visiting professor at the University of California at Berkeley and Stanford University, at the California Institute of Technology, and the Ecole des Hautes Etudes en Sciences Sociales (Paris), and visiting fellow at All Souls College, Oxford. His books include *Leibniz et la Formation de l'Esprit Capitaliste* (1975), *Logic and Society* (1978), *Ulysses and the Sirens* (1979), *Sour Grapes* (1983), and *Making Sense of Marx* (1985). He is currently engaged in a study of the mechanisms and criteria by which institutions in various societies allocate the scarce resources at their disposal.

I

Decision making by the flip of a coin, the toss of a die, and more generally by formal or informal lotteries is, I believe, largely perceived as a curiosity. Randomization is often mentioned in passing as a possible method for allocating resources, assigning tasks, and, more generally, for making social decisions. It is occasionally discussed in more detail with respect to specific types of decisions. Yet with the exception of Thomas Gataker's *On the Nature and Use of Lots* of 1619, it has not, to my knowledge, received sustained and systematic attention.[1] This lack of interest in decision making by lottery might, of course, be thought to suggest that the problem is inherently uninteresting. My aim in these lectures is to persuade you that this vacuum is not a "much needed gap" but one worth filling.

Many of the ideas in these lectures grow out of a research seminar at the Institute for Social Research in Oslo. During a discussion of child custody legislation some three years ago, Karl O. Moene suggested that custody disputes might be resolved by the flip of a coin. The proposal seemed intriguing and worth pursuing, not only as a way of resolving custody conflicts (see my article cited in note 58 below), but as a way of making decisions in a number of different contexts. Among the participants in the seminar, I am especially indebted to Fredrik Engelstad and Aanund Hylland for their constructive and critical contributions. Thanks are also due Torstein Eckhoff, Karl O. Moene, and Kirsten Sandberg. I received many useful comments when presenting earlier versions of these lectures at seminars at the University of California at Davis, the University of Pittsburgh, Yale University, and the University of Miami. Earlier drafts have also been read by Akhil Amar, Robert Bartlett, John Broome, G. A. Cohen, J. Gregory Dees, Gerald Dworkin, Ed Green, Stephen Holmes, Mark Kishlansky, William Kruskal, Isaac Levi, Stephen Stigler, and Cass Sunstein. I am grateful to them all for their comments and suggestions. I also thank King K. Tsao for competent research assistance.

[1] Page references to Gataker's work are to the second edition, 1627. An important exception is some recent work done at the Yale Law School. See notably H. Greely, "The Equality of Allocation by Lot," *Harvard Civil Rights-Civil Liberties Review* 12 (1977): 113–41, and A. R. Amar, "Choosing Representatives by Lottery Voting," *Yale Law Journal* 93 (1984): 1283–1308.

There are two main questions we can ask ourselves with respect to the use of lotteries.[2] First, when are lotteries actually used
to make decisions and to allocate tasks, resources, and burdens?
This is the main topic of parts I and II. Second, under which conditions would they seem to be normatively allowed or prescribed
on grounds of individual rationality or social justice? This is the
question I shall address in part III. There is no reason, of course,
to expect the answers to these questions to coincide. Hence we
can generate two further questions, which are also addressed in
part III. What explains the adoption of lotteries in situations
where normative arguments seem to point against them? What
explains the nonadoption of lotteries in situations where they
would seem to be normatively compelling? This last question is
perhaps the most intriguing and instructive one. I shall argue
that we have a strong reluctance to admit uncertainty and indeterminacy in human affairs. Rather than accept the limits of
reason we prefer the rituals of reason.

The use of lotteries to make decisions itself requires the decision to use this decision mechanism rather than another. As
emphasized by Gataker (pp. 55–56), lotteries reflect an intentional choice to make the decision by a nonintentional mechanism.[3]
To explain and justify the decision to randomize (or not to randomize) requires a study of this higher-order decision. Who
makes it? How is it made? It can be made by an individual facing a choice between several courses of action. Seeking my way
out of the forest, I may decide to toss a coin when the road bifur-

----

[2] I shall not discuss ordinary lotteries, that is, the betting on numbers, as a
source of income for the state. It seems misleading to subsume this practice under
the rubric of "referring potentially contentious decisions to lot," as does K. Thomas,
Religion and the Decline of Magic (Harmondsworth: Penguin 1973), p. 140. It
should be noted, however, that ordinary lotteries have their origin in the selection by
lot of political representatives in Genoa. Initially people made bets on the candidates, whose names were later replaced by numbers.

[3] In J. Elster, *Ulysses and the Sirens*, rev. ed. (Cambridge: Cambridge University Press, 1984), pp. 13–17. I discuss two-stage decision problems where one inten-
tionally decides to solve a decision problem by trial and error rather than by consciously directed search.

cates. It can be made by a group of individuals who agree by unanimity, by majority decision, or in some other accepted way to allocate goods, burdens, or tasks among themselves in this manner. A divorcing couple who must decide on custody of the children, may agree to make the decision by the flip of a coin. It can be made, finally, by an administrative, legal, or political agency. Hospital administrators may decide to use a lottery to allocate kidneys for transplantation.

There is a second decision that has to be made before the decision by lottery can take effect: one must decide how the possible actions should be matched with the various outcomes that can be generated by the randomizing device. Clearly, the general solution cannot be to assign actions to outcomes by means of another lottery. At some stage, the assignment will have to be done by "picking" rather than "choosing." [4] Neglect of the need for this preliminary decision led Gataker (pp. 185–86) to propose the following invalid argument against the interpretation of lotteries as showing God's particular will or "special providence." He observed, correctly, that men often use past (unknown) events as elements in the lottery which is to guide their decisions. From this he concluded that, since even God cannot alter the past, the outcome of lotteries cannot in general reflect his special providence. The inference fails, since God's intervention might well come in the contemporaneous stage of matching actions with outcomes. Using his knowledge of past events he could influence the matching so as to bring about his particular will.

The use of lotteries is associated with uncertainty, indifference, indeterminacy, and incommensurability. In the absence of reasons for choosing one alternative, one candidate, one recipient, or one victim rather than another, we might as well select one at random. These lectures will to a large extent be an elaboration of this statement.

[4] On this point, see E. Ullman-Margalit and S. Morgenbesser, "Picking and Choosing," *Social Research* 44 (1977): 757–85.

The relation between uncertainty and lotteries is, however, more complex than one might suspect at first glance. Generally speaking, we tend to see uncertainty as an unmitigated ill. Uncertainty prevents us from planning for the future. Even more important, it prevents us from making choices that we can justify to ourselves and others as grounded in reason. This leads us to adopt tactics for uncertainty-avoidance and uncertainty-reduction. Usually, we do not want to cope with indeterminacy but to avoid it. The use of lotteries to resolve decision problems under uncertainty presupposes an unusual willingness to admit the limits of reason.

Sometimes, however, we welcome an element of uncertainty, and even create it if necessary. It is true that uncertainty makes it difficult to plan for the future, but without uncertainty we might not even want to plan for the future at all. It is not easy to imagine how we would feel and behave if we knew the exact day on which we would die, but a backward induction argument similar to that of the finitely iterated Prisoner's Dilemma might apply.[5] If life today has meaning only because there is a prospect of further meaningful days in the future, then the knowledge that on one specific day there will be no more meaning would retroactively remove meaning from all earlier days. This argument is, inevitably, speculative. For myself, I am quite sure that I would prefer a shorter life expectancy with a larger spread to a longer life with no spread at all. If I had the choice, on this issue, between an unfair lottery and a sure thing, I would take the lottery.[6]

Our life span is substantially outside our control. Here, we do not have the choice between certainty and uncertainty. In other domains, where we do have this choice, we might want to set up a lottery. By removing the knowledge about who will do what or

---

[5] R. D. Luce and H. Raiffa, *Games and Decisions* (New York: Wiley, 1957), pp. 98ff.

[6] Formally, this is a form of preference for risk. The underlying reasons, however, are quite different. If I prefer the smaller average with the larger dispersion, it is not because I gamble on a long life but, as stated, because the certainty would be intolerable.

get what at which times, one also removes incentives for opportunistic and wasteful behavior. Since lotteries also remove the opportunity for long-term planning, their net effect may be positive or negative. I shall discuss cases of both kinds. Here I only want to insist on the variety of attitudes we adopt toward uncertainty. Sometimes we face it squarely; sometimes we seek to avoid or reduce it. We may welcome uncertainty and even actively promote it.

I shall now proceed as follows. I first discuss the nature of randomness and random choice, to bring out some conceptual and practical difficulties associated with lotteries. I then consider, very briefly, the use of lotteries as an aid to individual decision making. In the remaining part of the lectures I look at some varieties of social lotteries. After an overview of actual or proposed social lotteries, I go on to consider the use of lotteries to allocate goods and burdens and to compare them with other allocation mechanisms. In part II, I discuss a variety of political and legal lotteries. In part III, I sketch some tentative answers to the questions stated at the beginning: When are lotteries used? When ought they to be used? When and why do the answers to these two questions differ?

In most contexts, we want lotteries to be fair, in the sense of being truly random and unbiased. To implement this goal, we would want to have at our disposal a truly randomizing device which gave each outcome the same probability of being realized. The problem lies in the construction of a physical device of this kind. As John von Neumann once observed, "anyone who considers arithmetical methods of producing random digits is, of course, in a state of sin." [7] Tables of random numbers have had to be modified because they turned out to have undesirable regularity properties. [8] Such revisions are hard to justify, since any

[7] Cited in H. Goldstine, *The Computer from Pascal to von Neumann* (Princeton: Princeton University Press, 1972), p. 297.

[8] L. Lopes, "Doing the Impossible: A Note on the Induction and Experience of Randomness," in H. R. Arles and K. R. Hammond, eds., *Judgment and Decision Making* (Cambridge: Cambridge University Press, 1986), pp. 720–38.

sufficiently long random sequence is virtually certain to have some regular looking chunks or runs. By eliminating them, one approaches the nonrandom case of intentional mixing.[9] There is (casual) evidence that the selection of questions from different subdisciplines by university examiners in successive years is a form of intentional mixing rather than random selection. In theory, students should be able to exploit this practice to their advantage.

Could one appeal instead to the inherent randomness of the selections actually generated by the device, as distinct from patterns in the hypothetical long-run sequence? Here again we run into problems. The notion of inherent randomness is quite deep and may ultimately defy analysis for reasons related to Kurt Gödel's incompleteness theorem.[10] Although one may sometimes be able to prove that a given sequence of numbers is random or that it is not random, no computer program can prove, for any given sequence, whether it is random or not. The notion of randomness invoked here can be brought out by comparing the following sequences:

$$0\,1\,0\,1\,0\,1\,0\,1\,0\,1\,0\,1\,0\,1\,0\,1\,0\,1\,0\,1$$
$$0\,1\,1\,0\,1\,1\,0\,0\,1\,1\,0\,1\,1\,1\,1\,0\,0\,0\,1\,0$$

The first sequence can be generated by the program "Print 0 1 ten times." The simplest program that can generate the second is "Print 0 1 1 0 1 1 0 0 1 1 0 1 1 1 1 0 0 0 1 0." This "incompressibility," which is used to define inherent randomness, corresponds to the intuitive idea that in a random sequence there will not be any obvious patterns. A truly random mechanism, on the other hand, would be one that has an equal likelihood of realizing any twenty-digit sentence of 0's and 1's. It would, therefore, sometimes pick a sequence which is not inherently random, although most se-

[9] W. Feller, *An Introduction to Probability Theory and Its Applications*, 3d ed. (New York: Wiley, 1968), vol. 1, p. 204.

[10] The following discussion draws heavily on G. C. Chaitin, "Randomness and Mathematical Proof," *Scientific American* 232 (May 1975): 47–52.

quences generated by a truly random device will themselves be fairly random, in a sense that can be made precise.[11]

Inherent randomness is neither necessary nor sufficient for justice by lottery.[12] Imagine that in a class of twenty pupils only ten can receive some good, and that they are matched in alphabetical order with an inherently random sequence constrained to have ten 0's and ten 1's. If the choice of this particular random sequence among others equally random was not itself made randomly, the pupils might well suspect some favoritism in the choice. Conversely, if an unbiased mechanical device happened to come up with a sequence of alternating 0's and 1's, the ensuing distribution would be quite acceptable once the pupils had satisfied themselves that the mechanism was truly random. For purposes of fairness what matters is that the randomizing device be thought to be unbiased.

Nevertheless when people have no direct knowledge about the generating mechanism, they have to judge the randomness of the draw by looking at its outcome. We have seen that this assessment is problematic even if they can observe many successive draws, and it is even more tenuous when inspection of a single outcome is used to judge how likely it is to come up. There are two closely related fallacies involved here. The first is that people misperceive inherent randomness. William Feller, referring to the pattern of German bombing over Britain in the Second World War, writes, "To the untrained eye, randomness appears as a regularity or tendency to cluster."[13] Similarly, Daniel Kahneman and Amos Tversky write, "Among the 20 possible sequences (disregarding direction and label) of six tosses of a coin, for example, we venture that only HTTHTH appears really random. For four tosses, there may not be any."[14]

[11] *Ibid.*

[12] On this point, see also I. Levi, "Direct Inference and Randomization," *PSA* 2 (1982): 447–63, at 453.

[13] Feller, *Introduction to Probability Theory*, p. 161.

[14] D. Kahneman and A. Tversky, "Subjective Probability: A Judgment of Representativeness," in D. Kahneman, P. Slovic, and A. Tversky, eds., *Judgment under Uncertainty* (Cambridge: Cambridge University Press, 1982), pp. 32–47, at p. 37.

Second, people believe that a given inherently random sequence is a more likely outcome of a random process than a given regular sequence. Kahneman and Tversky cite an experiment concerning the distribution of twenty marbles to five children, each marble being randomly allocated to one of them. Subjects stated that the outcome 4-4-4-4-4 was less likely to be the outcome of a random process than the outcome 4-4-5-4-3, in the sense that it would occur less frequently in repeated distributions. Yet the uniform distribution is actually more likely to occur.[15] As Kahneman and Tversky note elsewhere, "a slightly uneven outcome represents both the fairness of the coin and the randomness of tossing, which is not at all represented by the exactly even result."[16]

Even disregarding these problems, randomness is not easy to implement. In the 1940 draft lottery of American soldiers, out of serial numbers from 1 to 9,000, "no serial number between 300 and 600 was drawn in the first 2,400 draws. By pure chance, this would occur less than once in 15×10^{40} times."[17] Insufficiently good physical mixing led to a similar result in the 1970 draft lottery.[18] The 1971 draft lottery finally got it right.[19] The process of selecting jurors at random can be even more tortuous and difficult. In the recent case of *State v. Long* the defense successfully claimed that the process of jury selection in Atlantic City did not give each person the same chance to be selected for jury service.[20] For instance, the source list used for the random draw had about 180,000 names on it, whereas there were only 130,000 people in

[15] *Ibid.*, pp. 35–36. Subjects act as if they compare classes of distributions (equal distribution versus one child getting three marbles, one getting five, and the others getting four) rather than individual distributions.

[16] D. Kahneman and A. Tversky, "Variants of Uncertainty," in Kahneman, Slovic, and Tversky, *Judgment under Uncertainty*, pp. 509–20, at p. 514.

[17] S. Fienberg, "Randomization and Social Affairs: The 1970 Draft Lottery," *Science* 171 (1971): 255–61.

[18] Ibid.

[19] J. Rosenblatt and J. Filliben, "Randomization and the Draft Lottery, *Science* 171 (1971): 306–308.

[20] 499 A.2d 264 (N.J. Super L. 1985).

the relevant age group. Hence almost 40 percent of the people had double opportunity to be selected for jury duty. Also, the use of fifth-letter alphabetization as a criterion of selection "meant that many people in the same panel would have the same fifth letter in their last name. This explained how some panels had large numbers of Jewish names (e.g. Wise*m*an, Feld*m*an) or Italian names (e.g. Fera*r*ro, Dina*r*do)." [21] These practices were held to violate the defendant's constitutional right to a jury drawn from a representative cross section of the community. The value of this right is further examined in part II.

The belief that a process of selection is truly or objectively random is sufficient but not necessary for its perceived fairness. Epistemic randomness, that is, the fact that all outcomes are equally likely as far as one knows, may also be sufficient to ensure perceived fairness. [22] One may use natural lotteries, in which the decision is made contingent upon an event which is not specially arranged for the purpose and about which the parties have no special information. Gataker (p. 16) gives these examples: "Suppose two by the way contending which way they shall take, put themselves upon the flight of the next fowle that crosseth them, or upon the turning of a stranger, whom they see ride before them, to the right hand or to the left." The flight of the bird is subject to natural necessity and the turn of the stranger to intentional choice, but since these events are insulated from the information and control of the parties, they are random as far as they know.

[21] V. P. Hans and N. Vidmar, *Judging the Jury* (New York: Plenum Press, 1986), p. 57. First names are no more reliable. "In the town of Mannheim, for example, statistics were compiled regarding the number of children in each family. The sample comprised the families whose names had the initial letters A, B and M. It turned out, however, that names with these initials were especially numerous among Jewish families, and as the children of Jewish families were particularly numerous, the enquiry gave a misleading result" (A. Jensen, "The Representative Method in Practice," *Bulletin of the International Statistical Institute* 22 [1926]: 381–439, at pp. 429–30).

[22] On this point, see also G. Sher, "What Makes a Lottery Fair?" *Nous* 14 (1980): 203–16, at p. 206.

The problem is how to make sure that the events are really thus insulated. Often one party is better able to predict the natural event, or he may be in a position to influence it. When Darius and his competitors agreed to settle the empire on him whose horse should first neigh when they met in a given place on a given day, he rigged the natural lottery in his favor by arranging for his horse to have been in that place with a mare so that it could be expected to neigh.[23] The information problem can be solved by an analogy to the "divide and choose" principle. If one person proposes to have a decision made by a certain natural event, another shall have the right of matching outcomes with decisions.[24] The manipulation problem can be solved by using a past event to make the decision. By combining these solutions, we can ensure the epistemic randomness of natural lotteries.

I said that in *most* contexts we would want to use fair lotteries, in which each person has the same chance of being selected, at least as far as anyone knows. Although equiprobability is the rule, there are exceptions.[25] In Georgia's land lottery of 1832 "each citizen was entitled to one chance, unless he belonged to a favoured group — orphans, Revolutionary War Veterans, head of a family and the like — in which case he was given two chances." [26] Presumably the authorities did not want a settlement whose population was composed exclusively of orphans, veterans, and heads of families. Another example is provided by the West German procedure of admission to medical school. Applicants are rated on a point system, with probability of admission proportional to the number of points. The idea, presumably, is to strike a compromise between individual need and social utility, equity,

23 Herodotus, *The History*, 3.84–87.

24 For a related proposal, see Sher, "What Makes a Lottery Fair?" p. 207.

25 P. Fishburn, "Even-chance Lotteries in Social Choice," *Theory and Decision* 3 (1972): 18–40, at p. 19.

26 D. C. Wilms, "Georgia's Land Lottery of 1832," *Chronicles of Oklahoma* 52 (1974): 52–60, at p. 54.

and efficiency. Selective law enforcement could similarly be organized as a weighted lottery, with the more serious crimes having the greater likelihood of being pursued, without smaller offenders knowing that they could go about their business with no risk of punishment. Perhaps this is how police attention actually *is* allocated.

We should consider, finally, a very different interpretation of selection by lot, as the revelation of God's will. Proverbs 16:33 has it that "The lot is cast into the lap; but the whole disposing thereof is of the Lord." From the Old Testament until the early modern age, divinatory, divisory, and consultory lotteries were often used for the purpose of discovering God's will.[27] A late example is from 1653, when "a London congregation proposed that a new Parliament should be selected from nominees chosen by each religious congregation "by lot after solemn prayer (a way much used and owned by God in the scriptures)." [28] In this function, lotteries, whether formal or informal,[29] are but one of many equivalent devices used to force God's hand, the best-known alternatives being the ordeal and the duel.[30] On this interpreta-

[27] For an extremely full survey see Gataker, *On the Nature and Use of Lots*; also see J. Lindblom, "Lot-casting in the Old Testament," *Vetus Testamentum* 12 (1964): 164–78.

[28] Thomas, *Religion and the Decline of Magic*, p. 141.

[29] An instance of an informal lottery is opening the Bible at random in the hope that the selected verse might offer guidance to action. See Thomas, *Religion and the Decline of Magic*, p. 139; also see B. Donagan, "Godly Choice: Puritan Decision-making in Seventeenth-century England," *Harvard Theological Review* 76 (1983): 307–34, who refers to an instance where "by a Catch-22 argument, a randomly opened Bible on one occasion forbade the practice itself" (p. 317). (Gataker, *On the Nature and Use of Lots*, p. 346, refers to a similar self-undermining consultation by Saint Francis.) The practice goes back to the *sortes Virgilianae* of the classical world, amusingly described in Rabelais, *Gargantua and Pantagruel*, 3.11–12. Rabelais brings out the large scope for discretionary interpretation of the randomly selected texts.

[30] This distinction is slightly misleading, as witnessed by the existence of "ordeal by lot." For surveys of these techniques for revealing God's will, see H. Nottarp, *Gottesurteilstudien* (Munich: Kösel Verlag, 1956); H. C. Lea, *The Ordeal* (Philadelphia: University of Pennsylvania Press, 1973); H. C. Lea, *The Duel and the Oath* (Philadelphia: University of Pennsylvania Press, 1974), p. 195; R. Bartlett, *Trial by Fire and Water* (New York: Oxford University Press, 1986).

tion, there is no need to make lotteries fair, since God's hand could always steer the die or the coin so as to make the right side come up, just as he could ensure the victory of the weaker party in a duel. Nor would there be any need to take great care in selecting the pool of eligibles for a lottery. "If a lot were God's sentence, what need men be so curious in examining and trying the fitness and unfitness of those that they admit to a lot?" [31] That people did in fact care about these procedural matters testifies to their ambiguous attitude toward the methods.

Gataker's view was that the use of lotteries to reveal God's will was lawful only when expressly commanded by God.[32] Instances are the command to use lotteries to divide the land of Israel (for example, Num. 26:52–56) or to detect the guilty (Josh. 7). Otherwise the use of lotteries to reveal God's will is a blasphemous and superstitious tempting of God. Saint Thomas Aquinas, while holding broadly the same position, had a slightly more lenient view. "If, however, there be urgent necessity it is lawful to seek the divine judgment by casting lots, provided due reverence is observed." [33] To support his view Aquinas cites Augustine (*Ep. Ad Honor* 180): "If, at a time of persecution, the ministers of God do not agree as to which of them is to remain at his post lest all should flee, and which of them is to flee, lest all die and the Church be forsaken, should there be no other means of coming to an agreement, so far as I can see, they must be chosen by lot." Gataker's interpretation of this passage from Augustine seems more plausible. One should decide by lot who should "retire and reserve themselves for better times; that so neither those that stayed might be taxed of presumption, nor those that retired themselves be condemned for cowardice" (p. 66).[34]

---

[31] Gataker, *On the Nature and Use of Lots*, p. 200.

[32] Ibid., pp. 14–25.

[33] Saint Thomas Aquinas, *Summa Theologica*, pt. II–II, qu. 95, art. 8.

[34] The same argument applies to the other text from Augustine cited by Aquinas in support of his view: "If thou aboundest in that which it behooves thee

To discuss the use of lotteries in individual decision making, I shall distinguish between parametric and strategic decisions. The latter are characterized by a strong form of interdependence of decisions: to make up my mind I must anticipate what others will do, knowing that they are similarly deciding on the basis of anticipating my decision. In the former, the environment, including the behavior of other people, can be taken as given or at least as dependent only on my actual behavior, not on anticipations about my behavior. Both types of decisions have scope for randomization. Parametric decisions call for a lottery when the agent is indifferent or his preferences are indeterminate. Strategic decisions call for a lottery when there is no equilibrium point in pure strategies. In a parametric decision, decision by lot is rarely if ever rationally prescribed, although sometimes rationally allowed. (The habit of always using lotteries to resolve parametric decisions when they are rationally allowed may, however, be rationally prescribed as a means of economizing on costs of decision.) In a strategic decision randomization is sometimes rationally prescribed.

In parametric decisions, or "games against nature," decision by lot would seem useful when we are unable to make up our mind about what to do, or when the effort required to make up our mind does not seem worthwhile, or when it has good incentive effects. The last reason, while very important in social lotteries, has only a minor role to play in individual decisions. The most important example is probably randomization in designing experiments. "The medical experimenter who selects which patients are to receive a new treatment for a disease and which are to receive the standard treatment or none at all can unconsciously select for the new treatment patients that are healthier and have therefore

---

to give to him who hath not, and which cannot be given to two; should two come to you, neither of whom surpasses the other either in need or in some claim on thee, thou couldst not act more justly than in choosing by lot to whom thou shalt give that which thou canst not give to both." Again nothing supports the view that Augustine was recommending the lottery as a means to find the divine judgment. Indeed, the phrase "thou couldst not act more justly" directly suggests the other interpretation.

a better chance of recovery. Randomization prevents the exercise of such bias." [35] This is almost a two-person problem, in which a conscious self, seeking truth, uses a lottery to prevent an unconscious self, seeking success, from succumbing to the pleasure principle.

More important, we could use lotteries when there are several options that are equally and maximally good. These options may be indistinguishable, as in the choice between identical cans of Campbell's tomato soup, or they may differ in ways that exactly offset each other so as to leave us indifferent between them. Next, we could use lotteries when the top-ranked options are incommensurable, for either of two reasons. In some contexts we may be unable to rank or compare the outcomes of the various actions we can take. If the outcomes differ along several dimensions, we may find ourselves unable to make the necessary trade-offs. In other contexts we may be able to attach values but not numerical probabilities to the outcomes. Both are forms of uncertainty, about matters of value or preference or about matters of fact. The situation may also be more complex. The top-ranked options may be equally good as far as we know. We may be confident that one of them would prove superior if we took the time and effort to find out more about them. Yet it may not be rational to make the investment, because the difference is expected to be small compared with the cost of acquiring the additional information. [36] Since these conditions obtain quite often, we might expect lotteries to be widely used in making individual decisions. For reasons discussed in part III, they are actually quite rare.

Consider next lotteries in strategic decision making. Here, the purpose of randomization is not to resolve indeterminacy but to keep other people uncertain about what one is doing. A simple

---

[35] P. Suppes, *Probabilistic Metaphysics* (Oxford: Blackwell, 1984), p. 211.

[36] Strictly speaking, the first category, of choice under indifference, should be subsumed under this heading, since ties could always be broken by finding out more about the options.

example is randomized bluffing in poker.[37] A more complex example is taken from the hunting practices of the Naskapi, an Indian tribe in the Labradorian peninsula.[38] To determine the direction in which to hunt, they take the shoulder blade of a caribou and burn it over a fire so as to make appear cracks and spots in it. The blade is then held in a predetermined position with reference to the local topography, and the cracks and spots are used to indicate the direction. It has been conjectured that a useful effect of this randomized procedure is to prevent regularities in the hunting patterns, which might be detected by the hunted.[39] Although the randomizing device is probably biased, in that cracks and spots are more likely to form in certain ways than others, the "regularity stemming from this source may to some extent be lessened because the Naskapi change campsites." [40] This effect, if indeed it exists, might or might not explain the practice itself, depending on the presence of either intentionality or feedback in the process.

Randomization is most plausible in two-person zero-sum games, in which one person's gain is always another person's loss. Since military conflicts often approximate the zero-sum condition, it is not surprising that we find mixed strategies being used in the deployment of troops. On the other hand, nobody cares much about *ex ante* rationality. *Ex post* success is what counts. "Imagine a congressional investigation of a military commander, or an agency chief, who has adopted a specific pure strategy which has been ruinous. What would be the reaction if his defense hinged on the fact that he adopted this pure strategy by the throw of

[37] As Al Roth has pointed out to me, one can also use pure strategies to decide when to bluff, for example, by bluffing if and only if one is dealt the two of diamonds. Here one random event, the dealing of the cards, is used for two different purposes.

[38] The following discussion draws upon O. K. Moore, "Divination: A New Perspective," *American Anthropologist* 59 (1957): 69–74.

[39] Ibid., p. 71.

[40] Ibid., p. 72.

dice?" [41] If the commander or agency chief acts out of self-interest, he would be best advised to use the maximum pure strategy, even knowing that this may not be optimal against what the opponent will do. In nonzero-sum games randomization is much less plausible, for reasons that I cannot explore here.

I now turn to social lotteries, and begin with a list of cases in which lotteries are currently used to allocate tasks, scarce goods, or necessary burdens to individuals, or in which they have been used in the past for these purposes, or in which their use has been seriously proposed or at least envisaged. In parts II and III, I discuss some of these examples in greater detail.

There are not many instances of social decision making by lot in contemporary Western societies. The two major examples are the draft and the selection of jurors.[42] Lotteries have been used occasionally to allocate scarce medical resources such as kidney machines, and they play a role in regulating inheritance in some countries.[43] Lotteries play a somewhat trivial role as tie-breakers in various political contexts.[44] In the United States, oil drilling leases are partly allocated by lotteries.[45] In several countries, admission to high schools, universities, and professional schools sometimes used random drawing, within a pool formed by substantive criteria. Lotteries are frequently used in sports and

---

[41] Luce and Raiffa, *Games and Decisions*, p. 76.

[42] For a survey of randomization in the draft, see S. A. Fienberg, "Randomization in Social Affairs"; an eloquent argument for lotteries in the draft is found in Harvard Study Group, "On the Draft," *Public Interest* 9 (1967): 93–99. For a full discussion of American jury selection, see Hans and Vidmar, *Judging the Jury*.

[43] "Scarce Medical Resources," *Columbia Law Review* 69 (1969): 621–92, at p. 660; M. Herzfeld, "Social Tension and Inheritance by Lot in Three Greek Villages," *Anthropological Quarterly* 53 (1980): 91–100.

[44] South Dakota uses lotteries to break ties in congressional elections. In Tennessee the choice between two candidates with the same number of votes is left to the governor. In Massachusetts equality of votes means that no candidate is elected, and the situation is treated as if the incumbent had died in office. If the election is very close, courts will sometimes order a new election.

[45] A. Haspel, "Drilling for Dollars: The Federal Oil-lease Lottery Program," *Regulation: American Enterprise Journal for Government and Society* 9 (July–August 1985): 25–31.

games, to decide who plays first, to match teams with each other, or to match teams with players.[46] Lotteries and similar procedures are sometimes used to select questions in school and university examinations. Spot checks by the Internal Revenue Service and similar institutions are sometimes done on a quasi-randomized basis.[47] Public housing is allocated by lotteries in several countries. In Israel, for example, applicants for housing are ranked on a point system that takes account of dependents, present housing, and other variables. Those with many points participate in lotteries for the best housing, those with fewer points in lotteries for the less attractive housing.

In the past lotteries have been used more widely. The best-known cases are probably the choice of political representatives by lot in the Greek and Italian city-states.[48] Lotteries also played a role in Roman elections. The selection of jurors by lot was introduced in Athens in the fifth century B.C., and the random assignment of magistrates to cases a century later.[49] The selection

[46] In the United States, more complex sports lotteries include the following. In the National Basketball Association, it was formerly the case that the team that finished last in a given season had the first choice of players for the next season, the next to last had the second choice, and so on. Because of the incentives to lose created by this practice, the order is now determined by a lottery among the bottom eight teams. In the supplementary draft for the National Football League, the rights to choose players are allocated by an inverse weighted lottery. The World Champions get their name placed in a hat once. The last-place team (twenty-eighth) get their name placed in the hat twenty-eight times. (I am indebted to Mark Kishlansky for information about these practices.)

[47] Institutions of this kind face two optimization problems. First, what pattern of randomization should it announce to the public to achieve maximal deterrence? Second, what pattern of randomization should it actually use to maximize revenue from fines and payment of unpaid taxes? Because these institutions are allowed to proceed secretly, and because the public does not have the information to infer the true pattern from observed behavior, the two patterns are not constrained to coincide.

[48] J. W. Headlam, *Election by Lot at Athens* (Cambridge: Cambridge University Press, 1891); E. S. Staveley, *Greek and Roman Voting and Elections* (London: Thames and Hudson, 1972). On Italian city-states see especially J. Najemy, *Corporatism and Consensus in Florentine Electoral Politics, 1280–1400* (Chapel Hill: University of North Carolina Press, 1982).

[49] D. M. MacDowell, *The Law in Classical Athens* (Ithaca, N.Y.: Cornell University Press, 1978).

of religious officials and the assignment of sacred offices has been carried out by lot in many societies, the best-known being the selection by lot of the apostle to succeed Judas (Acts 1:26). The allocation of land to settlers by means of a lottery was a regular practice in the United States in the nineteenth century and is reported at several places in the Old Testament (for example, Num. 26:52–56 and 33:54).[50] Various kinds of draft lotteries were common in France from the late-seventeenth to the late-nineteenth centuries.[51] The practice of decimation, that is, killing one hostage or one treacherous soldier out of ten, has been very frequent. Often, the choice has been left to the victims themselves, as illustrated in Graham Greene's *The Tenth Man*. It was always part of the custom of the sea to choose the victim of cannibalism by lottery when the situation was desperate enough to justify this step.[52]

Gataker reports the following examples, among many others. According to Origen, angels have their place in heaven assigned to them by lot (p. 61). In Geneva, priests are selected by lot "to visit the infected at the pesthouse in times of general infection by epidemic disease" (p. 66). "In desperate cases, [the Jews] decided sometimes by lot who should slay each other" (p. 89). "In Egypt it is reported that they were wont yearly by lot to assign each man or each kindred what land they should till" (p. 104). Cambises' army "for want of victuals by lot sequestred a tenth part of themselves to make meat of" (p. 110). A Nestorian abbot cast lots to decide "between his heretical monks and the orthodox bishops, to

---

[50] For a description of one case of allocation of land by lottery, see E. E. Dale, "Oklahoma's Great Land Lottery," *Great Plains Journal* 22 (1983): 2–41. The procedure used was a combination of lottery, choice, and queuing.

[51] G. Sturgill, "Le tirage au sort de la milice en 1726 ou le début de la décadence de la royauté en France," *Revue Historique des Armées* 31 (1975): 26–38; A. Badeau, *Le village sous l'ancien régime* (Paris: Didier 1882), pp. 289ff.; F. Choisel, "Du tirage au sort au service universel," *Revue Historique des Armées* 37 (1981): 43–60.

[52] A. W. B. Simpson, *Cannibalism and the Common Law* (Chicago: University of Chicago Press, 1984), p. 140.

be thereby informed whether of them held the truth: which being cast, says the story, it went with the bishops, whereupon he and his monks, the most of them, came home unto them" (p. 330).

There have also been many proposals to use lotteries to regulate choices that are now made on other grounds. It has been seriously argued that political representatives should be chosen by random drawings among the votes, to facilitate the representation of minorities.[53] Similarly, the proposal has been made that when there are cycling majorities one alternative should be selected at random.[54] Also, by allowing the alternatives themselves to take the form of lotteries, certain perverse decisions can be avoided, although the procedure also creates problems of its own.[55] It has been suggested that randomly switching babies among families at birth, although undesirable because of the implied violation of family autonomy, would have the good effect of ensuring equality of opportunity.[56] It has been proposed, furthermore, that broadcasting licenses and procreation rights might be allocated in this way.[57] Various writers have argued that employers should use lotteries to choose among minimally qualified applicants for jobs, that layoffs should be decided by lottery, that elections should be randomly timed, that congressmen should be randomly assigned to committees, that custody of children in disputed cases should be decided randomly, and that the allocation of medical resources should rely on lotteries as a main mechanism.[58]

---

[53] B. Ackerman, *Social Justice in the Liberal State* (New Haven: Yale University Press, 1980), 286ff.; Amar, "Choosing Representatives by Lottery Voting."

[54] Ackerman, *Social Justice in the Liberal State*, pp. 291ff.

[55] R. Zeckhauser, "Majority Rule with Lotteries on Alternatives," *Quarterly Journal of Economics* 83 (1969): 696–703.

[56] J. Fishkin, *Justice, Equal Opportunity, and the Family* (New Haven: Yale University Press, 1983), p. 57.

[57] Greely, "Equality of Allocation by Lot."

[58] On minimally qualified applicants, F. Hapgood, "Chances of a Lifetime," *Working Papers for a New Society* 3 (1975): 37–42; T. M. Divine, "Women in the Academy: Sex Discrimination in University Faculty Hiring and Promotion," *Journal of Law and Education* 5 (1976): 429–51. On layoffs, Greely, "Equality of

There are two famous lotteries in fiction. Shirley Jackson's short story "The Lottery" describes, in chillingly trivial detail, a small New England village in which the inhabitants each June choose, by a multistage lottery, one among themselves to be stoned to death. The impact of the story comes from the utter lack of any perceived point in the sacrificial lottery, except for the mumblings of an old man that the harvest would be bad were they to give up the lottery, as other villages are said to be doing. The biblical ancestors of this story would seem to be the choice by lot of a scapegoat in Lev. 16:7–10 and the lot by which Jonah was selected to be thrown overboard as responsible for the tempest threatening the ship (Jon. 1:7). The analogies are imperfect, however. The goat to be sacrificed was not the scapegoat but the other goat upon which the Lord's lot fell. Rather, the scapegoat was driven into the wilderness, as were most human scapegoats in classical Greece.[59] When human scapegoats were actually sacrificed, there is no evidence that they were chosen by lot among the population at large.[60] Rather, the victims tend to be criminals or poor or otherwise repulsive persons. Being like dirt, they symbolize the dirt which is to be wiped out. The story of Jonah, on the

---

Allocation by Lot," p. 125; N. J. Ireland and P. J. Law, *The Economics of Labour-Managed Enterprises* (London: Croom Helm, 1982), pp. 19ff. On randomly timed elections, A. Lindbeck, "Stabilization Policy in Open Economies with Endogenous Politicians," *American Economic Review: Papers and Proceedings* 66 (1976): 1–19. On assigning congressmen to committees, R. Thaler, "The Mirages of Public Policy," *Public Interest* 73 (1983): 61–74. On custody of children, see J. Elster, "Solomonic Judgments: Against the Best Interest of the Child," *University of Chicago Law Review* 54 (1987): 1–45. On the allocation of medical resources, J. F. Kilner, "A Moral Allocation of Scarce Lifesaving Medical Resources," *Journal of Religious Ethics* 9 (1981): 245–71; for a very specific proposal of this kind, involving alternate stages of lotteries and selection on medical criteria, see A. Katz, "Process Design for Selection of Hemodialysis and Organ Transplant Recipients," *Buffalo Law Review* 22 (1973): 373–418.

[59] W. Burkert, *Greek Religion* (Cambridge, Mass.: Harvard University Press, 1985), pp. 82–83.

[60] A possible exception is provided by J. Frazer, *The Golden Bough* (New York: Collier Books, 1963), p. 660, who cites a text that "the human victim chosen for sacrifice . . . may be either a freeborn or a slave, a person of noble or wealthy parentage, or one of humble birth." The actual choice mechanism is not explained, however.

other hand, refers to a specific crisis, not to a periodically recurring sacrifice as in Shirley Jackson's story. Moreover, Jonah was not a scapegoat in the sense of a symbolic victim: he was actually believed to be guilty of something. Hence Shirley Jackson's story unites elements which, as far as I know, have never been found together in actual societies: the periodical character of the sacrifice, the selection of the victim from an unrestricted pool, the use of a lottery to select the victim, the subsequent killing of the victim, and the purely symbolic (nonretributive) significance of the rite.

Jorge Luis Borges's short story "The Lottery in Babylon" describes a society in which virtually all matters are left to chance, including the use of the chance mechanism itself.[61] The very operation of lotteries is tainted by randomness, uncertainty, secrecy, and fraud, until all members of society become their co-victims and co-perpetrators. The story is probably inspired by the story of Heliogabalus, described as follows by Gataker: "that monster of men, Heliogabalus, a second Nero, used to propound to whom he pleased, both in public and private, certain mixed lots, some matter of gift, some matter of charge, of such extreme inequality, that some were neither mended nor impaired at all, but mocked only, some were made, as we say, and others utterly undone" (p. 157). A modern Heliogabalus is described in Graham Greene's *Doctor Fischer of Geneva, or the Bomb Party*. The rich Dr. Fischer likes to humiliate his guests by offering them Christmas crackers which have either a large check or a small bomb in them. In these stories, lotteries are synonymous with capricious and arbitrary behavior, in contrast to Shirley Jackson's story in which they are part and parcel of the social order. These are indeed the two faces of social lotteries, which combine the regularity of an institution with unpredictability of outcome. The great advantage, and sometimes the great disadvantage, of lot-

---

[61] For an attempt to draw some lessons for political theory from this story, see B. Goodwin, "Justice and the Lottery," *Political Studies* 32 (1984): 190–202.

teries is that one can count on not being able to count on the outcome.

As conclusion to part I, I consider some examples in which lotteries have been used to allocate scarce goods and necessary burdens. To bring out the reasons for using chance devices, I shall compare them with other allocative mechanisms. The alternatives I shall consider are equal division; allocation according to need, productivity, or contribution; and market mechanisms. There are other mechanisms too, such as queuing, rotation, or status, which I do not have the space to consider here.

The first and obvious alternative is equal physical division. When a good can be infinitely divided without loss of value, it is often divided equally among all applicants or potential beneficiaries. When it cannot be thus divided, the principle of absolute equality dictates that it should not be given to anyone. Solomon's first decision, to cut the disputed child in half, followed the principle of absolute equality at the expense of efficiency. Usually, however, the principle of absolute equality is not applied when the good cannot be divided without loss of value. Instead, lotteries offer themselves as a natural alternative, substituting equality of chance for equality of outcomes. A clear example is in John 19:23–24: "Then the soldiers, when they had crucified Jesus, took his garments and made four parts, to every soldier a part, and also his coat: now the coat was without seam, woven from the top throughout. They said therefore among themselves, Let us not rend it, but cast lots for it, whose it shall be."

Lotteries are preferred to physical division when division reduces the value of that which is to be divided. Cutting a child in two would reduce its value to nothing. Cutting a seamless coat in four parts would reduce its value substantially. It is often more efficient to have half the age group perform two years of military service than to have the whole group do service for one year. In some cases, division reduces not only the value but the amount of that which is to be divided. To many people, it would seem obvious that work-sharing is a better solution to the unemployment problem than random layoffs, yet under quite reasonable conditions a shorter working day could lead to increased unemployment.[62]

In many cases, it might seem obvious that scarce resources should be allocated by *need* rather than by a lottery. Medical resources, unlike grace, should not fall impartially on barren and on fertile ground, but should be directed to the persons whom they can most benefit. To use chance instead of reason is "an abdication of moral responsibility."[63] A general answer to this argument, further discussed in part III, is that the abdication of reason can be a most rational procedure. It remains to be shown, of course, that the answer applies in the present kind of case. To show that it might apply, consider first decision costs. Fine-tuned considerations of differential needs for medical resources might, even when feasible, be excessively expensive for the community.[64] The temptation to reject such reasoning as inhumane should be resisted. The selection of which patients to treat is a costly element of the medical process which has to be assessed in terms of its benefits no less than any other element in the process, such as costly diagnostical procedures that are used to decide whether or not to treat a given patient.[65] Another, less controversial kind of decision cost involves costs to the patients rather than to the community. If the selection process is long and time-consuming, there is a risk that patients might die who otherwise would have survived or, at the very least, that they will suffer considerably and

---

[62] M. Hoel, "Employment and Allocation Effects of Reducing the Length of the Workday," *Economica* 53 (1986): 75–85.

[63] R. A. Belliotti, "Moral Assessment and the Allocation of Scarce Medical Resources," *Man and Medicine: The Journal of Values and Ethics in Health Care* 5 (1980): 251–62, at p. 255. Belliotti does not suggest that the patient's need be the sole criterion. Instead he advocates the use of a point system.

[64] This is one of the arguments for random selection in Katz, "Process Design," p. 401.

[65] See, for instance, P. T. Mentzel, *Medical Costs, Moral Choices* (New Haven: Yale University Press, 1983).

needlessly while waiting. I argue in part II that a similar argument applies to child custody decisions. In such cases more coarse-grained methods of selection, such as random choice, might be preferable. Even then, of course, one would usually have to take some account of need in forming the pool of eligibles among whom to draw lots for the scarce good.[66]

A more fundamental problem arises from the indeterminacy of the very notion of need. First, there is a conceptual indeterminacy. Does allocation according to need mean that one should give the good to the persons who would benefit most from it? Or that it should be given to those at the lowest welfare levels? The two criteria, the first in terms of marginal needs satisfaction and the second in terms of levels of need satisfaction, coincide under some circumstances, but not always.[67] Some people who are at a very low welfare level because of a handicap that reduces their productive efficiency may also, because of the same handicap, be inefficient converters of goods to welfare. Second, hard problems arise concerning interpersonal comparisons of welfare.[68] In addition to the usual sort of obstacles to such comparisons, a special difficulty arises in the case of life-saving medical resources. Assuming, for the sake of argument, that a newborn infant may benefit more from life-saving medication than a twenty-year-old person, many would feel that the latter should nevertheless have priority

[66] An elaborate four-stage procedure of this kind is proposed by Katz, "Process Design." A three-stage procedure is proposed by N. Rescher, "The Allocation of Exotic Lifesaving Therapy," in S. Gorowitz et al., eds., *Moral Problems in Medicine* (Englewood Cliffs, N.J.: Prentice-Hall, 1976).

[67] They coincide if all individuals derive the same amount of welfare from a given material situation and if their marginal welfare is always decreasing with increasing amounts of goods.

[68] These problems arise both in comparing welfare levels and in comparing welfare increments. Those who believe that levels are more easily compared than increments might prefer something like the maximin criterion. Those who believe that increments lend themselves better to comparison might prefer utilitarianism. See, for instance, A. Sen, "Interpersonal Comparisons of Welfare," in his *Choice, Welfare, and Measurement* (Oxford: Blackwell, 1982), chap. 12.

because he has more to lose.[69] Finally, the preference revelation problems associated with the measurement of welfare suggest that we would often find it impossible in practice to carry out finely grained comparisons of needs. These ambiguities suggest random choice as a good procedure in some cases. In many cases, of course, the differences in need are uncontroversial. A person who will die of cancer within a week is a less worthy candidate for a kidney transplant than a young and otherwise healthy person.

One can allocate the scarce resources where they do most good for society, as distinct from allocating them to the person who has the greatest need for them. It might be the case that X has greater need than Y for higher education, in either of the senses distinguished above, but that Y, because of his or her superior resources, would be able to use the education more productively. One person might have greater need for military exemption and yet be chosen for service because of his fighting skills. One worker might have a greater need for her job and still be laid off if she is less efficient than another. From the social point of view, the use of chance rather than productivity might also seem to be an abdication of moral responsibility.[70] Yet, assuming that we do take that point of view, several difficulties remain. Costs of decision might make it pointless to use very-fine-tuned methods of screening for productivity, even assuming them to be reliable. Moreover, the reliability of screening is quite dubious. Tests for school admission are often bad predictors of school performance and of later job performance.[71] The selection of research proposals according to their scientific merit does somewhat better than random selection but is very far from perfect.[72] Hence there

---

[69] Some arguments for abortion seem to assume a similar asymmetry.

[70] This position is strongly argued by M. Basson, "Choosing among Candidates for Scarce Medical Resources," *Journal of Medicine and Philosophy* 4 (1979): 313–33.

[71] Hapgood, "Chances of a Lifetime."

[72] S. Cole, J. R. Cole, and G. A. Simon, "Chance and Consensus in Peer Review," *Science* 214 (1981): 881–86.

is something to be said for first forming a pool of those who pass minimal levels of qualification and then selecting randomly within it. Not much is lost by way of efficiency, and much is gained by way of fairness. If necessary, the lottery could use weighted probabilities.

In addition, one may argue that productivity is not the proper criterion. The "Captain's Dilemma," invented by Lawrence Kohlberg, is intended to bring out this point.[73] In his story, one of three persons in a boat must be thrown overboard lest the boat should capsize and all die. Of the three, one is the captain, who is indispensable for navigating the boat. One is an old man with a broken shoulder. If he goes overboard, there is an 80 percent chance that the other two would survive. The third is a young and strong man in whose absence the others would merely stand a fifty-fifty chance. Kohlberg argues that the captain should draw straws between the old man and the young man. The lottery, while suboptimal from the efficiency perspective, is preferable on the Rawlsian grounds of enhancing the life prospect, as seen from behind the veil of ignorance, of the worst-off member of the group.

Although Kohlberg's reasoning is multiply confused, something like his conclusion does follow from the Rawlsian premise.[74]

---

[73] L. Kohlberg, *The Philosophy of Moral Development* (New York: Harper and Row, 1981): pp. 205ff.

[74] First, Kohlberg misstates Rawls's original position as one in which the parties know that they have "an equal probability of being the weak man or the strong man." On that interpretation of the veil of ignorance, the utilitarian conclusion, which he wants to avoid, follows unavoidably. Second, he gets his numbers wrong when he says that "if a lottery is used, the old man's probability of living is 50%." The correct number is 25 percent. Third, he inconsistently reintroduces utilitarian considerations when he says that the lottery is justified because "the strong man's chances of life decrease only 30 percent by the use of a lottery, compared to the 50 percent decrease in life chances of the weak man if he is ordered to go." Moreover, these numbers are also wrong: the strong man's chances decline by 40 percent, whereas the weak man's chances decrease by 25 percent. What follows from the Rawlsian premise is not that the parties would choose an even-chance lottery behind the veil of ignorance but that they would choose a lottery giving the weak man eight chances out of thirteen to remain in the boat and the strong man five.

My opinion, which I would not have the space to justify here even had I thought myself fully able to, which I don't, is that neither efficiency nor maximin is the right approach to distributive justice. The former gives too little protection to the vulnerable, the latter too much protection. Something in-between, like maximizing total utility subject to a floor constraint for each individual, seems to be called for. In this I seem to be in agreement with most non-philosophers, although philosophers understandably dislike the ad hocness of the proposal.[75] It does not follow, however, that lotteries could be justified to protect the worst-off if that is necessary to get their expected utility above a floor constraint. Protecting the worst-off makes sense if we are ensuring an actual minimal level of welfare. It is more dubious whether it also makes sense to ensure a minimum level of expected welfare when the potentially worst outcome is equally bad for all involved. Expected welfare is *not* a primary good: in fact, it is not any kind of good at all.[76]

Sometimes, goods are allocated according to earlier contributions. They serve, then, as a reward for good behavior (or as punishment for bad behavior). When the link between contribution and reward is established ahead of time so that the individuals concerned can count on it and plan accordingly, I shall refer to it as desert. Contribution and desert are backward-looking principles, unlike need and productivity, which are forward-looking. Reward according to desert may nevertheless have good effects on productivity by creating an incentive to good behavior. The allocation of grades to students or of bonuses to workers are examples. Also, a seniority system of layoffs creates an incentive for workers to stay in their firm, thus reducing turnover rates and increasing

[75] See M. Yaari and M. Bar-Hillel, "On Dividing Justly," *Social Choice and Welfare* 1 (1984): 1–25; J. Frohlich, J. Oppenheimer, and C. Eavey, "Laboratory Results on Rawls' Distributive Justice," *British Journal of Political Science* 17 (1987): 1–21.

[76] J. Broome, "Uncertainty and Fairness," *Economic Journal* 94 (1984): 624–32.

productivity.[77] These effects are not forthcoming when, as in the demobilization of American soldiers at the end of the Second World War, the system is not known in advance.[78] Here the order in which the soldiers were allowed to leave the army depended on how many points they scored on a composite scale in which contributions to the war effort — that is, length and danger of service — were a major component, together with number of family dependents. Another well-known example from the same war saw productivity take precedence over contribution, when scarce penicillin was given to soldiers with venereal disease to get them combat-ready rather than to soldiers who had been hurt in fighting.[79]

Lotteries may be used to supplement the principle of desert in the allocation of punishment for criminal behavior. When it is impossible or undesirable to prosecute all known or easily detectable offenders, the police should not be allowed discretionary power to select whom to prosecute, because they might use it to get back at personal enemies or to obtain favors.[80] Instead, they should use a nondiscriminatory procedure, such as selecting randomly whom to prosecute or proceeding on a first-come, first-served basis when that is more feasible. The age-old practice of decimation, that is, of executing every tenth soldier in cases of treason or desertion, is an example. The chosen individuals get (we assume) what they deserve, and hence the allocation follows

[77] R. B. Freeman and J. L. Medoff, *What Do Unions Do?* (New York: Basic Books, 1984), p. 107 (positive relation between seniority and turnover rates) and p. 174 (positive relation between turnover rates and productivity).

[78] S. Stouffer et al., *The American Soldier* (Princeton: Princeton University Press, 1949), vol. 2, chap. 11.

[79] H. K. Beecher, "Scarce Resources and Medical Advancement," *Daedalus* 98 (1969): 275–313, at pp. 279ff.

[80] K. C. Davies, *Discretionary Justice* (Urbana: University of Illinois Press, 1971), chap. 6. See also V. Aubert, "Chance in Social Affairs," in J. Dowie and P. Lefrere, eds., *Risk and Chance* (Milton Keynes: The Open University Press, 1980), pp. 74–97, at p. 91, and J. Feinberg, "Noncomparative Justice," in his *Rights, Justice, and the Bonds of Liberty* (Princeton: Princeton University Press, 1980), pp. 265–306, at p. 282.

the principle of desert; yet the choice of whom to select for this treatment is random. Similarly, we have the authority of Augustine and Aquinas for the legitimacy of selecting recipients of charity by lot.

Most of the goods discussed above, including exemption from burdens, can be allocated by auctioning, that is, by creating a market system. This can be combined with a lottery in two ways. First, one can let people pay for a chance of being selected. This is the practice followed in the U.S. oil-lease lottery program. At the present, each person can buy only one lottery ticket for a given parcel of land, but it has been argued that the system could be improved by allowing any number of tickets to be bought, thus more closely approximating a market system.[81] Second, the people selected by lot may be able to sell their right to the good or buy exemption from an undesirable duty. The examples known to me fall in the second category. I do not know of cases in which a recipient of a randomly allocated good is allowed to sell it in the market. By contrast, there are instances in which those chosen by lot for some necessary but unpleasant task can buy someone to take their place. Where draft lotteries have been used, the practice of buying substitutes has sometimes been allowed, although often expressly forbidden.[82] Alternatively, citizens have been allowed to buy their way out by paying a tax, the proceeds from which were used to induce volunteers.[83] A striking example of combined market and lottery is Greene's *The Tenth Man*, in which one of three selected by lot to be shot by the Germans offers his

[81] Haspel, "Drilling for Dollars."

[82] Choisel, "Du tirage au sort," p. 46. In Norway between the two world wars military service was regulated by a two-stage lottery. In the first stage, about one-third of the age group was exempted by lot from the regular three-month service. In the second, some of the conscripts were chosen by lot for an additional three-week service, for which it was possible to buy a substitute. (I owe this information to Magne Skodvin.) On the forbidding of buying substitutes, Sturgill, "Le tirage au sort."

[83] In France this system was introduced by Napoleon in 1855. The system of substitutes was reintroduced in 1868 (Choisel, "Du tirage au sort").

whole fortune to anyone who is willing to take his place and finds
a volunteer who accepts the offer.

II

In this part, I shall discuss lotteries and randomization in political and legal contexts. To impose some structure on the examples,
we may think of the institutional structure of (democratic) societies as organized in five successive stages (see flow chart).

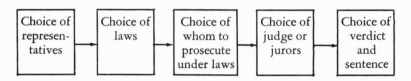

In this process, each stage except the second has occasionally
been organized as a lottery. Some have suggested that even the
second stage, the choice of laws, could be organized in this way.
Part I included some remarks about lotteries in the third stage.
The others are considered here.

Today, lotteries have virtually no role to play in the political
process beyond that of occasionally being used as tiebreakers. In
the past, however, they have been widely used to select members
of legislative or executive assemblies. Even today the proposal of
random selection of candidates is often discussed, and sometimes
advocated. Traditionally the unit of equiprobabilistic political
lotteries has been the candidate: each member of a given group
should have the same chance of being selected. In addition, lotteries were often used in elections to ensure the fairness of the
voting procedure. In modern discussions, by contrast, the unit is
the voter: each person should have the same chance of having his
or her preferred candidate selected.

Selections of representatives and officials by lot are mainly
confined to the Greek and Italian city-states. In Athens all officials
and council members were chosen by lot, with the exception of

generals and a small number of magistrates for whom special qualifications were needed. These were chosen by direct election. Excepting these technical tasks, virtually everyone was supposed to possess the competence required for governing the city.

The Athenian system is well known.[84] Rather than explaining it in detail, I shall say a few words about the more rarely discussed role of lotteries in Rome and then go on to consider an intriguing example of randomization in Italian politics.

Roman elections made subsidiary use of lotteries in two contexts, both of which were related to the fact that the Romans voted in tribes rather than individually.[85] They used lots to select the tribe in which should vote those Latins who happened to be present at Rome at the time of the vote. More important, they used lots to overcome flaws in the voting system. In some elections, the tribes voted successively, and the returns from certain tribes were announced before others were called to vote. Clearly, the former could easily exercise an influence on the latter. To prevent some tribes from having a systematic advantage over others, the order in which the tribes were called to vote was determined by lot.[86] In other elections, the tribes voted simultaneously, but the returns were declared successively until as many candidates as there were places to be filled had received a vote from the absolute majority of the tribes. At that point, the counting stopped and the returns from the remaining tribes were discarded. To ensure equality of influence, the order in which the tribes had their returns read was determined by lot. Clearly the problems could have been solved by more direct methods. When tribes voted successively, one tribe could have waited until all had voted before

[84] For a recent discussion which attempts to draw some lessons for democratic theory in general see R. G. Mulkan, "Lot as a Democratic Device of Selection," *Review of Politics* 46 (1984): 539–60.

[85] The following discussion draws upon Slaveley, *Greek and Roman Voting*, p. 152ff.

[86] This is a simplification, but not, I think, a misleading one for the present purposes.

reading out the results. When they voted simultaneously, one might have chosen the candidates with the greatest number of votes from all tribes. This patchwork solution may have served the goal of equalizing the influence of all tribes over time but hardly that of fairness toward the candidates, which may tell us something about the relative importance attached to these goals.

Fourteenth-century Florence was a society in search of, or at least in need of, constitutional constraints.[87] The development of the Florentine electoral system in this period could be summarized, perhaps, as the transformation of "instant politics," in which no institutions could ever be taken for granted, into (or at least toward) a regime capable of commanding durable assent. To understand the tensions which the political process was supposed to resolve, we can first note that Florentine society in this period was divided both vertically and horizontally. The vertical divisions were, first, between the aristocratic oligarchy and the guildsmen and, second, between various groups of guildsmen. The horizontal divisions were factions within the oligarchy, similar to if less violent than those between the Guelfs and the Ghibellines in the preceding century.

The object of electoral politics was the election of members to the city government (the Signoria) and to various committees. Every two months these bodies were appointed anew, by a process which in general included four stages. First, candidates had to be nominated; then, the nominated candidates had to be scrutinized for approval; then, among the approved candidates, a certain number had to be selected by lot; and finally, among the selected candidates, those were rejected who did not satisfy various conditions of eligibility, the main ones being that neither the candidates themselves nor their close relatives should recently have held office.

[87] The following discussion draws upon J. Najemy, *Corporatism and Consensus in Florentine Electoral Politics*.

The legislative assembly chose the mode of election of the government. In part of the period the assembly deliberated anew for each election, thus creating an extremely unstable system in which not only the set of officeholders but also the methods for electing them could change every two months. This extreme of untrammeled democracy was, however, the exception rather than the rule, since the assembly, or those to whom it delegated its authority, could in principle choose many successive governments with one fell stroke, as I shall now explain.

The important task was to overcome the destabilizing forces resulting from the short period of office and the high turnover of officeholders. The solution that came to be worked out was to have the officials for many successive governments nominated, approved, and selected simultaneously, with a selection process based on lottery. Disregarding numerous variations and qualifications, the system in force in the third quarter of the fourteenth century worked roughly as follows. Every three years various bodies, the most important of them the advisory colleges from the sixteen administrative districts, nominated candidates for office. The nomination process resulted in a large number of candidates, usually several thousand. These candidates were presented to a scrutiny committee of 144 members, most of whom were appointed directly by the existing government. The committee voted in secret on each candidate, a two-thirds majority being required for approval. The names of the approved candidates were then placed in bags, from which were drawn at random, every two months, those who would serve on the Signoria for the next period. Since the bags were not exhausted during the three-year period nor discarded after the end of the period, there were always several overlapping bags in existence. The rule was to start with the oldest bags and to proceed to the more recent as the oldest became exhausted or the candidates whose names were drawn were found to be ineligible for some reason. As a consequence there was a many-many correlation between governments and scrutinies, as distinct from the one-one correlation of modern elections.

The consequences of this complex arrangement were manifold. The fact that a large part of the citizenry was nominated for office contributed to the legitimacy of the system, especially since it was never made public who survived the scrutiny by the 144. The belief that "my turn may come" on some future extraction of names from the bags probably prevented many citizens from rocking the boat, even if in fact they had already been excluded. Here, epistemic randomness was what counted, not the objective chance of being selected. In addition, since the truly random element in the system prevented anyone from knowing who would hold office when, no faction could influence or bribe future officeholders. This was an important guarantee for the guilds against the powerful oligarchy, as were the restrictions on eligibility, which prevented individuals from the same family from holding office frequently. Moreover, the lack of clear correlation between scrutinies and governments ensured that electoral discontent lacked any obvious target of attack. Randomness in itself ensures that a corrupt government cannot be directly traced to a corrupt electoral mechanism, and the system of overlapping bags must have made it even more difficult to perceive any malevolent hand at work behind a bad outcome.

Against this, of course, both the temporal lag between nomination and officeholding and the element of randomness have clear inconveniences, well summarized by Leonardo Bruni in the early fifteenth century:

> Experience has shown that this practice was useful in eliminating the struggles that so frequently erupted among the citizens competing for elections [under the previous system]. But as much as extraction by lot is beneficial to the republic in this respect, just as much and even more is it harmful in another, namely, that because of the chance of the draw many unworthy persons are placed in the magistracy of the priorate. For the same care is not taken in staffing offices to be drawn in the

future as in electing present ones, and we certainly give more attentive consideration to present matters and tend to be more negligent in judging those things ordained for an uncertain future. This practice of extraction by lot also extinguishes any motivation for prudent conduct, since, if men were forced to compete in direct elections and openly put their reputations on the line, they would be much more circumspect [in their life and behavior].[88]

In other words, the system reduced the prescrutiny incentive of the nominated candidates to behave well, since the motive of the scrutinizers to pay attention to behavior was reduced by time and uncertainty. It also reduced their postscrutiny incentive, since in a random draw nothing they did could affect their probability of being chosen. For these reasons, perhaps, the procedure was later modified into a two-track system, in which nearly half of the government was drawn from another set of bags filled with names carefully selected by and from the oligarchy. With this final modification the system survived for another century. The de facto elite dominance ensured stability and continuity, as well as legitimacy among the oligarchy, while the broad popular participation made for legitimacy among the citizens at large.

Modern discussions of random elections emphasize the voter rather than the candidate as the unit of selection. An election should be decided by choosing a "random dictator" from the electorate. This proposal would appear strange, to say the least, yet there are a surprisingly large number of arguments to be made for it. Not surprisingly, however, the counterarguments are even stronger.

Perhaps the main argument for lottery voting, as I shall call it from now on, is that it reconciles honesty with self-interest.[89] It has been known for a long time that many methods of aggregating

---

[88] Cited in ibid., p. 313.

[89] I adapt this terminology from Amar, "Choosing Representatives by Lottery Voting."

individual votes into social decisions are plagued by the problem
that it can pay to be dishonest. By misreporting their preferences,
individuals may be able to ensure a social decision which is better — according to their true preferences — than the decision
which would be made if they reported them correctly. If people
follow their self-interest, however, they often have an incentive
to deviate from honesty. If they do, the social decision may be
disastrously bad, with no claim to being "the popular will."

Even if one denies, as I think one should, the assumption of
public-choice theorists that all behavior is based on opportunistic
self-interest, it would be desirable to have a political system that
economized on the need for honesty. Could one not design a system in which it is never in people's interest to misrepresent their
preferences? It turns out that lottery voting is the only system
which achieves this. Somewhat more precisely, the only voting
procedure which is Pareto-optimal, nondictatorial, and strategy-
proof is "random voting," the simplest case of which is when the
probability of an option's being chosen is equal to the proportion
of individuals who rank it as their first choice.[90]

A second advantage of lottery voting is that of reducing the
problem of the "wasted vote." Under a deterministic voting system there is little point in voting for a candidate whose victory is
confidently expected in any case, whence the traditionally low participation rates in the American South. Similarly, there is no point
in voting for a candidate who has virtually no chance of being
elected, whence the difficulties of new parties in attracting votes.
Sometimes, of course, one may want to increase the majority with
which one's candidate is elected, so as to give him or her the moral
authority or mandate needed to carry out major reforms. Similarly, a vote for a doomed candidate can give a show of respect-
ability to his or her cause. These, however, are second-decimal

---

[90] A. Gibbard, "Manipulation of Voting Schemes: A General Result," *Econometrica* 41 (1973): 587–601; Gibbard, "Manipulation of Voting Schemes That
Mix Voting with Chance," *Econometrica* 45 (1977): 665–81.

considerations. The problem of the wasted vote is real enough. It would be reduced by lottery voting, which ensures that each vote counts equally, that is, increases by the same amount the likelihood of the candidate's being elected. Under lottery voting, the power of an individual — measured by the probability of casting the decisive vote — is $1/n$ where n is the size of the electorate. Under deterministic majority voting, the power of an individual equals the chance that he or she will be pivotal, that is, that the other votes will be exactly evenly divided between the candidates. Under all plausible circumstances, this probability is much smaller than $1/n$.[91]

Another advantage of lottery voting is that it ensures that there will be no permanently unrepresented minorities. In many societies there exist minorities whose members differ from the majority along many of the critical political dimensions, such as race, religion, language, and wealth. If the creation of a separate polity is impossible because the numbers of the minority are too small or because its members are dispersed over the whole national territory, lottery voting can ensure that their voice is nevertheless heard.

Finally, lottery voting has the populist value of blocking the emergence of professional politicians. The system "would create a legislature of rotating citizen-legislators instead of a group of lifetime lawmakers." [92] The pressure from special-interest groups on legislators would be less effective because their ability to influence reelection chances would be reduced. Hence legislators would be freer to enact the public interest. Moreover, a steady stream of new representatives would improve the assembly's ability to perceive what that interest consists in, since it would largely be made up of people who have recently been active in community life.

[91] Estimations of that probability are given in G. Owen and B. Grofman, "To Vote or Not to Vote: The Paradox of Nonvoting," *Public Choice* 42 (1984): 311–25.

[92] Amar, "Choosing Representatives by Lottery Voting," p. 1298.

Against all these advantages, lottery voting has several disadvantages which explain why it has never been adopted and suggest that it never will be. Most obviously, the lack of continuity among the representatives counts against the proposal. Lottery voting would make it more difficult for representatives to learn from experience. What Alexis de Tocqueville identified as a major problem of democracies, that "each generation is a new people" and that "[a]fter one brief moment of power, officials are lost again amid the everchanging crowd," would be vastly exacerbated under a system of lottery voting.[93] Disproportionate power would accrue to the bureaucracy, which would, even more than today, be an element of stability in the ceaseless flux of politicians who come and go. On balance, therefore, populist goals would be badly served by the system.

Moreover, having to think about reelection is not simply a source of vulnerability to special-interest groups. It is also a form of accountability to the electorate without which the temptation to plunder the spoils of incumbency might be overwhelming. Furthermore, the predictable rise of numerous small parties would make the Fourth French Republic a paradigm of stability by comparison. With a combination of lottery voting and a large number of small parties, the laws of probability would ensure that even a large majority on a specific issue would often be reversed after the next election. The system might soon take on the surrealistic air of the "lottery in Babylon." Finally, the risk that some lunatic fringe might come into power is not acceptable, even if the chance would be very small. If we are concerned about the risk of nuclear accidents with a probability of about 10^{-7} of happening, we might well have reason to be afraid of less likely political accidents which could have disastrous effects on a much larger scale.

The second stage of the political and legal process could also be organized on a random basis. I do not know of any regime

93 A. de Tocqueville, *Democracy in America* (New York: Anchor Books, 1969), pp. 473, 207.

which has actually adopted this practice, but it is not inconceivable that the proposal might be implemented as a practical solution to the problem of cycling majorities. If an individual prefers *a* to *b*, *b* to *c*, and *c* to *a*, we would probably say that he hasn't thought carefully about the problem and that he would get his preferences straight by reconsidering. Ideally, one might want to say the same about an assembly of cyclical majorities. If the assembly gave itself more time for deliberation and rational discussion, it would achieve or at least approach unanimity.[94] In practice, for reasons that need not be spelled out in detail, this will not happen. There will often be a need to aggregate preferences which are sufficiently different from each other for cycles to arise. In such cases one might say that, for all practical purposes, the assembly has no preference and that one might as well choose one motion at random. This proposal would be certain to meet strong opposition. We have, I believe, a deep-rooted desire that the proximate causes of our decisions should be reasons. A similar and probably more acceptable device, one step removed, would be to have the order in which the alternatives are held up against each other set at random, to remove the possibility of agenda-manipulation. Since the motion finally adopted depends crucially on the order of voting, random agenda-setting effectively approximates random legislation.[95]

Consider two general arguments for democracy. On one conception, democracy is good because and to the extent that it allows expression of the popular will, or at least does so better than any other system. In light of the Arrow-McKelvey-Schofield impossibility theorems, this view cannot be defended, since the notion of the popular will is incoherent.[96] On another conception, democ-

---

[94] This view is notably associated wtih Jürgen Habermas. For a discussion, see my *Sour Grapes* (Cambridge: Cambridge University Press, 1983), chap. 1, sec. 5.

[95] For a summary of recent findings see W. Riker, *Liberalism against Populism* (San Francisco: Freeman, 1982), chap. 7, and P. C. Ordeshook, *Game Theory and Political Theory* (Cambridge: Cambridge University Press, 1986), chap. 6.

[96] Kenneth Arrow showed, loosely speaking, that no system of aggregating preferences can eliminate the possibility of cyclical social preferences. Richard

racy is to be recommended on procedural grounds, "as a way of picking out, without reference to inherently arguable claims to superior competence, a unique" decision.[97] Neither agenda manipulation nor random choice satisfies the first conception, since nothing does. Random choice, unlike agenda manipulation, satisfies the second conception of democracy.

I shall also consider, in increasing order of plausibility, three other proposals to randomize aspects of the political process. First, elections could be randomly timed, to prevent or dampen the "political business cycle" created by the tendency of each government to begin in potlatch and end in austerity.[98] Against this advantage one would have to consider the negative effects of lack of predictability. The government would be unable to plan effectively, and others would be unable to count on the (relative) stability of governmental action and policies. Also, governments might end up giving more rather than less thought to reelection, effectively acting as if each quarter were the last.

Second, the assignment of members of Congress to congressional committees might be done randomly.[99] Once again, the advantages and disadvantages are fairly obvious. On the one hand random assignment would break the system of entrenched power by seniority, which has been a major obstacle to rational policy making in the United States. On the other hand, there would be a loss of continuity and no possibility of matching committee membership with experience or inclination. On balance, the proposal might be a good idea, at least compared with current U.S.

McKelvey and Norman Schofield showed that this possibility is the rule rather than the exception and that, moreover, the cycles cover the whole policy space rather than being restricted to a small subset of it. See Riker, *Liberalism*, pp. 181ff.

[97] B. Barry, "Is Democracy Special?" in P. Laslett and J. Fishkin, eds., *Philosophy, Politics, and Society*, fifth series (Oxford: Blackwell, 1979), pp. 155–96, at p. 195.

[98] Lindbeck, "Stabilization Policy," p. 18n.

[99] Thaler, "The Mirages of Public Policy." M. Kishlansky, *Parliamentary Selection* (Cambridge: Cambridge University Press, 1986), p. 36, has a brief reference to a similar proposal in the seventeenth-century House of Commons.

practice. It might be a good thing for congressmen to get varied experience. They ought, after all, to be generalists rather than specialists. Being professional politicians with a trained staff, they would suffer smaller transition problems than most other people.

Third, one might consider random redesigning of electoral districts.[100] Ideally, reapportionment following population changes should be guided only by the principle of ensuring equal influence of all voters.[101] In practice, the parties in power can and do use reapportionment to increase their electoral chances. To avoid this, one could institute random redesigning of the districts whenever the inequality exceeds a certain level, constrained by the principle of equal influence and by topological considerations such as convexity. A good side effect of the random reapportionment could be the reshuffling of the political cards, so as to break the power of old alliances and create, on a small scale, the possibility for the periodical renewal of politics called for by Thomas Jefferson and others.

The final two stages in the flow chart set out above are the selection of judiciary decision makers and their decision making. The practice of choosing judges and jurors by a random device is frequently observed and easy to justify. The use of lotteries to choose a verdict or sentence has also been observed, although more infrequently. Although it might be thought to be inherently repulsive and irrational, I shall argue that there are cases in which the best way for courts to decide is by the flip of a coin or some similar device.

Compared with the choice of jurors, the assignment of judges and magistrates to cases is a little-discussed issue. Magistrates in

---

[100] As observed by Amar, "Choosing Representatives by Lottery Voting," p. 1294ff., lottery voting would also eliminate incentives to gerrymandering. The present proposal achieves the same aim without incurring the prohibitive costs of lottery voting.

[101] Behind this simple phrase lies a very complex reality. See J. W. Still, "Political Equality and Election Systems," *Ethics* 91 (1981): 375–94, and R. Rogowski, "Representation in Political Theory and in Law," *Ethics* 91 (1981): pp. 395–430.

Athens and judges in Rome were sometimes allocated by lot.[102] I briefly report some current Norwegian practices.[103] In one local court, each of three judges is assigned three or four of the numbers between 0 and 9. Cases are numbered in order of arrival and matched with judges by their last digit. For all practical purposes, this is a lottery system. In other courts the assignment is at the discretion of the chief magistrate. These practices are probably to be explained on grounds of convenience; at least nobody seems to attach any other significance to them. The assignment of judges to cases has been more consequential in the American context. Benjamin Cameron, a judge on the Fifth Circuit Court of Appeals, which dealt with a number of civil rights cases arising in the wake of *Brown v. Board of Education*, claimed that judges were systematically assigned to these cases in order to favor liberal and progressive views. Although the claim had little substance, it led to the development of a " 'fail-safe' system that separated the assignment of judges to panels from the scheduling of cases." [104] Assuming no communication between the judge who assigned panels to sit on designated dates in specific cities and the clerk who would calendar the cases, this is an epistemically random procedure.

Random selection of jurors is widely practiced. It was invented, together with the democratic jury itself, in Athens sometime before the middle of the fifth century B.C.[105] From those who volunteered, 6,000 were chosen by lot to be jurors for the year. Juries for the various courts were made up out of this list of 6,000. In the beginning each juror was allocated to one

---

[102] In Athens this practice was introduced well a century after the establishment of randomly selected jurors (MacDowell, *The Law in Classical Athens*, p. 40). For the Roman lotteries *inter collegas*, see Pauly-Wissowa, *Real-Encyclopädie des klassischen Altertums*, s.v. "Lösung," pp. 1497ff.

[103] I am indebted to Kirsten Sandberg for information about these practices.

[104] J. Bass, *Unlikely Heroes* (New York: Simon and Schuster, 1981), p. 241.

[105] The following discussion draws upon MacDowell, *The Law in Classical Athens*, pp. 33ff., 252ff.

court for the year. Later, probably because of trouble with corrupt juries, a different system was introduced. At the beginning of the year the 6,000 were divided into panels (probably ten), and each morning panels were randomly assigned to the various courts. Later still, the units of random assignment became the individual jurors, possibly because of the need to have an odd number of jurors so as to avoid ties.

Juries are widely, but not universally, used in modern Western societies. Their strongholds are in the Anglo-Saxon and the Scandinavian countries. In the United States, on which the following discussion will be concentrated, the process has at least two stages: selection of a panel of jurors and selection of the jury from the panel. Sometimes the panel itself is chosen from a larger subset of the adult citizens. In Norway, that larger subset is appointed nonrandomly by the municipal council. To settle the defendant's guilt or innocence, fourteen people are drawn at random from the subset, seven men and seven women. Of these, both the defense and the prosecution reject two, leaving a total of ten. The gender constraint does not operate in these challenges, so that in theory the final jury might have as much as a 7–3 bias. The four jurors selected to fix the sentence are, however, constrained by law to be two men and two women.

There are a number of arguments for choosing jurors at random. First, all citizens ought to have an equal chance to assume the privilege (or the burden) of jury service. Call this the *equal-chance argument*. If jury service is seen as a privilege, as it usually is, the equal-chance argument can be justified by the educative effects of jury service. As Tocqueville makes clear, one cannot take as a given that what is good for the citizens is also good for the parties in the case. "I do not know whether a jury is useful to the litigants, but I am sure it is very good for those who have to decide the case. I regard it as one of the most effective means of popular education at society's disposal." [106]

[106] *Tocqueville*, Democracy in America, p. 275.

Second, random selection of jurors has good incentive effects by making it more difficult to bribe or threaten those who have to decide the case. Call this the *incentive-effect argument*. This consideration has always been an important argument in jury selection, at least in societies with a generally high level of violence and corruption. Unlike the first argument, it is clearly grounded in concern for the goodness of the decision.

Third, random selection of jurors is often defended on the grounds that the defendant has a right to be judged by an impartial and representative group of his or her peers. Call this the *fairness argument*. It will be further discussed below. I shall assume, for the time being, that fairness requires the actual jury to be a representative cross section of the community and not simply drawn from a larger panel with this property.

To these three goals correspond three different concepts of randomness. The equal-chance argument requires an objectively random process in which each person has the same chance as any other of being selected. For the incentive-effect argument, epistemic randomness is sufficient. If the point of random selection of jurors is to eliminate the risk of bribery, the epistemic impossibility of knowing who will be selected is more important than objective equiprobability of being selected.[107] The fairness argument, as I have specified it, requires stratified randomization. In Norway this takes the form of selecting equal numbers of men and women, but on other dimensions of stratification the groups will not have equal representation. If the jury is stratified on race, for instance, the races will be represented in the jury according to their representation in the population. There is a clear hierarchy among these methods. Stratified randomization will achieve all three goals. Unstratified randomization will achieve the first and the second goals but not the third. An epistemically random process which is in fact biased will achieve only the second.

---

[107] See testimony by H. Zeisel, "Federal Jury Selection," Wednesday, March 20, 1967, U.S. Senate Subcommittee on improvements in the judicial machinery of the Committee of the Judiciary, p. 131.

I shall consider the fairness argument in more detail.[108] In American legal doctrine no defendant has a right to a representative jury, only the right to have a jury drawn from a representative cross section.[109] The process shall not be biased, although the end state may well be. Yet, often, end states are what we care about. To get the question in focus, I shall quote from the dissenting opinion of Justice Thurgood Marshall in the recent case of *Lockhart v. McCree*.[110]

> [T]here is no basis in either precedent or logic for the suggestion that a State law authorizing the prosecution before trial to exclude from jury service all, or even a substantial portion of a "distinctive group" would not constitute a clear infringement of the defendant's Sixth Amendment right. "The desired interaction of a cross section of the community does not take place within the venire; it is only effectuated by the jury that is selected and sworn to try the issues." . . . The right to have a particular group represented in the venire is of absolutely no value if every member of that group will automatically be excluded from service as soon as he is found to be a member of that group. Whether a violation of the fair cross section requirement has occurred can hardly turn on *when* the wholesale exclusion of a group has taken place.

It is clear, from the sentence quoted by Justice Marshall from a dissenting opinion he gave in an earlier case, that he wants to justify the right to a jury drawn from a fair cross section by end-

---

[108] I am indebted to Akhil Amar for clarifying my mind (or at least making it less confused) on these issues.

[109] See, for instance, John Ely, *Democracy and Distrust* (Cambridge, Mass.: Harvard University Press, 1980), p. 139. See also *Taylor v. Louisiana* 419 U.S. 522 (1974): "It should also be emphasized that in holding that petit juries must be drawn from a source fairly representative of the community we impose no requirement that petit juries actually chosen must mirror the community and reflect the various distinctive groups of the population. Defendants are not entitled to a jury of any particular composition . . . but the jury wheels, pools of names, panels, or venires from which juries are drawn must not systematically exclude distinctive groups in the community and thereby fail to be reasonably representative thereof" (majority opinion, Justice Marshall joining, Justices Rehnquist and Burger dissenting).

[110] 106 S. Ct. 1758 (1986).

state considerations.[111] The decision reached by the jury will be substantively better, and not simply procedurally more just, if the jury contains a variety of viewpoints. The effect of excluding "any large and identifiable segment of the community . . . is to remove from the jury room qualities of human nature and varieties of human experience." [112] A related but slightly different argument is the importance for defendants of having someone on the jury capable of understanding their situation, behavior, culture, and language. "What may appear to white jurors as a black defendant's implausible story may ring true to black jurors with a greater knowledge of the context and norms." [113]

From this it seems to follow that the jury should be a stratified random sample, ensuring that there will be some men and some women, or some whites and some blacks, proportionately to their presence in the community. To ensure the desired variety and communication, their presence on the jury itself, not simply on the earlier panels, would have to be guaranteed. This is especially true when juries are small.

The objection will be raised that a small jury can be stratified only along a small number of dimensions, whereas there is a potentially unlimited number of dimensions that could be relevant. No jury of ten or twelve can be a microcosm of a large community. To this I have three answers. First, the number of dimensions of stratification can exceed the number of people on the jury, if each person represents several dimensions. Instead of having, say, a young person, a black, and a woman on the jury, one might have a young black woman. Second, one might limit oneself to a small set of dimensions which historically have given rise to massive and systematic bias, race and gender being the most important. For civil-liberty reasons the set would probably have to be severely

[111] *McCray v. New York*, 461 U.S. 961 (1982).

[112] *Taylor v. Louisiana*, p. 532. The cited sentence is actually a quotation from the opinion of Justice Marshall in an earlier case.

[113] Hans and Vidmar, *Judging the Jury*, p. 50.

restricted in any case. One could hardly, for instance, ask people selected for the panel about their sexual orientation, even when this would be relevant to the case. Third, and this is my main reply, one might give the defendant the right to choose the dimension(s) of stratification.[114]

The conclusion that I draw from Justice Marshall's opinion is not the one he wants to draw himself. He was concerned exclusively with the *systematic* exclusion of certain groups, not with the exclusion that may happen through accidents of random selection. Yet if both kinds of exclusion can lead to the same end result, and if end results are what matter, how can the distinction be justified? The answer must be that biased end results will happen less frequently if the process is truly random. The reply might not satisfy the black defendant facing an all-white jury drawn in an impeccably random manner, but, or so the argument would go, in the long run the goals of the legal system are best served in this way. Against this I submit that a stratified random selection would have the same long-term benefits as unstratified selection, as well as being more fair in individual cases.

I turn now to the final stage of the legal system, that of legal decision making. By and large, of course, random selection is not allowed at this stage. When it occurs, it is punished. One example comes from England, where a "decision of 1665 allowed . . . juries to cast lots to resolve their differences as an alternative to a retrial when agreement could not be reached. (This decision was set aside eleven years later, however, and by the eighteenth century it had become a serious misdemeanour for juries to reach their decision in this way.)"[115] More recently, the Louisiana Judiciary Commission recommended disciplinary action against a Baton

[114] Would the same right have to be granted to the prosecution? I do not think so. The equal right of defense and prosecution to eliminate jurors does not imply an equal right to ensure the presence of jurors of a certain kind. The rationale for the defendant's right would be his need to have someone on the jury capable of understanding his language, culture, and norms. There is no corresponding rationale for the prosecution.

[115] Thomas, *Religion and the Decline of Magic*, p. 141.

Rouge city judge who gave the appearance of deciding cases by tossing coins, on the model of the judge in Rabelais who, after laborious and time-consuming presentation of evidence, invariably decides his cases by the fall of dice.[116] There are, nevertheless, civil-law cases in which the practice would seem to be justified. And there are several older cases in criminal law which show that random judgments have not always been perceived as abhorrent even if they would not be accepted today.

In a classic article John Coons discussed the curious lack of any place for compromise in the law, arguing that it is related to the "winner take all" attitude that underlies Western law, as distinct from the law of many other societies.[117] In the light of the possibility of random decisions, this cannot be quite right. A lottery is a form of compromise in which the winner does get all. Rather, resistance to compromise must be due to the resistance to acknowledge indeterminacy of fact or law. The elaborate system of the law presupposes that judges must and therefore can reach a clear-cut decision. The decision may be close but is not allowed to be indeterminate. As arguments for this principle, Coons mentions incentive effects on litigants, juries, and judges. More cases might be brought and each case might be less carefully considered if compromises were allowed. "Resolving factual issues against good men is often a distasteful duty. Remove that duty, and it is likely that more and more cases will begin to seem close." [118]

Nevertheless, there are cases in which compromises seem to be inevitable. Coons discusses the case of two men who are equally likely to be the father of a given child and says that under American law "precedents suggest" that one of them will be held solely

---

[116] P. Fishburn, "Acceptable Social Choice Lotteries," in H. W. Gottinger and W. Leinfellner, eds., *Decision Theory and Social Ethics* (Dordrecht: Reidel, 1978), 133–52, at p. 137; *Gargantua and Pantagruel*, 3.39–40.

[117] J. E. Coons, "Approaches to Court-imposed Compromise: The Uses of Doubt and Reason," *Northwestern University Law Review* 58 (1964): 750–94.

[118] Ibid., p. 762.

and fully responsible.[119] The selection of one rather than the other might be made by a lottery, but other considerations, such as income, could also be relevant.[120] In Sweden, however, the possible fathers share equally in the financial responsibility, thus substituting "an unvarying error of fifty per cent in all such judgments for an error of one hundred percent in half of these same judgments."[121] The Swedish practice seems to recommend itself on utilitarian grounds, assuming decreasing marginal utility of money and roughly similar utility functions.

If 50-50 chances of paternity call for a lottery or for equal division, what should we do in 51-49 cases? (I assume these to be reliable, objective probabilities.) Coons would apparently follow the mainstream and make the man with the slightly greater chance of paternity fully responsible. This, however, seems absurd. Rather, a 51-49 compromise should be imposed, whether a physical or a probabilistic one. A compromise would also be called for in 80–20 cases, since a 20 percent chance of innocence would certainly constitute "reasonable doubt" according to the usual criteria. In that case, however, a lottery might not be acceptable. If full responsibility was given to the man with only a 20 percent chance of being the father, he would probably think the decision monstrously unjust, whereas he might well accept to pay 20 percent of the child support.

Let us assume, however, that the latter option is not available, that is, that we are dealing with a case in which (*a*) we can assign unequal objective probabilities concerning the relevant facts and (*b*) no physical compromise is possible. In such cases, if there are any, a lottery using weighted probabilities might seem to recommend itself. As to the perceived injustice of the less probable

[119] Ibid., p. 758.

[120] Financial considerations are doubly relevant. Giving financial responsibility to the more affluent man is in the interest of the child (and of the mother). Also, under standard circumstances (see note 114, above) the more affluent man will be less hurt by the financial sacrifice.

[121] Coons, "Approaches to Court-imposed Compromise," p. 757 n. 4.

candidate's being chosen, we may appeal to an insightful observation by Francis Allen.[122] We should not ask, Who is the father? but Who engaged in illegitimate or illicit activity which was within the scope of risk, of which this little bundle now is the concrete manifestation? [123]

Another argument for legal lotteries arises in child custody litigation.[124] According to current legislation in most Western countries these cases are to be decided according to the best interest of the child. This is usually interpreted as the question of which parent is the most fit for raising the child. I believe, however, that this question is largely indeterminate, barring the small number of cases in which evidence of neglect, abuse, or psychiatric disorders shows one parent to be clearly unfit. In the majority of cases, there is no way of establishing the probabilities and value judgments that would allow us to say that the child's expected welfare will be higher with one parent than with the other. This indeterminacy is in itself an argument for using a lottery to award custody.

A more decisive argument, however, relies on the costs of legal decision making. Even assuming that fine-tuned distinctions of parental fitness can be made, the process of making them will be time-consuming and costly. I do not refer to the costs to the parents or to the legal system. Important as these may be, they should not prevent us from doing what is in the child's best interest. Rather, I have in mind the costs to the child of protracted litigation. Contested child custody cases usually lead to escalation of hostility between the parents, with devastating impact on the child's welfare. Trying to decide in the child's best interest may not be in the

---

[122] In the "Comments" on Coons's article, *Northwestern University Law Review* 58 (1964): 795–805, at p. 798.

[123] On the issue of "moral luck," which arises here, see B. Williams, *Moral Luck* (Cambridge: Cambridge University Press, 1981), chap. 2, and T. Nagel, *Mortal Questions* (Cambridge: Cambridge University Press, 1979), chap. 3.

[124] The following discussion draws heavily on Elster, "Solomonic Judgments."

child's best interest. Lotteries, by contrast, offer a swift, mechanical decision procedure that minimizes "process damage" to the child with no loss in "outcome value." Some have found the proposal to be "callous, an evasion of responsibilities both to children and to 'justice.' " [125] Others, with whom I sympathize more, have argued that "simplicity is the ultimate sophistication in deciding a child's placement." [126] I return to this argument in part III.

I conclude with some examples of how lotteries have been used in criminal cases. I do not think there are any arguments for incorporating lotteries in present-day criminal law. In old legal codes lotteries have nevertheless been used to decide the most serious cases, such as murder. An instance comes from old Frisian law.[127] When a man was killed by an unknown hand, a two-stage lottery was held among seven suspects selected by the accusers. In the first stage, an even-chance lottery was held to decide whether one of them was guilty, or whether all were innocent. If the lot showed one of them to be guilty, a second lottery was held to find the culprit. In all likelihood, the Frisians believed that the lottery was a divinely inspired method of proof, not just a man-made method of decision. Another intriguing case comes from "several Swedish and Finnish law cases from the 17th and 18th centuries in which by drawing lots it was decided who of several accused should be sentenced to death for murder. In those cases all those accused had attacked the victim but it was impossible to ascertain which of them had dealt the mortal blow." [128] The underlying idea probably was that of *lex talionis*: a life should be given for a life, but not more than one for one.

---

[125] D. Chambers, "Rethinking the Substantive Rules for Custody Disputes in Divorce," *University of Michigan Law Review* 83 (1984): 480–569, at p. 485.

[126] J. Goldstein, A. Freud, and A. J. Solnit, *Beyond the Best Interests of the Child*, 2d ed. (New York: Free Press, 1979), p. 116.

[127] Lea, *The Ordeal*, p. 107–108.

[128] T. Eckhoff, *Justice: Its Determinants in Social Interaction* (Rotterdam: Rotterdam University Press, 1974), p. 216.

III

I now turn to the four questions raised at the beginning of part I. The focus will be on social lotteries, with occasional references to individual decision making.

The first question concerned the factual problem: when have lotteries, in one form or another, actually been used to resolve individual or social decisions? [129] I have tried to provide a reasonably exhaustive answer to this question. I am sure there are cases that have escaped me, but I would be surprised if I had missed any major examples. The question is, What pattern, if any, emerges from the survey? Here are some rough generalizations.

First, as observed by Gataker (p. 68), "lotteries are most frequent in democracies or popular estates." The Italian city-states, though not democracies in our sense, provide an example. Here political lotteries were used to prevent or dampen conflicts among factions of the oligarchy and between the oligarchy and the guilds. Athenian democracy was different. Here, selection by lot was a natural compromise between the principle that the people should rule directly and the practical impossibility of having everybody involved in day-to-day matters of government. To Gataker's claim we have to add, however, that modern democracies invariably favor elections over lot. Lotteries may be more frequent in democracies than elsewhere, but they are not the most frequently used selection mechanism in democracies.

Second, lotteries are more common when they can be interpreted as the expression of God's will. In Athens itself the selection of officials by lot may have had a religious origin, although later it became a wholly secular institution.[130] Although official Christian doctrine after the twelfth century did not favor this interpretation of lotteries, it lived on for a long time. Thus under-

---

[129] Here I disregard cases in which lotteries have merely been proposed, to concentrate on those in which they have actually been used.

[130] Staveley, *Greek and Roman Voting*, pp. 56, 241 n. 90.

stood, the outcome of a lottery is not a random event but the result of an intentional act.

Third, the most pervasive uses of lotteries throughout history appear to be in assigning people to administrative legal and political tasks and in allocating burdens to people. The selection of jurors and of soldiers are recurring examples. The use of lotteries to allocate scarce goods is, by contrast, less frequent. I offer this generalization with some hesitation, but it seems to be supported by the facts I have surveyed. Although any allocation of a burden can also be represented as the allocation of a good — namely, exemption from the burden — there is a clear difference in practice between selecting one soldier from a village for military service and selecting one person from a large pool for a kidney transplant. There seems to be an asymmetry between using lotteries to allocate gains and using them to allocate losses.

The second question I raised concerned the normative justification of lotteries, in terms of individual rationality, economic efficiency, or social justice. Let me begin by discussing one frequently cited and in my view invalid reason for adopting lotteries: they prevent loss of self-esteem of those who are not chosen for the scarce good. It has often been noted that a perfect system of reward according to contribution, desert, or productivity can have bad effects on the self-perception of the losers.[131] It is easier to retain one's self-respect after a bad grade or failure of promotion if one can blame it on some nonrational element in the screening process, such as the selecting agent's bias, corruption, or incompetence. The denial of custody may not be felt as stigmatizing if the judge is obviously biased and irrational. Psychological studies suggest that procedural fairness together with an unfavorable outcome generates dissatisfaction, contrary to the frequently held view that people prefer losing fairly to losing unfairly.[132] (Later,

[131] Hapgood, "Chances of a Lifetime," p. 38; Greely, "Equality of Allocation by Lot," p. 120; "Scarce Medical Resources," p. 663.

[132] On dissatisfaction, L. Musante, "The Effects of Type of Evidence and Favorability of Verdict on Perceptions of Justice," *Justice of Applied Social Psy-*

however, I cite studies suggesting that the losers in lotteries experience loss of self-esteem.)

Arguments like these might seem to provide an argument for introducing a known element of randomness in the selection process, but a moment's reflection shows that this would hardly work. If a cheap and reliable system of screening according to the relevant criterion was available, the deliberate choice of an imperfect system for the purpose of enhancing the self-respect of the losers would not be acceptable. Imagine, for instance, that in a class of fifty students it is known that one out of ten A papers is randomly selected to receive the grade of B, in addition to the papers correctly graded B. Surely the knowledge that a prior, correct ranking had been made would make some of the B-grade students insist on getting the correct grades. By contrast, a naturally imperfect system, as distinct from one deliberately designed to be imperfect, might well have preservation of self-respect as a desirable side effect. If an employer uses a lottery because of the decision costs associated with fine-tuned screening, the applicants might welcome the procedure, but this is not the same as to say that they would ask him or her to use a lottery were there no such costs. Here, as elsewhere, self-respect is essentially a by-product that cannot be achieved by actions designed for the sole purpose of enhancing it.[133]

An apparent counterexample to this argument is found in the use of lotteries to avoid loss of esteem and self-esteem in seventeenth-century parliamentary elections in England. Mark Kishlansky argues that before the Civil War, a predominant con-

---

chology 14 (1985): 448–60. On the popular view that people prefer to lose fairly, J. L. Mashaw, *Due Process in the Administrative State* (New Haven: Yale University Press, 1985), pp. 162–63.

[133] For other arguments to this effect see Elster, *Sour Grapes*, chap. 2, sec. 8, and "Is There (or Should There Be) a Right to Work?" in A. Guttman, ed., *Democracy and the Welfare State* (Princeton: Princeton University Press, forthcoming).

cern of the electorate was to achieve consensus and avoid contests:

> The principle of parliamentary selection — and, judging from the available evidence, the reality as well — was unified choice. "By and with the whole advice, assent and consent," was how the town of Northampton put it when enrolling the selection of Christopher Sherland and Richard Spencer in 1626. Communities avoided division over parliamentary selections for all the obvious reasons — cost, trouble, fear of riot, challenge to magisterial authority — and for one other: The refusal to assent to the choice of an M.P. was an explicit statement of dishonor. Freely given by the will of the shire or the borough, a place in Parliament was a worthy distinction. Wrested away from competitors in a divisive contest, it diminished the worth of both victor and vanquished.[134]

Sometimes, nevertheless, consensus was not reached and election day approached with more candidates than seats to be filled. The local gentry would then, often successfully, try to persuade the candidates to get out of the impasse "by lot or hazard . . . or any other equal way." [135] When the number of candidates matched that of seats, disagreement might still arise over who was to have the first place. On one such occasion, "the justices explained to the two candidates, 'we have bethought ourselves of some mediation therein and such as can be no blemish to either of your reputations to consent unto.' They proposed that on the evening before the county day [the candidates] meet with the sheriff at Chelmsford and draw lots for the first place. 'And by that means fortune to be the director without touch to either of your credit.' " [136]

To be rejected by fortune was less dishonorable than to be rejected by the community. It could be inferior, nonetheless, to

---

[134] Kishlansky, *Parliamentary Selection*, pp. 16–17.

[135] Ibid., p. 78. The phrase is from a contemporary report on an election in 1614. On that particular occasion the offer to use a lottery was rejected by one of the candidates. For cases in which lotteries were successfully employed, see ibid., pp. 71, 141.

[136] Ibid., p. 68.

being selected by the community. One candidate, explaining why he refused the casting of lots proposed by the magistrates, said that he would not have it appear "that the freeholders of the said country had forborne to make election of him in regard of these rumors and reports." [137] Ideally, one would present oneself for office only if one was certain to be selected. When misunderstandings or lack of coordination led to a surfeit of candidates, a lottery might save the honor of all concerned, unless too many insults had been exchanged, for then nothing short of victory would do. The process was essentially noncompetitive, and lotteries were used only to resolve unwanted contests in a peaceful way. Hence they do not really constitute a counterexample to the claim that one cannot deliberately introduce a random element to console the losers in competitive processes.

Indeterminacy is a fundamental reason for using lotteries. The simplest form of indifference is equi-optimality. When there are several candidates who are equally and maximally good, one might as well toss a coin among them. In social decisions, this presupposes that "goodness" is measured in an objective, rigorous way. Counting votes to choose between political candidates is an example. Other examples are the point systems used for admission to medical school in several countries, for promotion in the U.S. Civil Service, or for demobilization in the U.S. Army in 1945. With equality of votes, or points, lotteries can be used as tie-breakers.

A more complex form of indeterminacy is equi-optimality within the limit of what it pays to find out. The costs of fine-tuned screening of candidates who pass a threshold of minimal qualification may be prohibitively high, compared with the social gains from choosing the best. If several candidates are equally good as far as one knows or would want to know, one might as well choose randomly. This argument works best when the selection criterion is productivity. Hiring workers, selecting soldiers,

---

[137] Cited in ibid., p. 81.

or admitting students to law school are choices properly guided by social gains rather than by the needs or deserts of the applicants. Exceptions, such as admitting women or members of minority groups, do not involve expensive screening. Similarly, in the choice of a custodial parent one should weigh the costs and the benefits to the child of fine-tuning, whereas parental rights or needs are secondary at best. Applicants who are rejected by the lottery may well think that their right to a fine-tuned evaluation has been violated, but I do not believe they have any such right. They have a right to equal concern and respect, and that right is not violated by the lottery. In principle, the decision-cost argument could also be applied when applicants are selected mainly according to their need, but in practice it will rarely be the case that the relevant welfare differences are large enough to be detectable and small enough to be offset by the cost of detecting them.

A third variety of indeterminacy is sometimes referred to as incommensurability. Here, comparison of the claims or the options is inherently impossible or unreliable, not just costly or difficult. In individual choice this situation can arise when preference orderings are incomplete or when it is impossible to assign numerical probabilities to the outcomes of action. In social allocation it can arise in several ways. First, within a given dimension of choice interpersonal comparisons may be inherently controversial. Consider the allocation of medical resources according to such proposed criteria as social utility, need, and past contributions to society. How do we compare the social utility of a tax lawyer and a public defender? [138] How do we compare a teenager and a middle-aged man with respect to levels or increments in needs satisfaction? How do we compare the past contributions to society of a general and a factory worker? I am not implying that such comparisons are always impossible, only that they often are. Second, there is in general no reliable, intersubjectively valid trade-off across these dimensions. The point system used for

[138] "Scarce Medical Resources," p. 662.

demobilization in the U.S. Army may seem to be an exception. The assignment of weights to the several dimensions, as well as the choice of the dimensions themselves, were made after a careful opinion survey among the civilian and noncivilian population.

It is unlikely, however, that the scheme could be duplicated in more complex settings, such as the selection of transplants or the drafts of soldiers for an ongoing war. The choice of observable proxies for contribution, productivity, and need would be highly controversial, as would the assignment of weights to these variables. In any case, Arrow's impossibility theorem tells us that we cannot in general expect to be able to construct a social ranking on the basis of individual rankings. Somewhat more precisely, we cannot hope to piece together the interpersonal comparisons made by different individuals into one consistent ranking with a claim to be *the* social comparison.[139] The demobilization scheme succeeded because the main variable, contribution to the war effort, was easily quantified, and because there was general agreement that this *was* the main variable. When consensus fails, we might as well use a lottery.

To say that we might as well use a lottery is not to say, however, that a lottery is rationally or morally required. If there is no detectable, relevant difference between the candidates, all are equally worthy, and hence it might appear that no wrong is done by using other methods of allocation. It has been proposed that one might select the most beautiful, the ugliest, the tallest, and (presumably) the shortest people in the pool.[140] One reason for preferring lotteries is their salience. Among the innumerable criteria that could be used in situations of indeterminacy, they stand out as being simple, mechanical, and universally applicable. An-

---

[139] This statement is made precise in unpublished work by Aanund Hylland, extending (and slightly weakening) Arrow's theorem to the problem of aggregating interpersonal comparisons.

[140] G. I. Mavrodes, "Choice and Chance in the Allocation of Medical Resources," *Journal of Religious Ethics* 12 (1984): 97–115.

other reason is that criteria related to manipulable properties of people create incentives to wasteful behavior. More generally, any given property may turn out to be highly correlated with other criteria that one would *not* want to use for allocating the scarce goods. Tall and beautiful people, for instance, tend to earn more. The general presumption against needless departures from equality counts against giving them preferential access. To prefer short and ugly people would reinforce the irrational social attitudes that define these traits as handicaps which justify compensation.

Another fundamental reason for using lotteries derives from incentive effects. The uncertainty surrounding the impact of lotteries on individuals cuts both ways. Ignorance of the future can remove the incentive for wasteful behavior — but also for socially useful behavior. Which effect dominates depends on the general level of honesty and on the complexity of social organization. For the Florentines it probably made sense to have political officials chosen randomly and to have them serve for a very short period, lest they use the office to enrich themselves or to consolidate their faction. The lottery may have prevented their society from degenerating into anarchy, given the general level of dishonesty and distrust.

Incentive effects can justify lotteries even when rational criteria are available and fully determinate. We may be confident that citizen X is more qualified than citizen Y to hold office and yet believe, assuming equal degrees of honesty, that a forwarned X would be more dangerous than an unforewarned Y and a fortiori more dangerous than an equal chance of an unforewarned X and an unforewarned Y. We might think that physical ability, an easily measurable factor, is the only relevant criterion in the selection for military service and yet use a lottery to reduce the incentive to self-mutilation. We might believe that people with professional experience ought to have some priority in the admission to medical school and yet use a lottery to prevent people from wasting years of their life accumulating points.

There are two sorts of undesirable incentive effects that are removed by lotteries. Consider the argument for choosing jurors and political officials by lot and the argument for random timing of elections. If the alternative to randomization is to have the decisions made by those who stand to profit from them, one would expect the prosecution to choose the jurors most likely to be favorable to them or the government to choose the date of election that maximizes its chances of winning. If, however, the alternative to randomization is to have the decisions made by an impartial mechanism that allows them to be anticipated, one would expect the defendant to bribe the jurors or the government to let the timing of economic policies be governed by the date of election. By creating maximal uncertainty about the outcome, on-the-spot randomization can be superior both to discretionary decision and to predetermined selection.

The incentive effects arise at several levels. Random selection prevents officials from using their discretionary power to play favorites, punish enemies, enrich themselves, or simply bask in the arbitrary exercise of power. In addition to this top-down effect there is a bottom-up effect that prevents potential appointees or recipients from bribing and threatening the officials. More generally, randomizing prevents recipients of scarce resources from trying to make themselves more eligible, at cost to themselves or to society. Self-mutilation to avoid military service is well known from many societies. Self-mutilation to increase the chance of medical treatment is at least conceivable. Finally, to the extent that the chosen individuals have themselves favor to dispense, randomization can deter third parties from extending bribes or threats. Often, the presence of third parties is the reason why officials and appointees would conspire in the first place, since they provide the kick back funds out of which both are paid.

On the other hand, uncertainty about who will do what and what will happen later can often be inefficient. Nobody has an incentive to invest time and effort to qualify themselves for positions which are assigned randomly. One might think that allocating research grants by random choice would not make much difference, since peer review is both costly and unreliable. That argument, however, assumes that the pool of applicants would remain the same in the random system, which it would obviously not if grants were known to be allocated in this manner. I have quoted Leonardi Bruni's comments on the Florentine electoral system, and notably his observation that the "practice of extraction . . . by lot extinguished any motivation for prudent conduct." Since the anticorruption and antifactionalism arguments for random assignment to office also presuppose that the term of office must be short, the system also removed the incentive for long-term planning in office.[141] It is similar in that respect to the systematic rotation of officials practiced in Imperial China to prevent them from forming alliances with the local gentry or to the Soviet practice of rotating managers.[142] Lotteries and rotation have better worse consequences and worse best consequences than a system that allows officials to form bonds with the local population. They would, therefore, be chosen by a constituent assembly acting on Hume's "maxim, that in contriving any system of government, and fixing the several checks and controls of the constitution, every man ought to be supposed to be a knave, and to have no other end, in all his actions, than private interest." [143] Yet in mature political systems, in which some measure of public-spiritedness in public officials can be counted on, the uncertainty has more bad effects than good ones.

Incentive-effect arguments also apply against John Harris's proposal to have a "survival lottery" that would allocate scarce

[141] This point is related to but distinct from Tocqueville's argument, cited above, that high turnover rates prevent officials from learning.

[142] G. W. Skinner, "Cities and the Hierarchy of Local Systems," in G. W. Skinner, ed., *The City in Late Imperial China* (Stanford: Stanford University Press, 1977): pp. 275–352, at p. 341.

[143] D. Hume, *Essays: Moral, Political, and Literary* (New York: Oxford University Press, 1963), p. 40.

resources for transplantation by choosing donors randomly in the population.[144] Each donor would give several organs, thus allowing many lives to be saved at the expense of one.[145] The proposal has met with numerous objections. On utilitarian grounds, which are also the basis for the proposal itself, it has been argued that the scheme would remove "the natural disincentives to imprudent action," since the potential recipients would know, for instance, that they can eat what they like without worrying about heart problems.[146]

As noted earlier, lotteries are sometimes used to regulate inheritance, but never to my knowledge to allocate the whole estate randomly to one heir.[147] One might ask why the latter practice has never been observed. Equal division of a property may be fair, while efficiency often requires a single heir, usually chosen by primogeniture. Would not random choice of the sole heir be a superior system, combining fairness and efficiency? The answer (or part of it) is that random choice would lack one of the two efficiency features of primogeniture. It would, like primogeniture, allow for economies of scale. It would not, however, give the heir time to prepare himself or herself for the job of running the family farm. In fact equal division may also be more efficient than random assignment of the whole estate to one person, if the inefficiency generated by uncertainty exceeds that generated by diseconomies of scale. The negative incentive effect that would be

[144] J. Harris, "The Survival Lottery," *Philosophy* 50 (1975): 81–87.

[145] A state of technology is assumed that allows all organs to be transplanted with certain success.

[146] P. Singer, "Utility and the Survival Lottery," *Philosophy* 52 (1977): 218–22.

[147] A partial exception is found in Danish law. When several heirs want the same object in the estate, it is allocated by a lottery. In the final accounting, the object thus allocated is evaluated below market value, so that the surplus is effectively allocated randomly (O. Krabbe, "Om lodtraekning i fortid og nutid" (On lotteries past and present), *Juristen* 1944, 157–75). The earlier law said that the whole estate should be divided into an equal number of equally valuable parts, to be allocated randomly. Presumably postallocation trade could reduce inefficiency in both cases.

created by lotteries may be the explanation why they are never observed in these cases.

Let me summarize the discussion up to this point. Lotteries are rationally allowed or permissible in cases of indeterminacy. Because of their simplicity and universal applicability, and because of the undesirable incentive effects that would be created by most other criteria, they are in fact rationally prescribed. Moreover, the presence of incentive effects can warrant the use of lotteries even when there is no indeterminacy. These are, it seems to me, the main arguments for using lotteries.

A final and frequently cited value of lotteries is that of promoting fairness.[148] It is difficult to assess this claim, because of the vagueness of the notion of fairness.[149] In most cases it probably reduces to the view that when there are no relevant differences among the candidates or applicants, one should use a lottery, since the alternative — that is, using irrelevant differences — would be unfair. Fairness, on this conception, simply means that relevantly like cases should be treated alike. But there could be a stronger version of the claim. It would argue that even when there are relevant differences, people should be treated alike. In a fundamental sense, which lexicographically dominates the relevant differences, all persons are equally worthy. Any human life, for instance, is as valuable as any other, irrespective of quantity (that is, expected life span) and quality (that is, ability to enjoy life). Hence any person should have equal access or, in cases of indivisibility, equal chance of receiving scarce resources.[150]

[148] We must distinguish between two issues. The first, discussed in part II, is, When is a lottery fair? The second, discussed below, is, When is it fair to use a lottery?

[149] For a useful discussion, see J. Broome, "Selecting People Randomly," *Ethics* 95 (1984): 38–55.

[150] Jewish ethic, for instance, endorses the premise of this claim (F. Rosner, *Modern Medicine and Jewish Ethics* (New York: Yeshiva University Press, 1986), p. 346). The conclusion drawn is not, however, that one ought to use a lottery. Rather the principle advocated is that of equal physical division, or when the good is indivisible, not giving it to anyone. For an explicit version of the strong fairness claim, see Kilner, "A Moral Allocation of Scarce Lifesaving Resources."

Thus starkly stated, the argument is unacceptable. At the very least it would have to be extended in a maximin direction: unequal access or unequal chances are acceptable if they increase the access or chances of those who are worst situated. "In a lifeboat, we may want especially to treat those without whom the boat will probably not reach shore. Similarly, in a disaster, the best course may be to treat first any one who can help treat others."[151] Using a weighted lottery could increase everybody's chance of getting the scarce good, if the inequality creates opportunities or incentives that in the end make it less scarce. The regulation of access to medical or technical education by a weighted lottery could be understood in this sense.

Even thus improved, the argument is unacceptable. Productivity is not the only reason to deviate from equality. We can and do and should make distinctions on grounds of need. A person who is sure to die in a few weeks should not be a candidate for a kidney transplant. We can and do and should make distinctions on grounds of contribution and desert. In many contexts, fairness as equity — to each according to contribution — is more plausible than fairness as equality.[152] There was nothing unfair about the demobilization scheme used by the American army.

In these cases, we might still ask whether the function relating individual properties such as need or contribution to allocation should be deterministic or probabilistic. John Broome has argued that when people have unequal claims to a scarce, indivisible good, fairness requires that their probability of receiving it should be proportional to the strength of their claim.[153] The claim of old people to a kidney transplant being weaker than that of young persons, they should have a smaller (but nonzero) chance of

[151] Kilner, ibid., p. 265.

[152] For this distinction see, for instance, M. Deutsch, "Equity, Equality, and Need: What Determines Which Value Will Be Used as the Basis of Distributive Justice?" *Journal of Social Issues* 31 (1975): 137–49.

[153] In the discussion following the Tanner Lectures.

receiving it. Lottery voting may also be interpreted in this way, as a way of matching strength of claims with probability of being chosen. Under Broome's proposal, all claims are respected, not in the sense of being satisfied, but in the sense of having a nonzero chance of being satisfied.

One objection to the proposal is that in small groups there is a nonnegligible chance that all or most winners would be people with weak claims. Here, fairness *ex post* would be violated at the expense of fairness *ex ante*. This difficulty could be removed by using stratified randomization. Assume that ten kidneys are to be allocated among twenty recipients, ten old people with an expected lifetime (with a kidney) of five years and ten young with an expected lifetime of twenty years. Using expected lifetime to weight the probabilities, each old person would have one chance in five of receiving a transplant and each young person four chances in five.[154] Under an unstratified weighted lottery, all or most recipients might turn out to be old. A stratified randomization would ensure that two old people and eight young people are selected.

Even thus modified, the fairness of the proposal is not obvious. Is it fair to select two old people at the expense of two young who (by assumption) are more needy? Tentatively, I would argue against Broome's proposal. Once we have decided to use need as the criterion for allocating the scarce resource, it seems perverse to adopt a procedure that withholds the good from some very needy persons while giving it to some who need it much less. The proposal lacks psychological stability, because it would appear monstrously unjust to the high-need persons who are denied the good. But the question needs further clarification.

[154] I assume that expected lifetime could be a measure of need. Similar arguments could of course be carried through using number of family dependents as a measure of need. One might also decide to use a different criterion altogether, such as length of combat service when the potential recipients are soldiers. Or one could use a point system incorporating several criteria. The argument presupposes only that society somehow has reached agreement on what the relevant considerations are for allocating the good.

The third question — what explains the use of lotteries in situations where normative reasoning counts against using them? — will be discussed briefly, since I do not believe there are many such cases. When lotteries were interpreted as God's will, there must have been occasions on which one consulted the die without the justification of indeterminacy. Although the church insisted that one should not ask God to spare one the trouble of acting prudentially, the warning was far from always heeded.[155]

Gataker argues (p. 68) that in democracies lotteries tend to be used "though such indifferency indeed be not always allowable, nor such equality stand ever with equity." The democratic passion for equality could force the use of (even-chance) lotteries even when need, contribution, productivity, or entitlement would point unambiguously to a different allocation. This argument might be taken in two ways. If it refers to claims grounded in the inherent superiority of some over others — the more virtuous over the less, the more worthy over the less — it is unacceptable. That democracy has removed references to inherent superiority from political argument, is all to the good. If thereby it has also increased the use of lotteries, it has not led to more unjustified lotteries. The argument might also be, however, that democracies lead to lotteries which are unjustified within the framework of democracy itself. The democratic way of assigning priority is by voting, not by reference to natural superiority. One might argue that democracy is subverted if excessive democratic zeal leads to equality of chances rather than equality of influence in determining inequalities. Against this we must remember that the democratic aggregation of individual rankings is not always feasible.

More conjecturally, there may be instances of misplaced use of lotteries that derive from overemphasis of the positive incentive effects created by uncertainty and neglect of the negative effects. I have alluded to this problem before, in the discussion of Florentine politics. I can well imagine that firms that make random spot

155 Thomas, *Religion and the Decline of Magic*, p. 99ff.

checks of their employees could neglect the negative "atmosphere effects" created by such practices.[156]

The final question is why lotteries are so rarely used when there are so many good arguments for using them. I shall discuss several closely related explanations. They are all connected with the argument from indeterminacy.

Visibly arbitrary chance is often repulsive. Even when we have no reason to decide one way or another, we would like the outcome to be determined by reasons. To have it both ways, we can tie our decision to natural causality in the hope that it will reflect some underlying purpose or pattern in the universe, such as fate, God's will, or the natural interconnections among all things. There is a large overlap between lotteries and the various forms of divination, from prayer through astrology to witchcraft, memorably described by Keith Thomas in *Religion and the Decline of Magic*. Theologians made clear distinctions among these practices. Some of them were legitimate, but most of them were blasphemous and superstitious. In the popular mind they all came together, in an undifferentiated belief that the universe was not random and that it was possible to unlock its secrets. The permutations were endless. Sometimes people used a lottery to choose the best time to consult the astrologer.[157] Sometimes it was held that "no prayer could be effective unless offered at an astrologically propitious moment," whereas one famous astrologer "said prayers before setting a figure." [158] According to Sir Thomas Browne, " 'Tis not a ridiculous devotion to say a prayer before a game at tables." [159] Several "went so far as to declare that astrological diagnosis was the only sure way in which witchcraft could be discovered." [160] And so on.

---

[156] For a discussion of such effects, see O. Williamson, *Markets and Hierarchies* (New York: Free Press, 1975), pp. 37–39.

[157] Thomas, *Religion and the Decline of Magic*, p. 402 n. 86.

[158] Ibid., pp. 432, 450.

[159] Quoted in ibid., p. 135.

[160] Ibid., p. 757.

The purpose of these techniques was partly cognitive, partly practical. In a world of uncertainty and misery — writing about seventeenth-century England, Thomas refers to "the hazards of an intensely insecure environment" — people want to know the causes of their misfortunes as well as what to do about them.[161] The idea that suffering can strike blindly and randomly is hard to tolerate. While the most satisfactory belief is perhaps that someone else is to blame for one's misfortunes, it may be better to think oneself blamable than to believe that nobody is to blame.[162] If people, for instance, believe that the world is basically just, we would expect them to devalue and derogate victims of purely chance events, such as the people selected by lot for military service. Indeed, we would expect the unfortunate victims also to blame themselves. There is some evidence for this view in the "just world" studies initiated by Melvin Lerner.[163] The explanation, even if unfavorable to oneself, at least provides a *meaning* for the events in question. Since human beings are meaning-seeking animals, they are uncomfortable with the idea that events are merely sound and fury, signifying nothing.[164]

Human beings are also reason-seeking animals. They want to have reasons for what they do, and they create reasons when none

[161] Ibid., p. 5.

[162] Thomas argues (ibid., p. 763) that the tendency of many of these practices, including witchcraft, to make the sufferer believe in his or her own guilt was also socially valuable. Although he does not explicitly say that the social benefits enter into the *explanation* of this tendency, this conclusion is almost irresistibly suggested by the highly functionalist bias of his book taken as a whole.

[163] See notably M. Lerner and D. T. Miller, "Just World Research and the Attribution Process: Looking Back and Looking Ahead," *Pyschological Bulletin* 85 (1978): 1030–51, and S. Rubin and A. Pepau, "Belief in a Just World and Reaction to Another's Lot: A Study of the Participants in the National Draft Lottery," *Journal of Social Issues* 29 (1973): 73–93. The strongest result in this article is not the reaction to the losers in the draft lottery but the reaction of the losers, who tended to lose self-esteem. Other findings point in different directions. E. Hoffman and M. H. Spitzer, "Entitlements, Rights, and Fairness: An Experimental Examination of Subjects' Concepts of Distributive Justice, *Journal of Legal Studies* 14 (1985): 159–97, did not find that lotteries generate moral entitlements that can serve as the disagreement point for bargaining games.

[164] See also chap. 2, sec. 10, of Elster, *Sour Grapes*.

exist. Moreover, they want the reasons to be clear and decisive, so as to make the decision easy rather than close. Several findings support this view. We do not like making close decisions, perhaps because of the potential regret associated with them. There is a tendency for the arguments that went into a close decision to be rearranged, in retrospect, so that the chosen option emerges as clearly superior to the others.[165] Sometimes this process of adjustment takes place before the choice, to permit avoidance of the unpleasant state of mind associated with a close race between the options. It has been suggested that in such cases one unconsciously looks around for a framework within which one option, no matter which, has a clear advantage over the others, and that, having found such a framework, one adopts it for the time being and chooses the option which it favors.[166]

Similar findings about the tension created by predecision ambiguity are reported in an unpublished work by Amos Tversky.[167] In his experiment, subjects were given a description of two apartments that differed in price and in distance from campus and were told that they could either choose one of them now or go on looking at some other apartments that might or might not be available. If they took the latter option, there was a risk that the two apartments might become unavailable. Some subjects were placed in a high-conflict condition, in which one apartment scored high on the first dimension and lower on the second, and vice versa for the other. Both apartments, however, were quite good on both dimensions. Other subjects were placed in a low-conflict condition, in which one apartment scored higher than the other on both

[165] See, for instance, J. Brehm, "Postdecision Changes in the Desirability of Alternatives," *Journal of Abnormal and Social Psychology* 52 (1956): 384–89; L. Festinger, *A Theory of Cognitive Dissonance* (Stanford: Stanford University Press, 1957); P. Veyne, *Le pain et le cirque* (Paris: Editions du Seuil, 1957), p. 708 and passim.

[166] R. N. Shepard, "On Subjectively Optimum Selection among Multiattribute Alternatives," in M. W. Shelley and G. L. Bryan, eds., *Human Judgment and Optimality* (New York: Wiley, 1964).

[167] Personal communication.

dimensions. Here, however, both apartments were relatively poor in both respects. In the first condition, more subjects decided to search further than in the second. The desire to resolve ambiguity and to make a clear-cut decision apparently mattered more than the desire for a good apartment.

Keith Thomas argues that one cause of the decline of magic in the late seventeenth century was the increased "ability to tolerate ignorance, which has been defined as an essential characteristic of the scientific attitude." [168] It follows that explicit lotteries should be more frequently used, with no attempt to dress them up as an expression of fate or God's will. But Thomas also suggests that people in contemporary societies are just as averse to the recognition of uncertainty, ignorance, and indeterminacy. "The investment programmes of modern industrial firms, for example, often require decisions to be taken about future policies at times when it is often impossible to form a rational view of their outcome. It is not surprising that industrialists sometimes use barely relevant statistical projects to justify what is essentially a leap in the dark." [169] Speculating along similar lines, I would suggest that Bayesian decision theory itself is an expression of the desire to have reasons for everything. The idea that in the absence of specific information all outcomes should be deemed equally probable cannot be justified in logic because of the problem of individuating states of the world. It does, however, have firm psychological foundations, in the desire to force a determinate solution to all decision problems. The toleration of ignorance, like the toleration of ambiguity more generally, does not come easily. [170]

People want to have reasons for what they do. [171] More specifically, they want reasons to be the proximate determinant of

---

[168] Thomas, *Religion and the Decline of Magic*, p. 790.

[169] Ibid., p. 791.

[170] S. J. Loevinger, *Ego Development* (San Francisco: Jossey-Bass, 1976).

[171] "[H]umans generally prefer to order their affairs through reason rather than through random or arbitrary action" (R. S. Summers, "Evaluating and Improv-

their choice. In the argument for using a lottery, reason also inter-
venes, but at an earlier stage in the decision process. The decision
not to use reason to make the final choice may be the most rational
one, as recognized in Pascal's "Il n'y a rien de si conforme à la
raison que ce désaveu de la raison" or Descartes's "La principale
finesse est de ne vouloir point du tout user de finesse." [172] In an
earlier work I have discussed other examples of this rational abdication of reason, using Ulysses binding himself to the mast and
addiction control as paradigm examples.[173] In that case, the argument for abdication was that one could not trust oneself to make
the right decision when the time comes to make it. Here, the
argument is that there is no right decision.

The two arguments are somewhat related. Sometimes we
know that we could find the decision that would have been optimal if found costlessly and instantaneously. By investing more
time, effort, and money we may be able to rank the options on the
relevant dimension of choice. We may also know, or be in a position to know, that the benefits from finding out are small compared with these costs. Yet because of what one might call *an
addiction to reason* we do not use a lottery but go on looking for
reasons, until triumphantly, we find one. I believe the child
custody case brings this out with special poignancy. To promote
the best interest of the child, the rationality addict searches for
evidence of fitness and unfitness of the parents while, in the mean-
time, the damage done to the child by the process of searching
exceeds the benefits to be expected from the search. It is more
rational, then, to resist the sirens of reason.

---

ing Legal Processes: A Plea for 'Process Values,' " *Cornell Law Review* 60 [1974]:
1–52, at p. 26). In Summers's view, procedural rationality is to be valued independently of the outcome to which it leads: "of two legal processes yielding more
or less the same results, only one of which is a rational process, we should generally
prefer the rational one" (ibid.).

172 B. Pascal, *Pensée* 272. R. Descartes, *Oeuvres complètes*, ed. Adam and
Tannery, vol. 4, p. 357.

173 Elster, *Ulysses and the Sirens* (Cambridge: Cambridge University Press,
1984), chap. 2.

People also dislike making close decisions, as shown by the evidence for prechoice and postchoice tension when the decision looks likely to be a close one. To reduce the tension, they adjust the weights of the various criteria so as to make one option appear clearly superior to the others. Fear and anticipation of regret may be the driving force in this mechanism.[174] The explicit and conscious use of a lottery implies that the decision is extremely close, and hence that there is a large likelihood for later regret if more becomes known about the situation. Again, this may lead to over-investment in the search for more information.

A further, related reason is the inability to keep the *ex ante* perspective firmly in mind. A decision that turns out to be wrong in an *ex post* sense may nevertheless have been the best that could be made at the time of choice. A military commander who chooses his plan of attack by the flip of a coin to confound the enemy may be harshly criticized if it goes wrong. To reduce anticipated blame, he may choose the pure strategy with the highest security level attached to it. Equality *ex ante* can also be a fragile motivation. It may seem acceptable as long as the coin is hovering in the air, but when it comes down the losing party may protest that he or she was never given a fair hearing.

The basic reason for using lotteries to make decisions is honesty. Honesty requires us to recognize the pervasive presence of uncertainty and incommensurability, rather than denying or avoiding it. Some decisions are going to be arbitrary and epistemically random no matter what we do, no matter how hard we try to base them on reasons. There is a remark of Dr. Johnson to Boswell that perfectly illustrates the point: "Life is not long, and too much of it must not pass in idle deliberation how it shall be spent:

[174] This language should not be taken to be as intentional as it may appear to be. I do not suggest that people consciously adjust the weights because they consciously anticipate regret. If they tried, they would not succeed, because they would still remember the unadjusted weights (see Elster, *Sour Grapes*, chap. 2). Rather, the experience of regret following close decisions sets up a reinforcement process which, unknown to the persons themselves, shapes their attitude in later decisions of this kind.

deliberation, which those who begin it by prudence, and continue it with subtlety, must, after long expence of thought, conclude by chance. To prefer one future mode of life to another, upon just reasons, requires faculties which it has not pleased our Creator to give to us." [175]

Chance will regulate a large part of our lives no matter how hard we try to avoid it. By *taming chance* we can bring the randomness of the universe under control as far as possible, and keep free from self-deception as well. The requirements of personal causation and of autonomy are reconciled by the conscious use of chance to make decisions when rational argument fails.[176] Although the bleakness of this vision may disturb us, it is preferable to a life built on the comforting falsehood that we can always know what to do.

---

[175] J. Boswell, *The Life of Samuel Johnson* A.D. 1766 (Aetat 57) — a letter from Johnson to Boswell dated 21 August 1766. I owe this reference to John Broome.

[176] R. De Charms, *Personal Causation* (New York: Academic Press, 1968), pp. 269ff. On the requirements of autonomy, see Elster, *Sour Grapes*, chap. 3.

Greek Ethics and Moral Theory

GISELA STRIKER

THE TANNER LECTURES ON HUMAN VALUES

Delivered at
Stanford University

May 14 and 19, 1987

GISELA STRIKER is professor of philosophy at Columbia University, New York City. She was born and educated in Germany, where she received her doctorate from the University of Göttingen in 1969. Until 1986 she taught philosophy at Göttingen. She also held visiting appointments at the universities of Stanford, Princeton, and Harvard. In 1984 she gave the Nellie Wallace lectures at Oxford University. She has published monographs and articles on various aspects of ancient philosophy, including a study of Plato's *Philebus* (*Peras und Apeiron*, 1970) and of the notion of a criterion of truth (*kritērion tēs alētheias*, 1974). In recent years, her work has focused mainly on Hellenistic epistemology and ethics.

Greek ethics has had a kind of renaissance in the last few years. A number of authors, tired, perhaps, of debates about forms of utilitarianism or technicalities of metaethics, have pointed to the classical Greek theories as offering a wider perspective. Three points in particular have been singled out for praise. First, Greek authors were usually concerned to provide an account of the good life for man — what they called *eudaimonia*, happiness — as opposed to focusing narrowly on right or good action. Second, this wider scope led them to treat seriously and without philistine prejudices the question of motives for morality, or reasons for wanting to be good — a question that has been an embarrassment to both Kantians and utilitarians. Finally, the Greek philosophers tended to be concerned with virtues of character, the traits that underlie or explain a disposition to act in the right way, more than with principles of right action. This is an advantage for two reasons. First, it would seem that our evaluations of people as distinct from actions must be based on a consideration of their character — indeed, even actions can hardly be understood or evaluated without regard to the agent's motives, and motives have more to do with character than with theoretical justification. Second, it seems that if ethics is to have some beneficial effect, preaching the rules of morality would be a most unpromising way of trying to achieve this. As Aristotle said perhaps most clearly, what people are apt to do depends first and foremost upon their character, not on any knowledge of moral or legal rules that they might possess. Hence we should study ex-

This is a considerably revised version of the lecture I gave at Stanford University. I have learned much from my commentators, Julia Annas, John Cooper, and Tony Long, though I could not attempt to do justice to all their suggestions. I am particularly grateful to John Cooper for letting me use his notes. Mary Mothersill has helped me throughout with encouragement and advice, and, last but not least, by correcting my English.

cellence of character, try to find out what it is and how it comes about, and avoid entanglement in discussions of moral epistemology or ethical foundationalism. The emphasis on virtue of character over action is connected with the theme of the good life, since, as the Greeks realized, what counts as a satisfactory life for a person will depend to a large extent on what she desires, and desires are more closely tied to character than to reasoning.

Still, such praise of ancient theories does not mean that we should simply return to them. Closer inspection usually shows that there were drawbacks as well as advantages. In fact, the same authors who praise ancient ethics tend to tell us also that there is no chance of return. The conclusion can be quite pessimistic: modern moral theory is hardly any good; ancient ethics was better but built upon assumptions that we can no longer accept. So perhaps it is time to abandon the project as a serious philosophical enterprise.[1]

Such radical skepticism, I think, is premature, and I propose to take a closer look at the development of Greek ethical theories in the hope of finding out how ancient and modern questions might hang together. It seems to me that an examination of ancient theories that goes beyond the two great classics Plato and Aristotle (usually, and wrongly, thought to represent all of Greek ethics) might help us to see a little more clearly what if anything we could learn from them. Obviously, I cannot do this in detail here. My remarks will be limited to a few fairly general points of strategy.

For a modern reader the classical Greek treatments of ethics are surprisingly reticent about what we have learned to consider as the most fundamental question — the justification of moral decisions or the foundation of moral rules. Saying that those philosophers started from a different perspective, asking questions about the good life, will not really help to explain why they seem

---

[1] See, for example, the postscript in Bernard Williams's *Ethics and the Limits of Philosophy* (Cambridge, Mass.: Harvard University Press, 1985).

to have paid so little attention to a central problem — one that must surely have been current in their time, given the fifth-century debates about, for example, the objectivity or relativity of moral and legal rules. Furthermore, modern ethics is after all a descendant of the same tradition, however complicated the historical development, and so one would expect there to be some connection. Hence we might ask, how could the question of the foundation of moral rules appear so unimportant at the beginning, and when and where did it arise? I am going to argue that our question did not get much attention in the early stages of Greek ethical thinking, partly because it was confused with other questions, and partly because morality was not considered to be a question of rules until the time of the Stoics. However, the question did arise — and it might be that the first explicit debate about the foundations of moral rules led to that split between questions about happiness and moral questions which is rightly deplored by modern writers.

I

First, a very general outline of the type of theory I shall call eudaimonist. I will look at the four best-documented versions of eudaimonism (Plato, Aristotle, Epicurus, and the Stoics) and ask where and how questions about the foundations of morality did or should have come up.

Greek ethical theories are theories about the good life; their starting point is Socrates' question in the *Gorgias* (472C–D) — how should we live to be happy? Greek philosophers after Socrates assume that happiness or living well is an object of desire for everyone. This might be taken in a fairly trivial sense, meaning no more than that everybody would rather be satisfied with their lives than otherwise. But these philosophers also assume that happiness is a goal of action. This is no longer trivial, and not just because one might believe that it is a matter of luck, not of one's own efforts, whether one is living well. The main problem arises from the assumption that it makes sense to consider happiness as one thing that we might try to achieve.

Might not living well consist, not in achieving a single end, but rather in achieving or getting lots of different things, so that a desire for happiness should be understood simply as a second-order desire to get what one wants most of the time, with no implications about objects of first-order desires? If so, happiness can hardly play the role of ultimate aim of action that the Greeks ascribed to it — that for the sake of which everything in one's life ought to be done, as the Stoics put it (see v. Arnim, *Stoic. Vet. Fragm.* 3.2, p. 3). For then to say that one does something "for the sake of happiness" is just to say that one does it because one wants to, and that is hardly an explanation. If happiness is to play the role of ultimate aim of desire and action, it must be something more concrete — either a certain life-pattern or else a life lived in a certain sort of way.[2] To say that happiness is the ultimate end of action, then, seems to presuppose (*a*) that there is a general answer to the question What sort of life can count as a good life for humans? (*b*) that every human being desires to live a good life, and (*c*) that we do or should plan all our actions in such a way that they lead or contribute to such a life.

All of these assumptions may seem dubious. The first has sometimes been rejected on the ground that there can be no general answer to the question about a good life because individuals differ so much in character, talent, and inclinations that it makes no sense to look for a recipe that fits everyone. This seems to me to be a rather superficial point and easy to refute. We need only to think of the notion of welfare to realize that there is probably quite a long list of generally necessary conditions for a satisfactory human life. A description of the good life in general will no

---

[2] The first is suggested by classifications of kinds of lives (*bioi*), such as money making, politics, or philosophy (see, e.g., Plato, *Republic* 9 581C-E; Aristotle, *Nicomachean Ethics* [EN] 1, 1095b14–1096a5); the second by Prodikos's famous parable about Herakles' choice between the lives of virtue and vice (Xenophon, *Memorabilia* 2.1, 21–34).

doubt have to make room for many individual differences, but this does not show that we could not try to find out what will be needed by way of necessary conditions for everyone. A theory of the human good can apply to individuals only as members of the species, but that does not mean that such a theory is useless or impossible. (I do not mean to suggest that it is easy to determine what counts as common and what does not. Obviously, a "daily schedule for the happy person" would be ridiculous, but should we include such things as education, opportunities to enjoy music or theater, traveling, and so on?)

The second thesis — that every human being desires to live a good life — should probably be interpreted to mean that every person who knows what the good life is will desire it as his or her ultimate aim (cf. Plato, *Philebus* 11D). But is this true? Some people, to all appearances, do *not* wish to have a good life in the required sense, for example, ascetics who deliberately deprive themselves of things that ordinary people would find indispensable, or monomaniacs who devote their lives to a single pursuit, like painting pictures or solving mathematical problems. It seems question-begging to insist that such persons have a wrongheaded idea of what is good for them, and that if they had been brought up in more enlightened ways, they would have realized that they "really" wanted to be prosperous, sociable human beings like everybody else. This objection should be taken seriously, but it does not show that it makes no sense to assume that people *normally* desire to lead a good human life, and indeed we seem to assume just that when we try to decide about how to treat others. For certainly even if some people do not want the things most of us desire, we do not feel justified in depriving them of the opportunity to have them. Thus ascetics and monomaniacs must be treated as exceptions that will not disprove the thesis that human beings generally desire to lead a good human life.

The last point — that all our actions are or should be directed toward the good life — is more difficult. Aristotle raises the question whether we should assume that there *is* a single ultimate end in the first chapter of his *Nicomachean Ethics*, but it is not clear whether he wishes to maintain, as a factual claim, that all deliberate human action aims at happiness as its ultimate goal or, rather, more modestly, that rational agents should try to organize their lives in such a way that they can be justified in terms of a true conception of the good life. Not all eudaimonist theorists are as cautious as Aristotle on this point. For Socrates, Epicurus, and the Stoics, the good for man is an end we pursue in all our actions, whether we know what it is or not, so that we will be unhappy or disappointed with our lives if we have a wrong conception of the good. If we find that claim difficult to accept, we may still study the Greek theories on the basis of the more limited interpretation suggested by Aristotle.

Given the basic assumption that there is an ultimate end of desire and action, to be called happiness or living well, the task of ethics will be to establish what this end is — what happiness consists in — and how we may best achieve it. I shall use the term "eudaimonism" to refer to theories that use this framework.

Philosophers vary in their views of how we determine the end. Aristotle relies on his natural teleology;[3] Plato and the two Hellenistic schools seem to start from a conception of the good, from which they then derive a definition of the good life. That definition largely determines the rest of the theory, which will consist in an investigation of the constituents of the good life and a discussion of how we may achieve the good life through action.

---

[3] This is not the doctrine that the natural world is governed by a rational planner who has arranged it in such a way that each part contributes to the good order of the whole. The Stoics, but not Aristotle, held such a view. Aristotle's teleology is the theory according to which natural things, and organisms in particular, have a specific form and activity that is their "end" (*telos*) in the sense that it is (*a*) the outcome of their normal development from seed to maturity and (*b*) the kind of life that their characteristic capacities, when fully developed, permit them to lead. The latter is what Aristotle calls the "function" (*ergon*) of an organism.

II

Now note that eudaimonism as described so far has as yet nothing to do with moral theory. The topic of virtue comes in by way of the question whether or not a good moral character is necessary for the best human life. Philosophers have tended to argue that it is indeed necessary — the Hellenistic schools even tried to defend the view that it is also sufficient. These arguments initially arose from a background of opposition or at least controversy: one of the earliest arguments in Greek ethics, that of Antiphon the sophist, purports to show that justice is a hindrance on the way to happiness. Hence from the time of Socrates on we find Greek philosophers defending justice and the other virtues as belonging to the good life — either as a means, or as a constituent, or even as identical with it.

It is important to notice at this point that a defense of virtue, or of justice in particular, need not have anything to do with questions about the foundations or principles of justice. In order to show that a person needs to be just to lead a happy life, one has to argue that the kind of character that makes one disposed to act in the right sort of way will be beneficial, or that lacking this virtue is apt to make one miserable. Such an argument may proceed on an implicit understanding of what right action is, because we need not appeal to specific principles of justice to show that one needs the virtue. Indeed such an appeal is unlikely to be of great help, since principles of justice, as we ordinarily think of them, are distinct from principles of self-interest. But some defenders of justice did try this line, by producing a quasi-historical account of the origin of legal systems as instruments of social peace and cooperation and then urging people to support these goals by obeying the law.[4] Such an account, if convincing, might show

---

[4] See, for example, the so-called Anonymous Iamblichi (Diels-Kranz, *Fragmente der Vorsokratiker* 2.89, 607, pp. 402–404), an author from the time of the sophists, or Protagoras in Plato's dialogue of this name, who argues (322D–323C) that every citizen must be minimally just for a city to survive.

that human communities need a legal order and hence some kind of justice, understood as obedience to law.

However, as Plato saw, this is not a good defense of justice as a requirement for an individual's happiness. Egoists who thought that they could be happier if they had more than their neighbors and were not restricted by legal rules could plausibly arrive at the conclusions of Antiphon, or Callicles, or Thrasymachus — the best situation for an individual is one where everybody else obeys the law, but you are free to break it. This is, I think, why Plato has nothing but contempt for the early version of a contract theory of justice cited by Glaucon in the *Republic* (2.358E–359B). Plato is right in pointing out that this theory is inadequate to answer the question Why should I be just? But it seems unfortunate that he did not pay more attention to the possibility of treating this theory, not as a defense of justice as a virtue, but rather as an explanation of the origin and principles of justice as represented by the legal order.[5] It may have been easy to overlook this point because the contract theory, and similar ones, were probably introduced as a defense of *justice* in the famous nature-versus-convention debate of the fifth century. Instead of showing why individuals should try to become just persons, such theories set out to argue that human society needs rules to survive; and by appealing to this function of a legal system, they also provide at least a rudimentary account of what the principles of such a

---

[5] This does not mean that Plato might then have accepted it. As John Cooper points out to me, he does implicitly rely on earlier theories of the origin of justice in his account of the development of the city, but he probably thinks that they are not sufficient, because a good state should do more than provide for the economic necessities and the safety of its citizens. What Plato eventually describes as justice in the city is an order of government designed to ensure that the most competent citizens rule and everybody is assigned their proper place and role in society. He seems to think that the contract theory invites the sort of reasoning exemplified by Thrasymachus's argument in book 1, and the story of Gyges (*Rep.* 2.359A–360D). This is, I think, quite unfair, since it supposes that the contract theory goes with the assumption that human beings are by nature ruthless egoists. (Thomas Hobbes, who combined a version of contract theory with an egoistic psychology, had great difficulties — and failed, I think — in refuting the egoist's objection. See *Leviathan*, pt. 1, chap. 15. But clearly the combination is not necessary.)

system should be: they should protect the members of communities from mutual harm and perhaps provide a framework for cooperation that would benefit everyone, if so we may understand the phrase "common good" (*koine sumpheron*).

It is a separate question whether individuals in a society should wish to have the kind of character that makes them reliable and law-abiding members of the community. Plato's arguments attempt to establish this second thesis by showing that the soul of a just person will possess the kind of internal order that is necessary for happiness, while an unjust person will be constantly plagued by fears and inner conflicts. Given the task he has set himself, Plato is right to concentrate on moral psychology and the role of virtue for happiness, and we can see why questions about the principles of just legislation or just action, as distinct from questions about a just form of government, play a minor role in the *Republic*. Not that there is no theory, but it is mostly implicit. A just society, according to Plato, will be one that exhibits the same internal order that he wishes to ascribe to the just soul — intellect will rule, and emotion and appetite will be so trained that they gladly follow reason's guidance. The *Republic* starts from the dubious assumption that justice is the same in a city and in an individual (368D–E), and Plato's just society, with its three classes, has the same structure as the just soul. This is, I think, the counterpart of what I take to be Plato's misunderstanding of the theories about the origin of justice: Plato rejects them as a defense of justice because he seems to think that social justice must be the same as individual justice — a virtue of society. It is not so surprising that he has difficulties in accommodating traditional Greek conceptions of social justice, such as the idea of equality, in this picture. I believe, in short, that Plato's assumption of univocity — that the same word must indicate the same sort of thing in each case — was wrong in the case of justice and that his neglect of the question of principles is due to his exclusive attention to justice as a virtue of character. If one wanted to extract a thesis about the justification of moral decisions from Plato's theory, one would presumably have to say that right decisions are made by the rulers on the basis of their knowledge of the Form of the good — which has remained a mystery ever since Plato wrote the *Republic*.

III

Aristotle's ethical theory follows the eudaimonist pattern set out by Plato. He is concerned with virtue as a constituent of the good life and so concentrates on moral psychology, working out what seems still to be one of the most insightful accounts of character traits and their genesis. However, he defines virtue of character as a disposition to make decisions that are adequate as determined by reason — and surely this makes one expect an account of the reasoning that precedes virtuous decisions, and in particular, of the first principles and premises of such reasoning.

Aristotle's notion of adequacy (the mean) would seem to require him to state his standards of adequacy, since he has expressly rejected Plato's postulated general theory of the good and hence can no longer explain adequacy in terms of "adequate for reaching a good result." But Aristotle nowhere produces an account of the principles of practical reasoning — presumably for the good reason that he thinks no clear and general account can be given. In his discussion of practical wisdom (*EN* bk6) he emphasizes above all the intelligent person's capacity to grasp what needs to be done in a particular case. He thinks that particular decisions and value judgments will have to precede the formulation of general rules that are derived from them by induction and will be in constant need of revision in the light of new situations. Aristotle's emphasis on the intelligent person's intuitive grasp of a particular situation as opposed to his knowledge of general rules may be quite correct — he might be right in thinking that for practical purposes experience without theory is more important than theory without experience (which he thinks is no use at all, since it won't influence action).

Yet one begins to wonder what it would be like to engage in a moral argument with an Aristotelian person of practical wisdom. "We must attend to the undemonstrated remarks and beliefs of experienced and older people or of intelligent people, no less than to demonstrations," Aristotle says (*EN* 1143b11–13).[6] He thinks that a person who has practical wisdom will be able to correct the law if a rigid application of it would lead to an unacceptable result. This may be quite true, but what if several such people disagree about what would be the right or just thing to do, or we find that we cannot agree with them? What reasons will they invoke to explain and justify their decisions, if challenged? It seems to me that Aristotle vastly underestimates the possibilities of disagreement here. Perhaps his readiness to give up on the possibility of general principles may be due to the idea that one would have to face the hopeless task of giving rules for each of the individual virtues. Aristotle seems to think that the good man's decisions will be guided by his correct conception of the end, and that, according to Aristotle, is an active life in accordance with virtue. Hence he says that a good legislator should prescribe action in accordance with all the virtues (see *EN* 5.1129b19–25 and 1130b22–24; *Politics* 7.1333b8–9). Any reader of Plato's early dialogues would have learned to be pessimistic about such a project. For time and again Socrates' interlocutors try to define one of the virtues in terms of a specific type of action, only to find themselves immediately refuted by counterexamples. The most famous of these is probably found in the *Republic* (1.331C–D): justice cannot consist in returning deposits, for who would find it just to return a weapon to a madman?[7] But all this might show is that spelling out rules for virtues is not the right way for finding principles of moral reasoning; it is not a proof that a different method could not succeed.

[6] Trans. Terence Irwin (Indianapolis: Hackett, 1985).

[7] See also *Laches* 190E–191D for courage as "standing one's ground"; *Meno* 73C–D for virtue as "ruling over people." It is interesting to note that "standing one's ground" is one of Aristotle's examples of good legislation at EN 5.1129b19.

Thus far I have tried to show that Plato's and Aristotle's apparent neglect of the central question of modern moral theory can indeed be explained but need not be seen as a repudiation of the whole problem nor as evidence of some deeper insight. On the other hand, it is wrong to suppose that eudaimonist theories leave no room for such questions. Although they do not arise at the very beginning, they are certainly invited by any account of human virtue that includes justice. Plato seems to have thought that he had or could find an answer if only he could fully explicate his theory of the good; Aristotle perhaps concluded that he had said as much as could be said, given the overwhelming complexity of the matter, but if he thought so, that is not really to his credit.

I will now try to show that later Hellenistic theories of happiness did address the question of justification in promising and illuminating ways. I hope that a consideration of the fate of the Stoic theory in particular might also indicate what went wrong when theories of happiness and theories of morality split up into the allegedly different fields of prudential and moral reasoning.

IV

Epicurus was perhaps the first philosopher who made a clear, if implicit, distinction between justice as the virtue of an individual and the justice of societies or legal order. With respect to legal justice, he adopted the old contract theory rejected by Plato. The nature of justice, he tells us, is "a guarantee of utility with a view to not harming one another and not being harmed" (*Principal Doctrine* 31).[8] Laws will be just only if they contribute to these goals (*P.D.* 37). It follows that a justification of legal rules, or rules of justice, must appeal to the purpose of the original contract, which, though obviously related, is not the same as happiness for the individual. Hence a separate argument is needed to

---

[8] Translation from A. A. Long and D. Sedley, *The Hellenistic Philosophers* (Cambridge: Cambridge University Press, 1987), vol. 1, p. 125.

show not only why rules of justice are useful for a community but also why individuals should want to be just persons. Here Epicurus's argument is complicated, as one might expect, since he needs to show why a person whose ultimate aim is a pleasant life for himself should take an interest in something that does not immediately contribute to this goal. Epicurus can argue, of course, that an Epicurean will wish to live in a peaceful society and be protected from attacks by other members of the group. But this is not enough, because it might invite the old conclusion exposed by Plato — let others be just, and prey on them if you can. But Epicurus also holds that a rational hedonist — of the peculiar Epicurean brand — has no motive for wanting to harm others. He knows that he can get all that he needs without having to take it away from his neighbors and that this will be enough to make him happy. Also, he values friendship (though it may be hard to account for this within the Epicurean system) and knows that this depends upon mutual trust (cf. Epicurus, *Vatican Sayings* 34). And if he should ever be tempted, say, to take what is not his, he will reason that injustice is not worth its consequences — the nagging fear of discovery and punishment (*P.D.* 34).

Epicurus does not claim that just action will directly contribute to one's happiness, but he believes that being a just person will — his is not an attempt to derive rules of morality from an account of individual happiness. But this important point was not much emphasized by Epicureans, and so it tended to be overlooked by unsympathetic critics like, for example, Cicero (in *De finibus* 2), who treats Epicurean ethics as a straightforward version of egoist hedonism and sets out to show that it is incompatible with virtue as commonly understood. Cicero's counterexamples, used to this day to demonstrate the untenability of egoism as a foundation for morality, are, I think, misguided, because Epicurus never maintained that rules of justice are identical with rules for maximizing individual pleasure. In any case, whether because of misunderstanding or lack of attention, this first attempt to separate questions about virtue from questions about social jusice did not lead to an extended debate about the foundations of morality.

V

The first installment of that debate, which continues to this day, seems to have occurred in the second century B.C., when the skeptic Carneades launched an attack on the Stoic theory of natural law. The Stoics, as is well known, tried to show that happiness is identical with virtue. They did this by arguing for a conception of the human good that makes it coincide with what they considered to be the fundamental principle of morality — conformity to the order of nature. The reasoning behind this thesis is too complicated to rehearse here, but I will need to state its main steps to show the force of Carneades' criticism.

Very briefly, the Stoics held that the good, universally speaking, was rational order, represented in its greatest perfection by the order of the universe. Humans, as rational animals, would lead the best possible life if they tried to follow that order, so that the good for man could be defined as "living in agreement with nature." We can discover nature's rules for human beings by studying the way nature has made us and finding out from this how she intends us to organize our lives.

According to the Stoics, nature has provided us with two primary impulses that determine our behavior long before we use reason to guide our actions; and if we use reason to follow up nature's intentions, the result will be virtuous conduct. The two primary impulses were said to be toward self-preservation on the one hand, toward sociability on the other. These instincts lead us to seek out what contributes to our physical welfare and normal development of capacities and also to care about and assist our neighbors; they also teach us to avoid what might lead to destruction or harm for ourselves and others. The natural law thus directs us, as the Stoics used to express it, to "select" what is natural, that is, an object of one of the primary impulses, and to reject what is contrary to them; and "appropriate action" consists in this selection.[9] Virtue and "right action" require, in addition, that selection should be exercised with the aim of conforming to the order of nature. So, for example, the virtue of justice, since it has to do with interactions among human agents, will be based on the impulse toward sociability and will be exercised in pursuing its objectives with the intention of living in agreement with nature.

Obviously, this *is* a theory about the foundation of moral rules, albeit a very general one, and it is interestingly close to what one might expect to find, but does not get, in Aristotle — an attempt to show that virtue is a perfection of human nature. But it is presented as a theory of happiness, not primarily as an explanation of the principles of morally good conduct. The Stoics expected that trying to achieve happiness by following the rules of nature would lead to virtuous conduct –– and this is, I think, the doctrine that was attacked in what must have been one of the most spectacular and entertaining episodes in the history of ancient philosophy: two speeches, given on two consecutive days, first defending, then attacking justice, by the Academic skeptic Carneades in Rome, 155 B.C.

We do not have any contemporary records, let alone writings by Carneades or indeed the Stoics he was criticizing; what we have is a mutilated and no doubt altered version of the negative speech in the fragmentary remains of Cicero's *De re publica* 3. Rather than try to reconstruct an outline of this speech, I will just state what I take to have been Carneades' main line of attack.[10] He

----

[9] The Stoics made a terminological distinction between "selection," which aims at the objects of the natural impulses, and "choice," which aims at virtue or agreement with nature, and a parallel distinction between "appropriate" and "right," or virtuous, action. "Natural things" are said to be "preferred," their opposites "dispreferred," while the predicates "good" and "bad" are reserved for virtue and moral evil.

[10] I assume that Carneades was arguing against the Stoics, not Plato or Aristotle, though these are cited as the main defenders of justice whom Carneades refuted, because the theory that is attacked is in fact Stoic. Cicero tends to believe, following his teacher Antiochus, that most of what the Stoics said was derived from, and in agreement with, the doctrines of Plato and Aristotle.

argued that the method of "selecting what is natural and rejecting what goes against nature," far from resulting in virtuous conduct, would lead to cunning and ruthless egoism, if not of individuals, then of groups — exemplified, if Cicero's report is correct, by the imperialism of Rome's successful and highly admired generals. Since the Stoics had identified rational selection with practical wisdom, Carneades ironically agreed with them that wisdom will lead the way to happiness — understood, however, as success in getting the objects of the natural impulses, rather than as trying to live in agreement with nature. On the other hand, just and virtuous conduct in the ordinary sense, since it is not likely to lead to material success, would have to be considered as the utmost folly. Carneades concluded that rules of justice could not be derived from natural human impulses; on the contrary, the existence of legal rules must be explained as an attempt to restrain our natural selfishness, keeping people from harming one another by the threat of punishment.

Carneades' devastating critique seems to have gone to the heart of Stoic theory and to have opened up a whole new field of inquiry and debate. What Carneades had pointed out was not only that it was doubtful, to say the least, whether the perfection of human nature would turn out to be virtue; what would have been more disturbing for the Stoics was the suggestion that the advantageous and the morally right, happiness and virtue, far from coinciding in the rational pursuit of objects of natural impulse, might actually be opposed to one another. Carneades' argument seemed to show that there was no preestablished harmony between self-preservation and sociability such that following one's natural impulses would always produce the right result, and it was unclear how one could possibly show that altruism would always take precedent over egoism in cases of conflict.

The effects of this new challenge to Stoic theory can be seen, I think, in Cicero's *De officiis*, a book that became very influential in the history of later moral thought. Cicero tells us that his model for this book was a treatise by the Stoic Panaetius, one generation after Carneades. Panaetius, according to Cicero, divided the topics of deliberation about appropriate action into three: first, we should ask whether an action is morally good or bad (*honestum, turpe*) : second, whether it is advantageous or otherwise (*utile, inutile*) ; third, we must consider cases where the morally good appears to conflict with what appears to be advantageous (*De off.* 1.9; 3.7). The word "appears" is probably important here, because Panaetius no doubt intended to argue that these conflicts were *only* apparent, since what is morally bad can never be advantageous. However, Panaetius never wrote the book that was to deal with this problem (*De off.* 3.8), and one wonders, indeed, how he could have done so. For the way in which the problem is set up seems to condemn any attempt at a solution to failure: Panaetius had to all appearances identified the morally good with altruistic values, the advantageous with egoistic ones, and so he would have had to argue, in effect, that altruistic action is never an unprofitable course to take for an egoist. One understands why other philosophers — one would suppose Stoics — protested that the proposed topic should not be treated at all, because the advantageous could not possibly conflict with the morally good, being identical with it (*De off.* 3.9–11). This follows, indeed, from the Stoic thesis that only the morally good (Greek *kalon*, Lat. *honestum*) is good at all — clearly nothing that is not good can be advantageous, and every good will be an advantage. The problem that Carneades had pointed out, and that Panaetius misdescribed, should be described in terms of conflicts between two sets of values that are the objects of our natural impulses. None of these objects counted as good or morally valuable for the Stoics, because goodness was to be found only in rational selection itself, not in obtaining the "natural things." If the Stoics wanted to defend their thesis that following nature results in virtue, they had to show somehow that nature also directs us to set the right priorities when we have to make a choice between things pertaining to self-preservation and to sociability.

Cicero, who bravely undertook to fill the gap left by Panaetius, succeeded only in giving a very clear statement of the problem, not in providing a solution. He offers a "formula" to deal with those "apparent conflicts," which runs: "To take away something from another, or for a man to promote his own advantage through the disadvantage of some other man, is more against nature than death or poverty or pain, or anything else that could happen either to the body or to external things" (*De off.* 3.21). That is indeed what the Stoics should have tried to prove, but the supporting argument is missing. It appears that this is where the debate remained. Instead of working out a theoretical justification, later Stoics seem to have been content to repeat claims like Cicero's about naturalness. And one might be inclined to think that the missing solution could hardly be found, because it might just not be true that nature, who gave us our basic impulses, also provided us with a natural way of bringing them into harmony, so that virtue can be seen as the rational perfection of a natural development of human impulses. In this respect, Carneades' criticism seems to me to have been well founded.

VI

Still, it appears that the discovery of those apparent conflicts between utility and virtue had the unfortunate effect of suggesting that the pursuit of happiness and the path of virtue are two distinct and separate things, to be dealt with independently of one another. For in those conflicts, it seemed that happiness was squarely on the side of utility. But this is in fact merely a consequence of another anti-Stoic argument by Carneades, to the effect that happiness must be success in getting the objects of natural impulse, and wisdom — *prudentia*, in Cicero's Latin — the art of being successful. There is no need, however, to conceive of happiness in this way, even if one grants the occurrence of real conflicts of values. Instead of describing these as conflicts between the goals of happiness and morality, one should describe them as situations in which one has to choose between goods of different kinds, both of which are required for happiness. It seems unproblematic to say that a person who values both her own and other people's well-being would not want to obtain an advantage by harming others. But even if a real sacrifice is needed for the sake of helping or not harming others, this need not be seen as a sacrifice of happiness for the sake of morality — rather, it is the choice of a lesser over a greater evil. It may well be the case, depending on the seriousness of the loss, that happiness is thereby ruled out (as when one has to sacrifice one's life) — but it is still not obviously true that happiness could have been preserved or gained by harming or omitting to help others. The choice will be justified by the consideration that one would become more unhappy by committing a crime, say, or abandoning a friend in need of help, than by giving up some material advantage.

Instead of this sort of account, however, we seem to have inherited a view which distinguishes sharply between prudence (the Latin translation of *phronesis*, wisdom), as concerned only with nonmoral utility, and moral considerations, concerned with a different sort of value not related to one's happiness. No wonder it has become a mystery how anyone whose aim is his own good, happiness, could ever be argued into wanting to be virtuous.

It might be salutary to realize that the distinction between prudence and morality, which appears so natural or even self-evident to us, quite possibly goes back to a very specific argument, and a very dubious conception of happiness, that we have no more reason to accept than its author did.

Whether or not Carneades — through Panaetius and Cicero — was behind the bifurcation of prudential and moral reasoning, it seems to have led to the misconception that eudaimonism and moral theory are rivals when in fact we should probably see them as complementing one another. If we take seriously the broader conceptions of happiness advocated by Plato and Aristotle, we may follow their lead in trying to find a motive for morality in moral psychology. Obviously, though, we cannot use such a conception of happiness as a starting point for the derivation of moral rules, since this would involve us in a circle: if happiness includes virtue, then we would be saying that in order to act virtuously, we should try to be virtuous. For the justification of moral rules we should perhaps, like Epicurus, look to the role they play in society, appealing to the functions of a social order — for example, protection from harm and promotion of mutually beneficial cooperation. The distinction we ought to preserve is not the contrast between prudence and morality but rather that between planning one's own life and setting up rules for the life of a community. Then if it is true, as it seems to be, that man is an eminently social animal, it should not be difficult to argue that we have good reasons to plan our lives within an acceptable social order. And that should mean, not that considerations of morality must override considerations of happiness, but that we can hardly hope for a truly happy human life unless we have the virtues that make us inclined to act in the ways we think we should.

The Dynamics of Reform and Revolt in Current South Africa

F. VAN ZYL SLABBERT

THE TANNER LECTURES ON HUMAN VALUES

Delivered at
Brasenose College, Oxford University

October 27 and 29 and November 5, 1987

FREDERIK VAN ZYL SLABBERT was born in Pretoria, South Africa, and completed his undergraduate and graduate work at Stellenbosch University. He has written widely in academic journals and co-authored two books, one with Professor David Welsh, *South Africa's Option: Strategies for Sharing Power*, and, with Professor J. Opland, *South Africa: Dilemma of Evolutionary Change*. He is also the author of *The Last White Parliament*. In addition to being a Professor and Head of the Department of Sociology at the University of the Witwatersrand, he is co-founder and Director of the Institute for a Democratic Alternative for South Africa.

I. FROM APARTHEID TO REFORM: THE IDEOLOGICAL PREPARATION FOR THE TOTAL ONSLAUGHT

INTRODUCTION

All the ingredients for a climactic eruption in South Africa have been present for decades. Even this potential remains unfulfilled. So much so that one rates doomsday scenarios not so much on predictive accuracy as on the originality and freshness of new assumptions. South Africa is waiting to become — a hovering society. Almost universal agreement on the untenability of the present is matched by equally deep differences on the pattern for the future. The conflict is also rooted in the divergence and diversity of hopes about what is to come. South Africa is not a hopeless society; perhaps that is why its central conflict appears to be so intractable. Some have what others want, and others are determined to monopolize what some want to get at. It is a deeply divided society where one side's dreams and expectations for the future becomes the other's threat to, and frustration of, the present. That is also why it is increasingly becoming a violent, bitter, and brutalized society. People are beginning to hate each other out of the future.

The question is, why? What is the underlying issue? Is it class, race, ethnicity? Obviously greed, intolerance, fear, are primordial emotions that run deep in South Africa, but they epitomize rather than explain the dilemma. South Africa escapes analytical precision and closure. It is a land of shifting paradigms: Marxists end up making concessions to race and ethnicity, liberals to class, and pluralists to almost anything that disturbs their train of thought. Very often residual categories in one framework pop up into prominence at the very moment their irrelevance has been defined.

[205]

Because analyses of South Africa are often so starkly divergent, it provides a fertile climate for ideological dogmatism. Differences of opinion, tactics and strategy, often blow up into major confrontations and are seized upon to pronounce on moral sanity, sincerity of commitment, or some anticipated state of grace or retribution. Ideological certainty depends on intellectual compromise, and South Africa is rife with compromised intellectuals who know better but refrain from saying so. The need for certainty is often the most compelling evidence for uncertainty. Sometimes ending on the loser's side is a greater sin than being right. It becomes easy to confuse silence for wisdom.

What then is the underlying issue? Perhaps it is easier, if not necessarily safer, to begin with elimination. Although South Africa shares many of the characteristics of a typical colonial society, it is not. It has the characteristics of a typical colonial society without the colonial options of external metropole intervention, or minority withdrawal toward it, or both. Algeria had France; Rhodesia, Britain; Mozambique and Angola, Portugal. South Africa has neither this kind of retreat nor intervenor. Anyone who plans strategy on the assumption that it has is preparing for a false confrontation. And it is not very helpful to view South Africa as "colonialism of a special kind," as some Marxist scholars do.[1] A civil war can be seen only as a stage in a "special" colonial struggle at enormous cost to human and natural resources before the error inevitably will have to be acknowledged. And yet, it is precisely South Africa's colonial past without the "normal" decolonialization option on the way to the future which makes the resolution of the present conflict so intractable and costly.

If South Africa is locked into a conventional class conflict, it so far stubbornly refuses to come to terms with it. At present there are simply too many "false consciousnesses" straying across

[1] A good overview of this debate is contained in an article by Peter Hudson, "The Freedom Charter and the Theory of National Democratic Revolution," *Transformation* 1 (1986): 6–39.

enemy lines. And yet, nobody can deny that South Africa has all the characteristics of a class struggle: extraordinary concentration of capital, collusion between state and business at key periods in its history, and a growing political and alienated working class. However, it is precisely because of the intransigence of racial and ethnic factors that good old-fashioned Marxists are tempted to look on South Africa as first having to resolve the struggle for "national liberation" (colonialism of a special kind) before settling down to the "real" class revolution.

It is difficult to find any black liberals among workers and working-class academics. This does not serve to inhibit the optimism of liberal economists that South Africa will inevitably "grow" itself out of its present crisis if only the philosophy and practice of free enterprise is allowed to have its way. Too often the "if only" qualification becomes an intellectual escape route. There is enough evidence from the past that growth without efficient political redistribution increases a sense of relative deprivation and compounds the conflict. At the same time, it is quite true that without growth in the economy the politics of redistribution dies on the vine. It is as futile to attempt to redistribute what society does not have as it is dangerous to refuse to distribute as equitably as possible what it does have. However, more than a few big businessmen's courage has failed them when they have had to face the political consequences of this kind of economic analysis. It is almost pointless to wax eloquent on the virtues of free enterprise in a politically unfree South Africa; it is not so pointless to ponder how well free enterprise will survive in a politically free South Africa. How compatible is freedom with the demand for equality?

The underlying issue is not really apartheid. Apartheid is simply the flare that illuminates the scene of battle. From South Africa's colonial past, in every class analysis which comes to grips with the complexities of the present as well as the source of tension in the liberal economist's attempt to reconcile growth and redistribution lies the issue of *white minority domination: socially, economically, and politically.*

Obviously colonial conquest created the social and political infrastructure for white domination, and British and Dutch trade and financial imperialism gave it economic context. Apartheid was Afrikaner-Nationalism's uniquely "South African way" of articulating white domination. It was also a futile and therefore brutal attempt to escape the pitfalls and consequences of continued colonialism. Whatever the case, it is on the fact and intractability of white minority domination where the paradigms of liberals, pluralists, and Marxists briefly converge before they go their separate ways to explain its significance and to predict its end.

And today, when international anger, outrage, and moral revulsion are mobilized to sanction the obstinacy of apartheid and domestic forces revolt to bring about its demise, what is at issue in the "total dismantling of apartheid" is not only doing away with racist legislation or giving "blacks a fair deal" or even "sharing political power" (whatever that implies). *It means a transfer of political power away from exclusive white domination and with the demonstrable support of the total adult population, no matter how this support is manifested or how long it will endure.* This is the central issue at stake in the international and domestic pressure building up against those in power in South Africa.

The South African state has responded to this pressure with a "program of reform"; this in turn has precipitated revolt on a scale not experienced before in this century. It is the purpose of these few lectures to stimulate some discussion on the current dynamics of reform and revolt in South Africa. I will try to do so in three talks, each one concentrating on a different perspective on the relationship between reform and revolt. First, I wish to discuss the ideological shift from apartheid to "reform," after which I wish to illustrate how this shift is reflected in policy, bureaucracy, and new institutions. Finally, I wish to look at the whole area of reaction or resistance to the reform, which I broadly refer to as revolt. I say broadly because I wish to discuss not only the political actions of domestic and exiled groups experiencing repression and reform but also wider responses to the South African community, such as international pressure through diplomatic isolation, sanctions, and so on.

Before I begin discussing the ideological shift from apartheid to reform, a brief methodological note could be useful. Throughout I will refer to those in power as the South African state, rather than the government or the regime or the Nationalist party. The reasons for this will become obvious as my analysis proceeds. At this stage, I only wish to say that I regard the South African state as an autonomous entity with its own goals, structure, and interests. I do not use it in any mystical, disembodied, or holistic sense but in the sense of a collective unit manned by real people with definable interests, where those interests cannot simply be seen as an extension or reflection of class interests or where they are simply the "disinterested" or "neutral" protectors of a state structure within which other interest groups pursue their goals. My use of the word "state" in analyzing the dynamics of reform and revolt is similar to that of Skocpol in her fascinating analysis of revolutions in Russia, France, and China, although I do not for one moment intend to embarrass her with the crudity of my own attempt.[2]

From Apartheid to Reform

There was, of course, a time when colonialism was fashionable and white domination unproblematical. It was a time, particularly between the two world wars of this century, when whites in South Africa and southern Africa had their heyday. South Africa belonged to the Commonwealth and its whites were decorated as war heroes, won Olympic medals, and had "representative" sporting tours to and from other countries; its political leaders could

---

[2] Theda Skocpol, *States and Social Revolutions* (Cambridge: Cambridge University Press, 1979).

even qualify as "statesmen" of international repute, as in the case of General Jan C. Smuts, a close confidant of Winston Churchill.

However, by the end of the Second World War, the West, in particular, was beginning to feel the impact of powerful philosophical and economic forces. Slavery, racism, and economic exploitation became anathema, and these, together with the declining economic fortunes of the former colonial powers, made decolonization a very attractive option. As this process gathered momentum, so the very idea of white domination became increasingly embarrassing and repugnant. Wherever there was majority domination — for example, in the United States of America, Canada, Australia, New Zealand — whites could successfully impose their own variations of liberal democratic governments and gradually, through force of circumstances, accommodate those who were not white into the arms of government and social and economic life. By the time the pressures for decolonization gathered momentum, these white-majority dominated societies, together with white-minority dominated South Africa, had, through various processes, gained independence. The drive for independence during the post–World War II period of decolonization was also a drive to get rid of white minority domination in India, Ghana, Nigeria, Northern Rhodesia, Tanganyika, Nyasaland, and so on. A last-minute desperate attempt to gain special "South African–like status" for white domination was Rhodesia's futile attempt at Unilateral Declaration of Independence on November 17, 1965.

South Africa had independence at the onset of decolonization after World War II. But the whites who elected the government were determined not to succumb to the same pressures which gave it momentum. Having had all the economic and political privileges of colonial administration without the option of imposing a majority solution on the domestic situation, or minority withdrawal to the metropole, most whites were determined to set themselves apart from the majority of people in their own country and continue to maintain a colonial lifestyle despite decolonization. Thus with the advent of Nationalist party rule in 1948 was born apartheid, or separateness. The first two Afrikaner Nationalist premiers, Daniel F. Malan and Johannes G. Strydom, were quite crude and unsophisticated about the racist measures with which they attempted to maintain the segregated privileges of whites. In their era, 1948–58, the basic legal infrastructure of apartheid was created: the Population Registration Act No. 30, 1950; Prohibition of Mixed Marriages Act No. 55, 1949; Immorality Amendment Act No. 21, 1950; Reservation of Separate Amenities Act No. 49 of 1953; Group Areas Act, No. 41, 1950, as well as the group of statutes, laws, and proclamations broadly known as the pass laws, which primarily affected the movement of black Africans. There was an absolute frenzy of legislative action during the first ten years without any coherent ideological justification other than the simple "Baasskap," a word coined by Strydom: in "his own" country the white man was going to be "boss."

Ironically, it took a Dutch-born naturalized Afrikaner, Hendrik F. Verwoerd, to realize the complete untenability of this approach in the prevailing African and international climate. He became prime minister after Strydom in 1958, and until his assassination in 1966, a torrent of energy was unleashed in Afrikaner academic and cultural circles to develop a coherent and intellectually defensible ideology for apartheid. It became "separate development." Verwoerd was its architect and supreme articulator. He defended it in international circles when he led South Africa out of the Commonwealth and into a republic, and with tireless zeal he convinced his supporters that separate development was not only morally just but the only way out of the problem and away from white domination. His white opponents in the old United party were defenseless against his attack that their alternative was simply a "softer" variation of white domination, and those opponents left of the United party were simply accused of exchanging one form of racial domination for another.

Verwoerd understood quite clearly that the challenge posed
by Africa's demand for independence had to be met also in South
Africa. For Africa generally, this demand meant that white
minorities had to relinquish exclusive political control or with-
draw to the mother country or both. Verwoerd was going to do
exactly the opposite — instead of getting rid of the whites, he was
going to get rid of the blacks. In fact, one of his protégés, Dr.
Connie Mulder, then minister of information and the crown prince
to succeed John Vorster as prime minister, could with a straight
face argue in the white parliament ten years later that once separate development had been fully implemented, there would be "no
black South Africans." From a very important perspective separate development was a massive exercise in social engineering
aimed at denationalizing the majority of South Africa's citizens.

South Africa, so the separate-development theory goes, is not
a land consisting of black and white people. It is a culturally
diverse population — in fact a plurality of cultural minorities.
There is not one nation in South Africa but many nations striving
for independence. Just as Europe and its colonial masters were
assisting African nations toward maturity and independence, so
the whites in South Africa had to assist the black ethnic tribes
(nations) in South Africa to their independence. The 1913 and
1936 Land Acts of South Africa had set aside traditional African
land for blacks. This should form the geographic basis where the
different black African nations would live out their political aspirations. As each one eventually took full independence so their
citizens would lose their South African citizenship and become
foreigners just like any other foreigner who visited what would
then be white South Africa. Once all these nations were "independent," the problem of white domination would have been
solved, because there would be no blacks to dominate.

Upon the existing racist legal infrastructure built to achieve
Malan and Strydom's goal of apartheid, Verwoerd now constructed a new legal superstructure called separate development.

Key elements of both structures were intimately related to one another, but there were many aspects of apartheid not necessary for separate development and vice versa. But that was for another era to discover — when "reforms" became fashionable. Initially Verwoerd was reluctant to go for "full independence" for blacks, feeling that this was an option forced on the white minority by the outside world, but by the time of his assassination in 1966, the Department of Bantu Administration was the major bureaucracy of government and most of the legislative underpinning for separate development in the pipeline. In fact, John Vorster, who succeeded Verwoerd, spent the next ten years (1966–76) primarily doing two things: giving content to Verwoerd's version of internal "independence" and creating an encompassing network of far-reaching security laws and measures in order to be able to act against those who did not comply.

The point I wish to emphasize about the period of apartheid and separate development, which has been thoroughly researched, is that the aim was to maintain white minority domination at a time when this was the distinctive feature of colonial administration and when every antislavery, anti-Nazi, antiracist and anti-capitalist exploitation lobby could cite this as an example of the ultimate evil. When, in a sense, the West was going one way, South African whites were going the other. This alone guaranteed that South Africa would remain controversial in international affairs for a long time to come.

But another point I wish to emphasize about the apartheid–separate-development era is of domestic or internal relevance. The whole exercise created a massive and pervasive bureaucracy — a new state structure which began to take on a life of its own. Not many countries can compare with South Africa where its size is concerned. By 1985 the political system had given birth to thirteen houses of Parliament or legislative assemblies, as well as the President's Council with quasi-legislative functions. There are three legislative chambers in the Central Parliament, six legislative assemblies in what are termed the "nonindependent black states," and four legislative assemblies in the "independent states."

Occupying seats in these fourteen bodies are 1,270 members, consisting of 308 members of the three houses of the Central Parliament; 60 members of the President's Council, 501 members of the legislative assemblies of the non-independent black states, and 401 members of the legislative assemblies of the independent black states of Transkei, Bophuthatswana, Venda, and Ciskei. Of the 1,270 persons, 121 are ministers of government (approximately one out of ten), and in addition, there are at least 21 deputy ministers.

Each of the legislative organs has government departmental structures which, by August 1986, had spawned 151 government departments in South Africa. These departments included 18 departments of health and welfare; 14 departments of education; 14 departments of finance and budget; 14 departments of agriculture and forestry; 12 departments of works and housing; 13 departments of urban affairs or local government; 9 departments of economic affairs or trade and industry, as well as 5 departments of foreign affairs, transport, posts and telegraphs, labor and manpower, law and order, defense or national security; 3 departments of justice, 1 department of mineral and energy affairs, 1 department of environmental affairs and tourism. Finally, these 140 departments were responsible to eleven presidents, prime ministers, or chief ministers in South Africa.

As M. Savage wryly observes: "This legislative network with 121 Ministers and 151 Government Departments is not cheap to run." [3] It may not be cheap to run, but it certainly provides security of income and many privileges for those who work for it. As time went by, those involved in it developed a powerful vested interest in keeping the whole system going, whatever the ideological goals it was supposed to pursue. The original idea, of course, was that

[3] M. Savage, "The Cost of Apartheid," Inaugural Lecture, University of Cape Town, 1986.

all these duplicated departments and legislative assemblies would reach a certain level of maturity, would take off and develop separately and independently. The South Africa would then have its own "commonwealth of sovereign nations," which could even broaden into a "confederation of Southern African States."

Vorster was the last National party prime minister who seriously tried to pursue the goals of old-style separate development and apartheid. But even during his period of office the cracks were beginning to show. The first right-wing breakaway occurred in the beginning of the 1970s because of concessions to multiracial sport; a parliamentary Commission of Inquiry into Homeland Consolidation concluded that it was a futile and economically unproductive exercise (thus undermining a cherished goal of separate development), and the Commission of Inquiry into the position of the Coloured population group concluded that it had to be accommodated on all levels of government in South Africa.

Separate development, which was essentially centrifugal by design, was also being eroded by powerful centripetal demographic and economic forces. The decade of the seventies saw an accelerated rate of overall but particularly black urbanization, increased economic integration, and far-reaching changes in black labor organizations. Black resistance and alienation was rapidly developing and exploded with the Soweto riots of 1976, when the compulsory instruction of Afrikaans was seized upon by black schoolchildren to symbolize their deep rejection of the goals of apartheid and separate development.

In 1987, eight years after P. W. Botha succeeded Vorster, most of the major goals of separate development as well as the philosophy of apartheid (an "outmoded concept" according to Botha) had been abandoned. Homeland independence was preferable, but not mandatory; blacks could "in principle" own land outside the homeland areas; consolidation was no longer a priority; blacks were entitled to South African citizenship. In fact, one cabinet minister, Chris Heunis, proudly announced, South

Africa should be "one country, with one citizenship and one government" and negotiation and consensus should be the political
style rather than unilateral decision making. Even some of the
old racist segregationist measures had been repealed, such as the
Prohibition of Mixed Marriages Act, the Immorality Act, aspects
of the Separate Amenities Act and the Improper Political Interference Act. The policy of influx control had been abandoned, and
systematic black urbanization was accepted as the desired alternative. Even the so-called Coloured Labour Preference Policy for
the Western Cape was repealed in the face of inevitable black
urbanization.

It was, however, the new tricameral constitution which became
the prize offering symbolizing the era of "reform." It was put to
a referendum for white approval only and succeeded in seducing
the majority of whites, businessmen, and some Western governments as a "step in the right direction." The blacks who were
excluded from it, and the so-called Coloureds and Indians who
were going to be the prime beneficiaries of the new constitution,
were not given the opportunity to express an opinion. The paradox
was that the new constitution, which was to herald in "reform"
and the beginning of the end of apartheid, also precipitated the
most widespread revolt the country has known — revolt from both
ends of the political spectrum. For the majority it became increasingly obvious that the government was going to abandon key
aspects of apartheid and separate development without sacrificing
white domination, and for right-wing whites it became clear that
this kind of concession was the thin end of the wedge which
would eventually lead to black rule. The tricameral Parliament
not only flushed out the right-wing Conservative party of Andries
Treurnicht, it also led to the creation of the United Democratic
Front (UDF).

Both Vorster and Botha were sensitive to right-wing electoral
threats. Vorster responded to it by simply doing nothing, or as
little as possible, to create the impression that apartheid or sepa-

rate development was being abandoned. Botha, however, had inherited a situation where it became more and more obvious that separate development and apartheid were coming unstuck. The ideological void which was beginning to develop because of the untenability of apartheid and separate development was slowly being filled by the concept of a "total onslaught," which necessitated a "total strategy" to cope with it. The whole bureaucratic edifice which had been created to achieve separate development was now going to become part of the total strategy to cope with the total onslaught. This onslaught also became the supreme justification for "reform." Thus security and domestic constitutional policy intersected and reinforced one another. Reform was necessary for security, but security was also necessary for reform. It was the historical responsibility of the dominant white minority not to lose control and thus disturb the delicate balance between the two. This, as Botha repeatedly stressed during the recent all-white election, would lead to "chaos and a communist dominated ANC [African National Congress] government." Botha won a handsome white mandate — to progressive whites he promised that security would not jeopardize reform, and to reactionary whites he could promise that reform would not jeopardize security.

The concept of a total onslaught did not materialize overnight. As minister of defense, P. W. Botha together with his then chief of staff, Magnus Malan, and chief of the army, Constand Viljoen, worked tirelessly to promote the idea.[4] If one could pinpoint a date which gave momentum to the idea of a total onslaught it would be April 25, 1974, when a coup in Lisbon led to the independence of Mozambique and Angola. For the first time, the cordon sanitaire of white minority governments north of South Africa had been broken. Rhodesia came under extreme pressure after that. Vorster's initial response was benign, almost indifferent

---

[4] All of them were deeply influenced by the work of André Beaufre, *Introduction to Strategy* (London: Faber and Faber, 1965), in which he related his experiences in World War II and the war in Indo-China. Therein he propagates the idea of a "total strategy" in conditions of "total war."

to a Marxist government in Luanda and Maputo. He reiterated the old foreign-policy principle of nonintervention and good neighborliness and even continued with limited initiatives elsewhere in Africa. Not so the Defence Department under P. W. Botha. Almost immediately they began to redefine the security interests of the Republic of South Africa. A year later, 1975, South Africa had penetrated militarily deep into Angola in an attempt to influence the composition of the government about to take over. Soon afterward South African security personnel began to involve themselves with Rhodesia's civil war. The principles of good neighborliness and nonintervention had to be sacrificed to cope with the total onslaught.

When Botha took over as prime minister and later as president, the whole security bureaucracy became the central focus of government administration. Not only did destabilization of neighboring countries become established practice, but the defense force was brought into townships to cope with domestic unrest on a "continuous basis." The total onslaught became standard propaganda fare on all government-controlled and supporting media. But at the same time, it could be used to explain why apartheid and separate development had to be abandoned and why reform was necessary. A careful look at what "reform" is all about will show how it inevitably had to precipitate revolt, because in the final analysis it was simply another, new way of extending white minority domination. The white minority was embarking on "reform" by looking for a way to share power without losing any. More about this in the next lecture.

II. THE DYNAMICS OF REFORM: CO-OPTIVE DOMINATION — SHARING POWER WITHOUT LOSING ANY

A great deal of confusion continues to surround the idea of reform in the present South African context. There is no point in arguing whether change or reform has taken place or not. Of

course it has. But how do we assess its significance? There is truth
in the assertion of government spokesmen that at the moment that
they introduced more reforms away from the policies of apartheid
and separate development than ever in the history of National
party government, they experienced the severest pressure and hostility from inside and outside the country. But this is so because
with the reforms the realization has crystallized that the South
African state is prepared to "negotiate," "broaden democracy,"
"dismantle apartheid," that is, to "reform," but only on *its* terms.

The tricameral Parliament is the continuing manifestation of
this kind of logic. Nothing precipitated domestic, and subsequently international, revolt against South African government
reforms more than its implementation. It more than anything
else demonstrated that those in control of the state were prepared
to adjust, "soften," and sophisticate the entrenchment of white
minority domination, but not get rid of it. It brought some of
those who are not white a little closer to the center of power,
while showing them how far away they are going to remain
from it.

There is nothing fundamentally new in the thinking which
accompanied the shift from a racist Westminster to a multiracial
tricameral system of Parliament. At the heart of it was the idea
that racial groups could be accommodated as predetermined political entities into a South African political system. Within the
logic of apartheid–separate development the shift was certainly
new, if not all that fundamental. Until 1983 the idea was that a
National party government could unilaterally partition racial
groups *away* from the political center and so preserve white "self-
determination," or domination. No one can sensibly deny the
reality of racial or ethnic groups in South Africa, but the Nationalist party government has seized on this reality to determine that
every South African individual shall participate in politics only as
a member of a racial or ethnic group. If one asks why, it is difficult
to escape the conclusion that it is done so that Afrikaner Nation-

alists, as the largest white ethnic group, can dominate the political system as part of a racial minority. Whatever P .W. Botha has in mind in the nature of reform, as the embodiment of the present Afrikaner Nationalist leadership, he certainly does not see an alternative where he or his party or both will not be firmly in political control of South Africa. And when he talks about negotiation, he certainly has no intention of talking himself, or his successor, out of a job.

This is the crux of the matter. On this issue, different agendas for "reform," "negotiation," "broadening democracy," and "transferring power" find their origin. That is why opposing groups very often use the same concepts with completely different meanings. As for those who dominate in South Africa, they are prepared to adjust the domination, but not to abolish it — this is their so-called bottom line for reform—whereas those who oppose domination demand the abolition of it before accepting the validity-legitimacy of reform. That is why the overwhelming response to the reform program of the government has been revolt — both domestically and internationally. The interaction between reform and revolt has trapped South Africa into a process of violent evolution which threatens to ravage its human natural resources.

A simple question needs to be answered: If the above is true, why reform at all? The conventional response to this question tends to identify various sources of pressure which in a sense "forced" the South African state to bring about certain reforms: international action, domestic political reaction, urbanization, and so on. No doubt these factors played an important part in influencing the National party government's actions, but these pressures have always been present in stronger or weaker form. In fact, Verwoerd's response to these pressures was precisely to shift the policy of apartheid to separate development. This policy shift must rank as one of the most massive attempts at social engineering of the twentieth century. It was done to maintain or preserve "white minority self-determination" in South Africa and to free it from the accusation of racial domination. The shift from separate development to reform is preoccupied with exactly the same problem. Again and in the final analysis reform is necessary to preserve white self-determination, and again it is intended to bring about a situation "where no one group must be in a position to dominate another or others."

Still, the scope and tempo of reform cannot be adequately understood in terms of a particular factor or group of factors supposedly influencing it or intended to bring it about, for example, sanctions, armed struggle, township unrest, diplomatic pressures. To the extent that this is done, it is easy to understand why reforms thus far have been dismissed as sham, cosmetic, too little, too late, and so on. The pattern and tempo of reform has to be understood in terms of how the white minority has defined its security interests, reshaped the security system, and coordinated the whole state bureaucracy to deal with any conceivable threat to its interests. In the process, it has developed a vast empire of patronage in which a diversity of clients has a very real vested interest in maintaining the South African state. In fact, without the compliance of a substantial number of people who are not white, white minority domination would be in very real difficulty indeed. Reform is intended to extend this system of patronage and thereby strengthen the security of the state as defined by the white minority in control. Security and reform go hand in hand, but it is only if one understands the priority that security interests enjoy that some of the confusion surrounding the reform program can be cleared up. It is almost impossible to make sense of the constitutional program of the National party government if it is viewed on its own as a "rational" or "reasonable" response to pressures for reform from, say, the ANC, UDF, EPG, Inkatha, or even white liberals. However, viewed against the background of the National Security Management System developed by the Botha government, the constitutional program interlocks quite efficiently

with the security system. It is true that P .W. Botha has "reformed" apartheid and separate development more than any other
National party leader before him. What is not often appreciated
is how extensively he reshaped the security system of South Africa
and the South African state bureaucracy, which made it possible
to bring about those reforms but also limited him and those around
him in how far those reforms could go. A brief analysis of the
development of the security system will deepen our understanding
of the reform program and also reveal why it is almost inevitably
bound up with continuing revolt.

Before 1948, that is, before National party rule, conventional
military policy was based on the assumption that there was a clear
identity of interests between South Africa and the West. As during the two world wars and even the Korean war, it was accepted
that in any major international conflict South Africa would side
with the West. But as apartheid became official policy and South
Africa became increasingly isolated, the defense planners began to
accept that the West was embarrassed to be seen having South
Africa as an ally. Gradually the West was depicted as hostile to
the security interests of South Africa and later even as an unwitting ally of the expansionism effort of the Soviet Union, which
coveted South Africa as a "strategic jewel" of great importance.
Cut off from arms supply because of an international embargo
as well as facing increasing diplomatic isolation, security planners
turned to domestic resources to reshape the security system, first in
the area of armaments provision, and second in terms of manpower. Politically this refocusing of the security system involved
a massive propaganda campaign to sell the idea of total onslaught.

Before this became the major preoccupation of the security
planners, the bureaucracy involved with security-intelligence matters went through various changes as definitions and perceptions
of security matters changed. From 1948 to 1963 there was a
Special Branch of the Police that had to focus on any internal
security threat. The Security Police came into being in 1963 under

General Hendrik van den Bergh, a close confidant of John Vorster. A Directorate of Military Intelligence was organized in 1964 and a State Security Committee had to coordinate intelligence gathering and prevent overlapping as far as possible between Military Intelligence and the Security Police. There was always an uneasy relationship between these two branches of the intelligence community, and in 1969 a Bureau for State Security (BOSS) was created under the same General van den Bergh with the following terms of reference: "(1) Investigate all matters affecting the security of the State, to correlate and evaluate the information collected and, where necessary, to inform and advise the Government, interested Government departments and other bodies in regard thereto; and (2) perform such other functions and responsibilities as may be determined from time to time." [5]

At this stage, there were actually three departments involved with security-intelligence matters: the Security Police, Military Intelligence, and the Bureau for State Security. Bureaucratic envy, one-upmanship, and overlapping remained a problem. John Vorster appointed Justice H. J. Potgieter to head a commission of inquiry. He recommended the creation of a State Security Council (SSC), which came into effect through the Security Intelligence and State Security Council Act (No. 64 of 1972) with the following terms of reference: "(1) The formulation of *national policy* and strategy in relation to the security of the Republic and the manner in which such policy or strategy shall be implemented and executed; (2) a policy to combat any particular threat to the security of the Republic (and) . . . to determine intelligence priorities." The SSC broadened the basis of interaction between professionals and politicians on security matters. It also enabled P. W. Botha, as minister of defense, to have a greater say in security matters and to try to limit the influence of General van den Bergh of BOSS, with whom he had a personally hostile relationship. Botha was also intensely jealous of any encroachment on military matters,

[5] Government Notice 808 of 1969 (No. 86 of 1969).

and given the wide scope of BOSS's terms of reference, it was almost inevitable that clashes of interests would arise. Van den Bergh had the inside track with Prime Minister John Vorster, and therefore his view on security matters tended to prevail. In any case, Vorster gave van den Bergh almost carte blanche in this respect. Van den Bergh, together with Dr. Connie Mulder, minister of information and the most likely successor to Vorster, embarked on an aggressive campaign to sell South Africa (that is, separate development) to the international community and to Africa. For this they established a number of secret funds unaccountable to parliament. One such source was within the Department of Defence, much to the discomfort of P. W. Botha. Botha's view on the security interests of South Africa differed quite sharply from those of van den Bergh and Mulder. Instead of selling separate development to an unwilling outside world, South Africa should be preparing itself for the total onslaught.

Botha and his top generals, particularly Magnus Malan (later to become minister of defense himself), were profoundly influenced by *Introduction to Strategy*, by General André Beaufre, a French militarist who wrote about his experiences in World War II and the war in Indo-China.[6] Beaufre wrote about the need for a "total strategy" in order to cope with a "total war." This book also formed the basis of lectures at the Joint Defence College and became required reading for "red stream" staff officers in civil-military relations. Botha's thinking on the issue of total onslaught, which remains unchanged even today, is reflected in his introduction to the Department of Defence white paper tabled in parliament in 1973:

> The RSA [Republic of South Africa] is a target for international communism and its cohorts — leftists, activists, exaggerated humanism, permissiveness, materialism and related ideologies. In addition, the RSA has been singled out as a special target for the by products of their ideologies such as

[6] Beaufre, *Introduction to Strategy*.

black radicalism, exaggerated individual freedom, one-man-one-vote, and a host of other slogans employed against us on the basis of double standards.

It is against this global background that the Government is developing its policy. Traditionally, a country's policy' structure comprises three basic elements — internal policy, foreign policy and defence policy. The last is determined by the preceding two, but these in turn cannot be developed properly unless they are sustained by a sound and adequate defence policy. These basic elements must therefore be closely coordinated and integrated; this is of vital importance, particularly in the present international climate which is typified by total strategy and which obliges us to face the onslaught of monolithic organisations which are in absolute control of all the means available to their states.[7]

From the outset, Botha's idea of a total strategy to cope with the total onslaught (shared by all his top officers) drew no distinction between defense-security interests and domestic and foreign policy. The 1977 white paper on defense, tabled in Parliament, fully developed the idea of a total national strategy. It recommended that the State Security Council should be assisted by a *permanent work committee* drawn from a dozen or more state departments. Within the ambit of a total national strategy, the white paper identified certain goals for the state. These included:

the orderly development and maintenance of the body politic;

the preservation of the identity, dignity, the right to self-determination and the integrity of all population groups;

the identification, prevention and countering of revolution, subversion and any other form of unconstitutional action;

the maintenance of a sound balance of military power in relation to neighbouring states and other states in Southern Africa;

aiming for the greatest possible measure of economic and social development, and the maximum self-sufficiency;

[7] P. W. Botha, *Republic of SA White Paper on Defence*, 1973, p. 1.

the creation of friendly relations and political and economic co-operation with the states of Southern Africa; and

planning the total national strategy at Government level for co-ordinated action between all Government departments, Government institutions and other authorities to counter the multi-dimensional onslaught against the RSA in the ideological, military, economic, social, psychological, cultural, political and diplomatic fields[8]

From 1948 to 1979, almost thirty years of National party rule, the changes in the internal security structures were the result of a long and convoluted interaction between the various security intelligence agencies in South Africa. There was confusion about goals and functions, overlapping, and interdepartmental rivalry. However, ever since P. W. Botha took over as minister of defense in 1966, he was determined to make the South African Defence Force (SADF) militarily strong and self-sufficient. He responded to the arms embargo by developing Armscor, a state-controlled arms production industry, into an impressive arms exporting industry — one of the ten largest in the world. His defense philosophy encompassed both foreign and regional policy and reached far into most aspects of domestic policy. It was Botha who masterminded the military intervention into Angola in 1974–75, thus sacrificing the principle of noninterference in the internal affairs of other countries and introducing a policy of destabilization for neighboring states. And long before he became prime minister, he argued tirelessly for a national total strategy to ward off the total onslaught. It is fascinating to speculate on what would have happened to the ideology of total strategy-total onslaught if Dr. Connie Mulder and General van den Bergh had not been eliminated from security-intelligence influence as a result of the so-called information scandal from 1974 to 1979. Until then, Botha was not considered a very serious contender for the position of prime minister. When Vorster resigned, Connie Mulder seemed

[8] *Republic of SA White Paper on Defence*, WPF-1977, p. 5.

earmarked for the position. The information scandal revealed a massive misappropriation of secret funds. Mulder and van den Bergh were deeply implicated, and even Vorster came out of it with deep political scars. Botha and his supporters moved swiftly; the caucus of the National party elected him to succeed Vorster and it was not long before Mulder, van den Bergh, and Vorster were out of the picture. For the first time, P. W. Botha was in a position to implement his security policy without any other departmental competitors or strong personalities to challenge him. He lost no time — he promised "clean administration" and a rationalization of the civil service. But the country, as well as the state bureaucracy, had to be educated on the total onslaught as well.

In the 1979 white paper on defense (the year that P. W. Botha became prime minister), it was bluntly stated that "the total onslaught as is being waged against South Africa" requires "highly co-ordinated action" if it is to be successfully counteracted.[9]

The following year, General Magnus Malan, who was soon to move from being a professional soldier to minister of defense in the Botha cabinet, spoke at the Institute for Strategic Studies at the University of Pretoria, and said:

> The design of a total onslaught, masterfully controlled by Russia, robs the intended victim of the luxury of preparation from mobilization to conventional warfare. The RSA realised the necessity of a state of continued preparedness to cope with the onslaught on its power bases. For this a total strategy is necessary, because a total onslaught against the RSA can only be overcome by a co-ordinated application of all the means at the RSA's disposal.[10]

In a special series of articles in *Paratus*, the official Defence Force magazine widely distributed to conscripts, Permanent Force mem-

---

[9] *Republic of SA White Paper on Defence Armaments Supply*, WPF-1979, p. 1.

[10] W. A. de M. Malan, "Die Aanslag teen SA," Institute for Strategic Studies, University of Pretoria, *Strategic Review*, Nov. 1980.

bers, and all arms of the civil service, the SADF argued the need
for "total involvement" because

> the enemies of the RSA will eventually try to deliver the *coup
> de grâce* by means of a conventional onslaught from one or
> more of the neighbouring states. . . . This onslaught would
> include maritime action and be accompanied by large scale
> internal unrest. The USSR is for this reason using the so-
> called threat that South Africa's military potential holds for
> its neighbouring states as an excuse to supply huge quantities
> of arms to those countries. This build up also includes the
> gradual increase in involvement by Soviet-bloc military per-
> sonnel as well as the development of those countries' infra-
> structure for war.[11]

Notice again how the description of the total onslaught-total
strategy interaction involves coordinated action in the areas of
international, regional, and domestic policy. The period 1979–87
saw the militarization of the South African society on an un-
precedented scale. The 1982 Defence Department white paper
sets, as one of the goals of the SADF, the policy of militarizing the
entire society. "It is policy that all population groups be involved
in defending the RSA. This means the representation of all population groups in the SADF, in other words, a Defence Force of the
People for the People." [12]

There already existed an Indian and Cape Coloured Corps
and the idea was to establish battalions in each of the so-called
National States. There is no compulsory conscription for those
who are not white, but the SADF has no difficulty in recruiting
more than the required volunteers that it can accommodate. It is
important to realize that the "total involvement" of other population groups in the defense of the Republic of South Africa also
serves as a powerful rationale for "dismantling apartheid" and
legitimizing "reform."

[11] "Total Involvement," *Paratus* 33, no. 5 (May 1982): 22.
[12] *White Paper on Defence and Armament Supply*, WPM-1982, p. 2.

One of the first things Botha did when he became prime minister was to reduce the number of cabinet committees and to coordinate their agendas. One of them, the State Security Council, was elevated into a position of special prominence. It enjoyed statutory recognition, and Botha, as prime minister, was its chairman. In terms of its scope of activities a National Security Management System (NSMS) was adopted on August 16, 1979. The NSMS has created a formidable apparatus, drawing together officials and politicians who wield extraordinary power and influence in South Africa. Not only has it effected a very high degree of coordination in the civil service, it has also induced a much higher degree of efficiency in coping with perceived security threats and has infused in a new generation of public servants and other beneficiaries of state patronage an awareness of total onslaught and a commitment to total strategy as a means of coping with it.

The NSMS is deployed on the central, regional, and local level of state administration. On the central level of administration there are five major components:

1. The *cabinet* together with the president forms the link between political and security interests.

2. The *state security council* has the state president (formerly the prime minister) as chairman and includes the senior minister in the cabinet, the ministers of foreign affairs, defense, justice, and police as well as the director of the National Intelligence Service (NIS has replaced BOSS), the chief of the SADF, the commissioner of the South African Police, the secretary of foreign affairs, and the secretary of justice. Additional members can be co-opted as circumstances may require. The SSC meets every fortnight before the cabinet and overviews security and intelligence matters. The state president then reports to the cabinet on such matters.

3. A *permanent working committee* consists of the heads of departments represented on the SSC as well as the chairmen of the other cabinet committees. Its functions are to meet every fortnight before the SSC meets to discuss the agenda of the SSC and to make recommendations on advice of the SSC to the cabinet.

4. The *Secretariat of the SSC* consists entirely of civil servants (approximately 100), who serve there either permanently or on secondment. The representation from government departments is: 11 percent Foreign Affairs; 1 percent Prison Services, 11 percent Security Police, 5 percent Railway Police, 16 percent SADF, and 56 percent NIS (that is, 89 percent of the representation comes from security-intelligence agencies). The Secretariat has four branches:

> The *Administrative Branch*, whose functions are self-evident

> The *National Intelligence Interpretation Branch*, which provides intelligence reports and interprets national intelligence

> The *Strategic Communication Branch*, whose main task is to devise strategies to counteract negative propaganda and to promote positive propaganda

> The *Strategy Branch*, which formulates total strategies and coordinates policies of interdepartmental committees.

5. *Interdepartmental Committees.* The Departments involved are Manpower, Security Services, Civil Defence, Transport, National Supplies and Resources, Government Funding, National Economy, Telecommunications and Electrical Power Supply, Service and Technology, Community Services, Culture, and Political Affairs. These interdepartmental committees are the key to the Strategy Branch of the Secretariat. They provide departmental strategies which

the Strategy Branch of the Secretariat coordinates into a total strategy to deal with an overall security threat.

On the regional level of administration there are twelve Joint Management Centres (JMCs) located conveniently at the twelve SADF command headquarters in Durban, Kimberley, Pretoria, Port Elizabeth, Bloemfontein, Oudtshoorn, Walvis Bay, Johannesburg, Cape Town, Potchefstroom, Pietersburg, Nelspruit. Eventually it is intended to let them correspond to the nine economic development regions that have been identified. Each JMC consists of between forty and sixty officials drawn from government departments with an "interest in the activities of the JMC," and each JMC has three standing committees.[13]

A *Joint Intelligence Standing Committee* (GIK) evaluates intelligence reports in the region.

A *Constitutional, Economic and Social Standing Committee* (SEMKOM) formulates joint strategies on a regional level to counteract security threats identified by the GIK.

A *Communications Standing Committee* (KOMKOM) disseminates accurate information (propaganda) or disinforms opponents.

(Notice how the three standing committees dovetail in terms of functions on a *regional* level with the functions of the three branches of the Secretariat on the *central* level.)

Each JMC has an executive which consists of the chairman of the JMC (in all cases so far it is a brigadier of the SADF or the South African Police, SAP) and the chairman of the three standing committees.

---

[13] Much of the detailed information on the structure of the NSMS depends on the unpublished thesis for a master's degree in political science by J. Selfe, "The Total Onslaught and the Total Strategy," University of Cape Town, 1986, chapter 111.

The formal terms of reference of the JMCs are "to ensure the necessary co-ordination on security matters at regional and local levels through the Departments concerned," but as General Piet van der Westhuizen, current secretary-general of the SSC put it, the JMCs are the eyes and ears of the NSMS and they monitor the implementation of total strategies. Their prime objective is "the lowering of the revolutionary climate; the prevention/defusing of unrest, and combatting terrorism and other revolutionary actions." [14]

The JMCs bring together in one organization all the top officials in the respective regions and they also control formidable executive powers. The total strategy applied to "external onslaught" at least provides the civil service and army with the fiction that this is in the interest of all South Africans and is therefore "non-political action." However, countering the "internal onslaught" or "lowering the revolutionary climate" brings the organs of state into direct political controversy, which destroys any pretense at political neutrality. The South African state becomes both the agent for "reform" to meet the onslaught as well as the source of counterrevolutionary action to undermine it.

If those who are supposed to be the beneficiaries of reform are also part of the total onslaught, it is not difficult to see how reform and revolt are inextricably linked to one another.

On the local level of administration there are 60 *sub-management centers* corresponding roughly to the 57 regional services councils that have been delimited and a further 350 *mini management centers* covering most of the towns of the RSA. It is on the local level of the NSMS administration where civilians become involved in the total strategy for the first time. Leading local personalities or office-bearers of local interest groups are co-opted into these management centers and their activities co-ordinated into strategies defined by the JMCs at the regional and professional level of the NSMS. Activities at the local level can

---

[14] General P. van der Westhuizen, *Die Burger*, May 27, 1986.

cover a wide range of activities which relate to security and intelligence matters: civil defense, emergency action, antiterrorist
training, first aid, distress relief action, and so on.

In tracing how the security interests of the Republic of South
Africa as defined by those in control of the state have changed
over time, one is able to see how it became possible to abandon
key aspects of apartheid–separate development in favor of a total
onslaught-total strategy alternative. The National party government under P. W. Botha shifted from proactively motivating
whites in favor of apartheid–separate development, as was the
case under Malan, Strydom, Verwoerd, and Vorster, to reactively
motivating them against the total onslaught. That is why the
values of security and stability have begun to lose their instrumental character and have become ends in themselves. The NSMS
of the P. W. Botha era provides the policy framework within
which the resources of the South African state are organized in a
total strategy to combat "the threat."

Any person or movement that questions the state's perceptions
of "the threat" is defined as part of it, and similarly, those who
resist being co-opted into the total strategy, become defined as its
legitimate targets. It is an ideology with a built-in self-fulfilling
logic. As long as the right of those who define "the onslaught"
and "manage the strategy" is not questioned or threatened, they
will tolerate, even encourage "reform," the "broadening of
democracy," and "negotiation." The moment it is questioned,
even by implication, as happened during the visits of the EPG and
Sir Geoffrey Howe, National party government spokesmen use
concepts such as "suicide," "surrender," "chaos," "disintegration,"
to conjure up alternative possibilities to their own continued control. The propaganda import is obvious — if a future strategy
could lead to "suicide," or some apocalyptic equivalent, the continued costs of the present one remain bearable. Divergent, even
hostile interest groups find themselves somehow trapped into

arguing within this propaganda framework — from right-wing racists to businessmen — even to some liberal newspaper editors. The morality and logic which argues that the fight for survival respects no rules is perfectly compatible with the argument "better the devil you know, than the one you don't." It is in this ideological context that the South African state's international, regional, and domestic policies have to be understood. Actions of the government which "normally" don't make sense become coherent — for example, the raid on neighboring territories during the EPG visit and while Ronald Reagan and Margaret Thatcher were fighting desperate rearguard actions against sanctions. The EPG, Reagan, Thatcher, and Howe all came with the same message: dismantle apartheid, release political prisoners, unban organizations, and negotiate. The obvious question of what was to be negotiated once apartheid had been dismantled was answered by P. W. Botha at the 1986 Transvaal Congress of the National party when he accused "the outside world of confusing reform with surrender." Similarly, the South African state's regional policy does not hesitate to defy convention, use subterfuge, lies, and uncomplicated force if it serves the total strategy in its fight against the onslaught.

The NSMS is the policy which gives effect to the ideology of total strategy versus total onslaught. It also destroys any pretense at neutrality or nonpartisanship. The idea of a neutral civil service loyally and disinterestedly serving whichever government happened to be in power was still a strong tradition when the National party took over in 1948. However, as Afrikaner nationalism consolidated itself and the civil service became the major channel of Afrikaner economic mobility, the partisan nature of the state bureaucracy became increasingly evident. Furthermore, new and vast bureaucracies were created in order to give effect to what was essentially a party political doctrine, that is, apartheid and separate development. With the implementation of a total strategy, which draws on "all the available resources" to meet the onslaught, no competing and, especially, contradictory ideologies or political programs can be tolerated. Thus, P. W. Botha, by redefining the security interests of the South African state, has given it a coherence and unity of purpose which it has not had before; it has developed a common ideology, a common set of goals and strategies, and an overall policy in terms of which to implement them. Every state structure, including Parliament, homeland governments, independent states and neighboring countries, are subservient to the goals and logic of the total strategy. Even reform.

On the domestic front, the crisp issue of reform is how to jettison apartheid–separate development without losing control and still mobilize enough support for the total strategy. Constitutionally the response has been a massive and sustained erosion of accountable politics in favor of co-optive decision making. At the central and key points, the control the white minority has ensures that its will cannot be challenged by popular rejection. The quid pro quo for co-optive control has been to multiracialize political participation. As the 1986 white paper on defense made clear, whites alone cannot implement the total strategy. The other population groups have to make their contribution as well. At present the South African state is planning to regulate this contribution in the constitutional area. It appears that what the leaders have in mind is a multiracial constitution making provision for the group representation of homeland, urban, and rural blacks, as well as Coloureds, Asians, and whites, with the white minority at the apex of control.

Those in control have no objections to popular elections, provided they occur within structures determined by them and provided that at the vital areas of decision making no headcount will determine the outcome where the government's own representation is in the minority. This pattern of representation is evident in the tricameral Parliament, the regional services councils, the members of the executive council (MECs) of the former pro-

vincial councils, and, in the latest development, the National
Council, which provides for elected blacks outside the homeland
and independent territories. The overall structure could very well
be a quasi-representative multiracial autocracy with the white
minority in firm control over political decision making and national security. For propaganda purposes it will be presented as
a government of national unity — the South African people's
response to the total onslaught. While conceding that it may not
be perfect, South Africa is responding in a unique way to a unique
problem, and it is preferable to what would happen under a
"one-man-one-vote ANC and Communist controlled State."

The viability of this system of co-optive domination will
depend primarily on two things: the South African state's continuing power of patronage and a sufficient degree of cooperation
from other population groups. It is important to realize that
co-optive domination does not depend on legitimacy and/or
majority support to work (too often people tend to think that
by demonstrating the illegitimacy of a regime they have also predicted its collapse); it simply needs enough people to participate
in it. This is where the battle is raging at its fiercest in urban
black communities. The South African state is determined to
find "good," "responsible," "peace-loving" blacks, and townships
are torn between cooperating and rejecting any form of collabora-
tion. Almost every aspect of black community life has become
politicized, so that everyday normal activities and issues become
topics of heated debate. It appears to be slowly crystallizing into
an ideological division between a multiracial autocracy versus a
nonracial or "socialist" democracy. By defining those who argue
or struggle for a popular democracy based on the free association
of individuals as subversive, the South African state has brought
the total onslaught into the domestic arena. Its own counter-
strategy is to offer multiracial patronage as part and parcel of its
"reform" program. That is why the state's reform program has

to be accompanied by a massive extension of coercion or repression. For the state to allow genuine accountability politics, it would have to face the risk of popular rejection of its whole total strategy and eventually of the position of minority domination for the whites. As P. W. Botha has so bluntly stated to the British foreign minister: "this could be political suicide."

The constitutional reform package which thus dovetails with the NSMS depends on co-optive participation at various levels of civilian government. At the *central level*, it includes (*a*) a confederation of states between South Africa and the TBVC countries (Transkei, Bophuthatswana, Venda, and Ciskei); (*b*) a National Council consisting of nine black representatives elected in each of the nine economic regions delimited by the state: representatives from the homeland governments as well as the state president, a few cabinet ministers and nine others nominated by the state president; and (*c*) a tricameral Parliament for whites, Coloureds, and Asians. At the *regional level* it includes: (*a*) MECs of the former Provincial Council; (*b*) nine electoral divisions for blacks from the nine economic development areas; and (*c*) homeland areas. At the *local level* it includes: (*a*) regional service councils; (*b*) local governments; and (*c*) management committees.

At each level an element of the NSMS is at hand to coordinate security strategies with political reform programs. The state is determined to channel all forms of political participation into these predetermined co-optive structures and then to "negotiate" further constitutional developments. Any dissent that tries to manifest itself outside of these structures is treated as an unwitting or witting agent of the total onslaught and can expect the full force of the state's repressive measures to act against it. It is against this background that one has to understand the structures, organizations, and strategies for resistance, opposition, or revolt and assess their chances of success. This is what the final lecture is all about.

III. THE DYNAMICS OF REFORM:
PATTERNS OF RESISTANCE AND REVOLT

On July 21, 1985, P. W. Botha announced a state of emergency
which has twice been renewed and endures to the present. In
terms of the proclamation, extraordinary powers were conferred
on officers of the security forces to deal with the unrest in the
townships. This was preceded by a decision of the state to use
the SADF on a continuous basis to assist the SAP to cope with
internal unrest. The first large-scale operation of this kind was in
Sebokeng in August 1984. Since then, this kind of operation has
become commonplace. The SAP has also been supplemented by
the introduction of "kitskonstables" (literally, "instant con-
stables") into the townships — police recruits with minimum training over a three-month period who are given sjamboks (whips)
and guns and who patrol urban black communities. The state has
used "black vigilante" groups to assist it in imposing coercive
control. In fact, South Africa has had the most extensive imposition of repressive control since Union in 1910. Six months after
the first announcement of a state of emergency, it was estimated
that about 7,500 people had been detained or arrested. By mid-
1986 detentions or arrests were estimated to be in the region of
12,000. The numbers have decreased significantly since then and
are now considered to be about 1,500. Included in this 1,500 are
a vast number of community leaders and some prisoners awaiting
trial. It is difficult to be exact because the state does not regard
it to be in the "public interest" to make this kind of information
available.

The manner in which the state of emergency was implemented
and the incidents of unrest, mob violence, and massive funerals
made South Africa prime-time viewing on most of the television
stations of the world. As a news item South Africa was one of
the ten most popular news items of 1985 and 1986.[15] The state

---

[15] *World Press Review*, February 1987, p. 8.

soon put a stop to this by forbidding entry into townships to television crews (particularly foreign ones) and laying down stringent conditions for reporting on unrest. It set up its own unrest information liaison structure, which carefully monitored news on the events of each day. Soon South Africa was off the front pages and editorial columns of newspapers, and particularly inside South Africa and for whites the impression was created that "normality" had returned and that everything was under control.

But there was a time during the height of the revolt and resistance when extraordinary and extravagant claims were being made about the imminence of the South African state's collapse. Confident predictions about the efficacy of sanctions, boycotts, strikes, liberated zones, and mass mobilization were commonplace. This kind of euphoria about the imminence of radical change has all but disappeared, but at its height, a climate existed in which there was a great deal of instant postapartheid scenario building. This inevitably focused attention on opposition movements and strategies and their relative significance in the widespread revolt that took place. In looking at the patterns of resistance and revolt, it is useful to keep the distinction between movements and strategies, if only for the obvious reason that different movements, parties, and organizations may have different goals and agendas for change but share the same strategies or, conversely, may differ on strategies but share the same goals.

MOVEMENTS

THE UNITED DEMOCRATIC FRONT

In considering the interaction between reform and revolt, it is appropriate to begin with the UDF, not because it is the oldest opposition movement (it is not) or necessarily the first to respond to the state's reform proposals, but because the UDF managed to capture the highground in mobilizing domestic resistance against the implementation of the new tricameral constitution. In doing so, it highlighted the fundamental cleavages between parliamentary and extra-parliamentary politics and posed a crisis of legitimacy for all individuals or organizations who participated in state-created constitutional structures. The issue of black exclusion from the new tricameral constitution was effectively seized on to question the relevance of any participation in such structures and to highlight the co-optive nature of the state's constitutional program. The UDF was careful never to elevate the issue of nonparticipation into an inflexible principle, but at the same time it very actively encouraged people not to participate in, especially, tricameral politics for the present, while challenging those who did to demonstrate the relevance of such actions. This approach was so effective that it made a mockery of the first so-called Coloured and Indian elections, which registered a very low overall poll and presented those who were elected with an enduring crisis of credibility.

The UDF is not a monolithic party or organization but a front with approximately six hundred affiliates distributed across the country. Its initial objective was mass mobilization against tricameral politics, and this inevitably meant a heavy emphasis on protest politics. This objective was eventually broadened to include other areas of domestic politics. The diversity of organizations belonging to it, as well as the rapidity with which its membership increased, made it difficult to judge it in terms of a single policy or agenda. Gradually, however, "critical issues" emerged which became identified with a UDF position: the Freedom Charter, sanctions, nonracialism, and a very sympathetic stance toward the ANC, although the UDF was insistent that it was not an ANC front and was committed to nonviolent opposition. Nevertheless, it still campaigns vigorously for the unbanning of political organizations, such as the ANC, and for the release of political prisoners. There is no doubt that the effectiveness of the mass mobilization of the UDF managed to achieve two things which characterized the nature of the revolt that accompanied reform: first, it located the revolt as a struggle between an extra-parliamentary executive (that is, state president plus ssc plus security forces) and extra-parliamentary opposition groups, and second, it forced the South African state to propagandize the ANC as the vanguard of the total onslaught.

THE AFRICAN NATIONAL CONGRESS

The history of the ANC is well recorded in numerous publications.[16] It is the oldest and arguably the largest mass liberation movement of South Africa. For about two and a half decades it has been banned and its leadership has been in exile or in prison, but there can be no doubt that it exerts a major influence on the quality and extent of resistance politics to the South African state. In fact, it is not possible adequately to understand the relationship between reform and revolt without giving due recognition to the strategic position which the ANC occupies in this relationship. Two reasons can be given for this: first, the ANC is the oldest, broadest based liberation movement with a fairly comprehensive strategy and goal for the liberation of South Africa; and second, the South African state has targeted the ANC as its major opponent. The ANC and what it stands for, as well as its associates, epitomize the total onslaught for the South African state and is therefore the major rationale for the total strategy, which in turn legitimizes reform.

During June 16–23, 1985, there was a Second National Consultative Conference of the ANC in Lusaka. From its proceedings as documented in committee reports, a comprehensive picture of the ANC structures, code of conduct, strategies, tactics, and membership emerges. Essentially, it sees itself as a broadly based revolutionary movement with the following goals:

1. To strive to unite the people of South Africa, the Africans in particular, for the objective of the immediate seizure of

---

[16] A recent overview of the present state of the ANC as an organization can be found in T. Lodge, "State of Exile: The African National Congress of SA, 1976–1986," *Third World Quarterly*, 1987, pp. 1–27.

power from the racist colonial regime and its transfer to the people of South Africa as a whole.

2. To further strengthen the People's Army into a force capable of defeating the enemy and defending the gains of the revolution.

3. To create a united, non-racial and democratic South Africa based on the principles of the Freedom Charter.

4. To support the cause of National Liberation, world peace and the right to independence of nations of Africa and the rest of the world.[17]

The strategies and tactics to achieve these aims and objectives are spelled out in a separate report and include "a people's war or armed struggle, mass internal mobilization, setting up underground structures and international isolation."[18] These different strategies are seen to be intimately linked and dependent on one another for their respective degrees of success. The following descriptions of the "People's War" illustrate this point very clearly:

> A people's war is fought by the people with arms and all other forms and methods of struggle. Without the organized support of the people, armed struggle is in danger of being isolated and strangled. The enemy attempts to isolate us by launching campaigns to win the "hearts and minds" of the people — of our people, the oppressed and suffering workers and peasants. To defeat the enemy we must involve the entire people in the National Democratic Revolution.[19]

> The armed struggle must be based on, and grow out of, mass political support and must eventually involve all our people. All military activities must at every stage be guided and determined by the need to generate political mobilization, organisa-

---

17 "Report of Commission on National Structures, Constitutional Guidelines, and Codes of Conduct," ANC National Consultative Conference, June 1985, p. 6.

18 "Commission on Cadre Policy, Political and Ideological Work, Internal Commission Report, Commission on Strategy and Tactics," ANC National Consultative Conference, June 1985.

19 "Report of Commission on National Structures," p. 15.

tion and resistance, with the aim of progressively weakening the enemy's grip on his reins of political, economic, social and military power, by a combination of political and military action. The forms of political and military activities and the ways these activities relate to one another, go through different phases as the situation changes. It is therefore vital to have under continuous survey the changing tactical relationships between these two inter-dependent factors in our struggle and the place which political and military actions (in the narrow sense) occupy in each phase, both nationally and within each of our main regions.[20]

Given the encompassing nature of the ANC strategies, it is inevitable that it will become involved in any significant internal resistance and revolt and that ANC supporters-members will either openly or clandestinely be active across a wide spectrum of movements, fronts, organizations, and activities. That is why strikes, consumer and school boycotts, protest meetings, and the like initiated by other organizations but with the same issues at stake will enjoy ANC support and even active participation. In this sense, it sometimes becomes irrelevant whether the UDF is an ANC front or not. Oliver Tambo, the ANC president, makes this quite clear when he says:

> What the UDF has been doing is part of this growing resistance to the Apartheid system, the struggle to bring about a new order. We are happy with that. . . . I think the UDF represents the success of our appeals to our people to be organized and to unite in action. That doesn't make them ANC, but they have got to fight the struggle. The ANC is with them. The ANC is the people, not in terms of formations, branches and regional organisations, but it's with them and its political line is public, it is clear.[21]

The same applies to any other single-purpose organization pursuing a line of action that falls within the ANC's broad definition

[20] "Commission on Cadre Policy," p. 12.

[21] Interview with Oliver Tambo by Margaret A Novicki, *Africa Report*, July–August 1985, pp. 34 and 35.

of the struggle, whether it be the Black Sash, the End Conscription Campaign (ECC), a trade union, a church, or even the Progressive Federal Party (PFP). This is an important point to grasp because by choosing the ANC as its prime opponent the South African state, by implication, criminalizes or demonizes any opposition group or strategy whose actions correspond with goals or strategies of the ANC. In fact, given the goals and strategies of the South African state and the ANC, respectively, it is quite evident that they define each other as the prime targets of each other's total strategies. The total strategy of the South African state is the NSMS and reform versus the total strategy of the ANC, which is the National Democratic Revolution for a liberated South Africa. Each strategy's final objective is the destruction of the other. That is why reform and revolt will continue to interact with one another until this cycle is somehow broken.

An important consequence of the South African state's targeting the ANC as its major opponent is that it can propagandize against any other party or organization which shares values in common with ANC objectives. Thus one man, one vote; nonracial democracy; freedom of association; unbanning of organizations; the rule of law; and the civil liberties of the individual as opposed to the "rights of the group" are values which immediately make a party or organization who campaigns for them suspect as either "a useful idiot" or willing collaborators of the ANC. At the same time, the state can select those aspects of ANC strategy or structure which it regards as the most useful for demonizing purposes and through guilt by association tar any other opposition grouping with the same brush. "Terrorism," "violence," and "communism" are the three most common labels. It is particularly in the white political arena where this rather crude tactic is very effective. A 1985 Human Science Research Council (HSRC) survey of white voters indicated that 85 percent were in favor of "negotiating with blacks," and only 3.6 percent of respondents believed that negotiations should be held with the ANC.[22] White voters are not only conditioned to think that negotiation *need not* include the ANC but are constantly brainwashed to believe that any negotiations with the ANC should be avoided at all costs. The ANC is officially presented in South Africa as a gang of incorrigible villains and demons that must be eliminated and with which there should be no negotiations. This approach by the South African state more than anything else lies at the root of its inability to attract credible leaders into any of its co-optive structures in the center, such as the tricameral Parliament and the National Council. Any other party or organization that petitions for the unbanning of the ANC and negotiating with it is then rubbished as wanting to hobnob with "terrorists" and "communists."

OTHER NONPARTICIPATIVE OPPOSITION

A useful distinction to be made in discussing groups in opposition to the state is between those who, like the UDF and ANC, either as a matter of deliberate policy or through convention, do not participate in the constitutional structures sanctioned by the South African state and those who do. Other nonparticipative opposition groups would, for example, be:

PAC, BC, National Forum, NEUM. The Pan African Congress, the Black Conservatives, and the New Unity Movement fall outside the ANC support group and are also regarded as "non-Charterist" organizations (that is, do not subscribe to or support or adopt the Freedom Charter accepted by those who attended the 1955 Kliptown Congress of the People). Although members and/or supporters of these organizations differ strategically and in certain respects ideologically from the ANC they have in many cases felt the same impact of state repression and have also been active across a wide front in revolt against state reforms. The ANC is very sensitive to its

[22] W. Van Vuuren, "The Reaction Back Home," *UWC* [*University of the Western Cape*] *News*, September 1982, p. 8.

pole position in the liberation struggle being questioned and very often reacts sharply to the perceived role of these groupings in regional and community politics. Accusations of "diluting and struggle," "divisiveness," and "undermining unity of purpose" often reflect an underlying rivalry and a battle for hegemony in opposition. The South African state is quick to exploit these differences when and wherever it suits it to "divide and rule" or to fragment opposition to its policy and programs.

The Churches. A self-evident distinction can be drawn between an established church's position in the revolt in terms whether its membership is predominantly black or white. To the extent that its membership is predominantly black, the church will be drawn deeper into the revolt against the state's reforms or repression. An inevitable reason for this is that the church forms a vital institutional base for community organization and communication. As the state systematically narrowed down avenues of legitimate dissent so the churches became more and more involved in dealing with reaction to and consequences of community repression. Funerals became emotional and symbolic occasions for demonstrating not only community grief but also solidarity and determination to continue resistance. The state again acted against this by forbidding television crews to cover funerals and by severely restricting attendance as well as what could and could not be said. A number of clergy have been detained, even tortured, during the state of emergency. Quite distinct from any theological considerations, the church as a social institution is going through a fundamental redefinition of its role in the "total strategy." Recently the Free State Synod of the Dutch Reformed Church adopted a resolution forbidding discussions between its office-bearers and the ANC. At the same time, Bishop Desmond Tutu led a delegation to Lusaka precisely for such discussions.

The Press-Media. Again a distinction can be drawn between so-called "established" press and "alternative" press. The latter is openly partisan to nonparticipative extra-parliamentary opposition and consequently a very obvious target of state action. Recently yet another series of stringent press censorship measures was announced, giving the state's representatives carte blanche to decide whether a particular publication was assisting or contributing to a revolutionary climate. The "established" press can (broadly speaking) be divided into those publications that are supportive of government and those that are opposed, although opposition can vary from being mild to principled. None of them would take the same risk as "alternative" newspapers in identifying with a particular nonparticipative extra-parliamentary group. However, despite crippling restrictions on reporting on the unrest and state of emergency, some of them have managed to expose state irregularities and excesses. They remain under continued threat of state action as long as they nudge against the official threshold of tolerance. At the same time there are managers and editors of the "opposition press" who, although they feel strongly about certain principles such as freedom of the press and rule of law, are not all that averse to accepting the "reality" of the total onslaught and the need for a total strategy.

PARTICIPATIVE OPPOSITION

When discussing participative opposition the issue is not only participation in the political structures sanctioned by the state (for example, Parliament, legislative assemblies, regional services councils, community councils) but also other structures regarded by the state to be "constitutional" (trade unions, schools, universities). The issue of participative opposition is relevant to the extent that groups, parties, or movements regard participation in those structures as strategically significant in pursuing their goals. The issue of participation in particularly political structures has created a great deal of tension and even open hostility between organizations and movements opposed to the state, and needless to say these divisions have been systematically exploited by the state to keep fragmentation and disunity to its total strategy alive.

Parliamentary Opposition. If Parliament as a base for not only opposing those in power but unseating them is to be taken seriously, then it is most likely to be a white right-wing political party. The fact that the dominant party can always undercut such a threat by making concessions to white fears and prejudices makes this an unlikely prospect. The tricameral Parliament is tailormade for white right-wing opposition. The "revolt from the right" is often overlooked when the dynamics of reform and revolt are considered. Apart from the fact that right-wing views are strategically well represented throughout the state bureaucracy, particularly in the security structures, and are intimately involved in the deployment of the total strategy, Parliament provides the most prominent public forum for promoting right-wing views. To the extent that the National party as the dominant party wishes to promote reform, but at the same time demonizes the most important organizations and movements representing blacks who are supposed to be the prime beneficiaries of reform, the right-wing can exploit any "new reform measures," no matter how timid or incremental, as a sell-out or capitulation of white interest. The irony of the reform program as part of the total strategy is that it forces the National party government into the extra-parliamentary arena to make it work. It is not sufficient to induce Coloureds and Indians into Parliament, it is necessary to persuade blacks onto the "reform structures" created by the state. M. G. Buthelezi sums this dilemma up concisely:

> On the level of constitutional development, the State President can make no gains from doing things which blacks reject. He has to involve blacks in constitutional development. We as black leaders have the ultimate weapon of veto right over what the State President can achieve. He can

blunder without us, but he cannot succeed without us. The next two to three years is going to be a crucial time in which massive endeavours should be made to stop the State. President establishing political circuses in which he can be the ringmaster.[23]

On the other hand, if the state president moves too rapidly to do things which "blacks do not reject" in the extra-parliamentary terrain, it will run up against what whites are not prepared to accept in the parliamentary terrain. These are the inevitable constraints within which white party politics is forced to play itself out and which limit the tempo and quality of "constitutional" change. That is why white opposition from the left in Parliament is so vulnerable. The moment it identifies too strongly with a nonracial democracy; freedom of association; one man, one vote, it is defined as part of the total onslaught and subjected to the same propaganda onslaught reserved for the ANC. At the same time, it is in no position to compete with those to the right of it in promising "white security." Consequently, "left" participative opposition of whites in Parliament can have strategic but not substantive significance, that is, it cannot substantially threaten any dominant party in the House of Assembly. Strategically it can enter into an alliance or coalition with other parliamentary or extra-parliamentary opposition groups, but at the increased risk of electoral vulnerability. However, if such opposition has relinquished any designs on "going for power," it can have a significant protesting role. In this sense it has played a part in the dynamic between reform and revolt by focusing on arbitrary state action during the different states of emergency.

What is true for white "left" opposition in Parliament is generally true for those parties in the other two chambers of the tricameral Parliament. An additional strategic significance, however, is that they can, in specific cases, constitutionally frustrate the plans of the dominant white party in Parliament. The latest

23 M. G. Buthelezi, *Clarion Call* (Inkatha Institute, 1987), vol. 2, p. 3.

example is the resignation from the cabinet of the Labour party leader Alan Hendrickse and his declared intention to oppose a change of the constitution unless certain concessions come from the government. So far this kind of confrontationist horse trading has been rare, but it is certainly a strategic advantage available to those who participate in this manner. In the absence of its being used regularly and effectively, those who participate are under continuous pressure to "deliver the goods" and have to cope with a credibility crisis from those who reject participative opposition.

Extra-parliamentary Opposition. There is little doubt that Inkatha, a predominantly Zulu-based movement which professes a paid-up membership of more than one and a half million and is led by M. G. Buthelezi, occupies a strategically important position in the dynamic between reform and revolt. Its pattern of participative opposition thus far has consistently frustrated the co-optive designs of the state, but at the same time, this has also frustrated the scope of the ANC's National Democratic Revolution. At the height of the revolt in 1985–86, an intensely hostile relationship existed between the UDF-ANC and Inkatha, and each accused the other of murder and bloodshed. There is clear evidence of community violence between Inkatha and the UDF in a number of townships in Natal. Buthelezi differs strongly with the UDF-ANC on a number of areas of strategy and principle. Clearly committed to a system of free enterprise, he opposes sanctions actively, domestically and abroad, is dismissive of the armed struggle, and did not participate in the protests and mass mobilization led by the UDF. For this, he has been depicted as an "enemy of the struggle," a "collaborator and sell out" by the ANC and other nonparticipative opposition groups.

Undoubtedly Inkatha-Buthelezi's national support suffered from the onset of constitutional reform. The tricameral Parliament not only precipitated mass mobilization against it, but brought the ANC into prominence as the flagship of revolt and raised the issue of participative opposition on all levels. But Buthelezi's support in Natal remains formidable, and it is quite obvious that he can fundamentally affect the state's latest co-optive constitutional designs by deciding to participate or not. He is consistently using the threat of participation-nonparticipation as a bargaining chip for concessions from the state. For example:

> The State President will fail utterly if he follows a course of events in which he gives political roles to good boys and expects them to do an impossible job. I would negotiate with the State President tomorrow if the negotiating agenda would include the scrapping of the tricameral Parliament and would, for instance, make it possible for me to table a final version of the KwaZulu/Natal Indaba constitutional proposals. Obviously, black democracy must be unshackled to give black negotiators the prospects of carrying blacks with them. The only blacks worth negotiating with are blacks who would, in fact, increase their own power bases through negotiations. Of what value would I be to Mr. P. W. Botha, to black South Africa and South Africa as a whole, if I was by now located in the South African political rubbish heap because I had prematurely involved myself in discussions with the State President? [24]

If the state president "is thinking of the kind of future in which whites remain the final decision makers over all matters which add up to establishing domestic and foreign policy" Buthelezi declares himself not available.[25] In short, if the state is prepared to negotiate away white domination, he is on board. If not, he is prepared to wait. Given the fact that protecting white domination is the raison d'être of the total strategy, Buthelezi's detractors accuse him of waiting in comfort, but both he and his detractors fail to convince each other about the effectiveness of their competing strategies.

[24] Ibid., p. 3.
[25] Ibid., p. 5.

The kind of participative opposition which Inkatha represents, certainly differs from that of the nonparticipative kind on more levels than strategy and principle alone. Inkatha is essentially a constituency organization that can function legally. The leadership is thus more immediately accountable, and because it does cooperate in administering part of the state structure, it is involved in dispensing reward and patronage. This alone introduces constraints and vested interests which do not affect the quality of leadership of nonparticipative organizations. Buthelezi epitomizes the trials and tribulations of this kind of participative opposition, which is also the fate, to a lesser extent, of other homeland leaders who do not have his scope and depth of support.

Trade Unions. South African trade unionism is one of the best-documented developments of recent years.[26] Black unionism has made spectacular advances. One of the central characteristics of this development is the extent to which unions have used the industrial machinery created by the state to pursue goals unintended by those who set up the structures. Given the manner in which the state cut off other legitimate channels of political dissent, it was almost inevitable that the unions would begin to experience a "political overload." Because of this, trade unionism is an inherent part of the dynamic between reform and revolt. Although unions may differ on their affiliation-support for the UDF-ANC and whether they are "charterist" or "workerist," all of them are in some way or other part of the struggle for liberation. Consequently, the state has been particularly aggressive, even brutal, in the actions it has taken against unions. Many leaders have also been detained, tortured, and in some cases killed in mysterious circumstances.

Because of their participative nature, the unions are constitutional and legal and have opportunities denied to banned or other nonparticipative organizations and movements. There is no doubt

---

[26] For a comprehensive recent publication, see Steven Freedman, *Building Tomorrow Today* (Johannesburg: Ravan Press, 1987).

that their experience in bargaining, organizing, and disciplining membership has increased dramatically as industrial disputes have multiplied in recent years. An unknown factor is the extent to which unions will retain their independence when and if conditions of freedom of organization and association exist in South Africa. Will they become purely functional labor organizations or be subsumed under broader political movements? This is not purely an academic question, because this issue also lies at the heart of some unions' resistance to becoming too "involved in politics" or losing their independence to the hegemonic demands of a liberation movement. Whatever the answer, trade unions will increasingly become a force to be reckoned with as the state deepens its commitment to the total strategy. The fact that they straddle the economic and political demands of the workers will guarantee this.

Schools. Particularly since the school riots of June 16, 1976, black schoolchildren have symbolized the revolt against the reforms of the state. Their actions have convulsed urban communities, divided opposition groups, and posed fundamental questions of strategy and control. Given their location in community life, the black youth drew almost the entire spectrum of opposition groups into their struggle: parents, teachers, workers, political organizations, and churches. Understandably many of the extravagant demands and predictions originated from them, as well as some of the worst excesses at the height of the revolt. It was from them that the cry of "Education after Liberation" came as well as the gruesome "necklacing" of enemies of the struggle. Given their youth and anger with the present, it is to be expected that they constitute an enduring source of radicalism in revolt. It is also easy to romanticize or to overevaluate their claims in the broader scope of revolt. However, any opposition group, whether participatory or nonparticipatory, would be foolish to ignore them in planning any large-scale strategy of resistance.

It was also black youth that, perhaps inadvertently, illustrated a fundamental dilemma in the choice between participation and nonparticipation. At one stage during the revolt and in pursuing the goal of "people's education," it was decided to boycott schools and state education. The longer this was done, the more it became evident that an important base of organization and communication had been sacrificed and that there was a very real danger that a whole generation of children would get no education at all. Thus participation facilitated organization, communication, and the development of skills, whereas it lost the dramatic and confrontationist advantages of nonparticipation. At the same time, participation always held the danger of succumbing to co-optive control.

SUMMARY

Although this overview of movements, organizations, and parties involved in some way or other in the revolt against the reforms of the South African state is brief, even cursory, it is sufficient to allow a general juxtaposition between the nature of reform and revolt:

Reform	Revolt
1. Creates a *group* based democracy	1. Creates an *individually* based democracy
2. Concerned with reforming *in* state structures	2. Concerned with reforming *of* state structures
3. Broadens participation through *co-option*	3. Broadens participation through *negotiation*
4. Wants to *multiracialize* South Africa	4. Wants to *nonracialize* South Africa
5. *Adjusts* white domination	5. *Removes* white domination

The ultimate objective of reform is to establish a multiracial government of an autocratic nature; the ultimate objective of revolt is to establish a nonracial government of a *democratic* nature. Those caught up in revolt may differ among themselves about the nature of that democracy and the socioeconomic structure of society to accompany it, but there is unanimity of purpose that the alternative should be democratic and nonracial. Those concerned with reform and the total strategy may differ among themselves about the scope and quality of reform, but they have unanimity of purpose that white minority control must not be sacrificed under any circumstances. Although those involved with the state's total strategy and reform program are in the minority and lack legitimacy, they have control over powerful resources and are well organized and cohesive. Those who are caught up in revolt are in the majority and enjoy considerable legitimacy but are more divided and organizationally vulnerable. One course of vulnerability and division concerns fundamental differences in strategy.

DIFFERENT STRATEGIES OF RESISTANCE

Sometimes differences in strategies between opposition groupings are tolerable and reflect different histories and emphases. Given the wide range of opposition groupings involved in the revolt against the state policy, this is almost inevitable. But it is when specific strategies are elevated into differences of principle and become an issue on which potential allies in opposition to the state's policies are excommunicated or defined as part of the problem that a measure of the division and fragmentation of opposition can be gained. Very often adherence to a particular strategy reflects an inflexible and dogmatic commitment to a particular theory or agenda of change in South Africa. The reluctance to abandon or even be flexible on aspects of this agenda is transferred into a rigid insistence that a particular strategy is nonnegotiable and its acceptance and support a precondition for qualifying as part of the "democratic struggle" against the state. To the extent that this involves a number of competing strategies, a great deal of opposition energy is wasted in defining and redefining thresholds of commitment; questioning bona fides and formulating hidden agendas to co-opt and/or weaken perceived competitors in the struggle. A brief discussion of three opposition strategies will illustrate these problems in the current South African situation.

The "Armed Struggle." The reasons why the ANC committed itself to the armed struggle are familiar. It was only after it had pursued all available peaceful means over a period of fifty years and these channels had been systematically removed by the state as well as their organization banned and its leadership incarcerated that the ANC turned to violence. Initially the armed struggle was extremely limited and circumscribed, but gradually the theater of conflict widened and today ANC rhetoric on the armed struggle depicts it as a full-scale "people's war" against the South African state as the enemy. As such, it has become a powerful and symbolic source of mobilization, particularly for black youth in the townships. Anyone who has attended a funeral or protest meeting in one of them and observed the youth "toi-toi-ing" (dancing) and simulating battles and scenes of confrontation, can verify how much this kind of militancy has become part of the culture of resistance.

For a number of reasons, it would be unreasonable to expect the ANC unconditionally to renounce violence — unreasonable in the sense that no political organization would consciously pursue a course of action that would weaken its support or undermine its bargaining ability. At the recent Dakar conference the ANC made it clear again that unless the conditions which led it to embrace the armed struggle were removed, there was no way in which it would reconsider, such conditions being the existence of apartheid–separate-development laws, continued banning of the organization, and imprisonment of the leadership. As Oliver Tambo said before then: "It has been suggested that the regime will talk to us if we abandon violence. Well, this is not serious because it is the regime which is violent and always has been. It is their violence which has resulted in us embracing violence. Unless they stop their violence, which is very difficult because it is the violence of the apartheid system itself, then it would be unreasonable to expect us to stop our violence." [27]

There is no question that if the ANC should abandon violence in the absence of major concessions from the state, this would lead to considerable loss of standing among the militant youth in the townships where the call for arms has become louder and more persistent. It is often not appreciated that the source of radicalization and increasing militancy of the ANC is much more domestic than external, and the manner in which the state of emergency has been handled by the state added momentum.

However, it is one thing to accept the armed struggle as part of the unfortunate reality of the South African conflict. It is quite another to insist that its acceptance and support is a precondition for participation in any effective opposition to the state's policies. For example, a significant number of white South Africans have abandoned apartheid and any variation of white domination and are willing to oppose co-option and repression and work for a democratic alternative, but these same people drift into a state of immobilized confusion if told that the only way to organize for it is through a commitment to a "people's war" or an "armed struggle."

How central and nonnegotiable is the armed struggle in the National Democratic Revolution of the ANC? How does the manner in which it is conducted exclude or affect other strategies of resistance or opposition? Consider the rhetoric of the following extract from Radio Freedom (Addis Abbaba) and reflect on what a white who wishes to persuade other whites to participate in the democratic opposition must do:

> The first and most important things to do at this time is to organise all combatants and militants into underground cells of the ANC. These cells must consist of a very few persons

[27] Interview with Oliver Tambo by Steven Freedman, ibid., p. 33.

who know one another very well. These cells must then organise ways of obtaining weapons of war.

We have to realise also that these weapons that are in our country today are meant to commit massacres against our nation. They are there to murder our people. The privileged white community is armed to the teeth. Those weapons also are meant to mow down our people. . . . Those weapons in white hands have to be transferred. We have to use all means available to get them.

In this regard, we call on our compatriots who are working as domestic servants to take a leading role. They know where their employers keep their weapons and they are the ones who can devise plans of transferring the ownership of the weapons. . . . These weapons must be removed from the hands of these trigger-happy murderers. . . .

It is high time now that we put paid to the notion that our struggle will remain confined to the black areas. We who have started confronting the enemy in all directions must make plans of extending our activities into the white areas. The regime's police and soldiers who have been massacring our people in millions over these years still return to their homes and spend comfortable nights in the warmth of their beds.[28]

One can place this kind of rhetoric within the context of a rapidly polarizing situation and dismiss the extravagance of the language as a consequence of brutalizing experiences by those on the receiving end of the state's repressive measures. But it would be shortsighted to underestimate the extent to which Radio Freedom and *Sechaba* (ANC journal) are being used by the state as counterpropaganda instruments for white consumption. As I said earlier, the fact that 85 percent of the whites agreed that there had to be negotiation with blacks but 83 percent said not with the ANC must be seen in this context. At the same time, it is clear that without ANC participation no negotiations can succeed.

---

[28] Winrich Kuhne, "Black Politics in South Africa and the Outlook for Meaningful Negotiations," *Stiftung Wissenschaft und Politik*, conference report SWP-k2524, p. 19.

Quite apart from moral considerations concerning the armed struggle, or even the question of its legitimacy, its effectiveness in opposing the state should not be put beyond debate. This point was stressed, in particular by André Du Toit at the recent Dakar talks.

> The State is relying on the gun, but the power of the gun is limited in what it can achieve. You cannot get children to go to school or get people to pay their rent or choose local governments at the point of a gun.
>
> What then must we make of this paradox? I submit that when we begin to think about strategies of political opposition and resistance, we should not look to a coercive showdown with the State. We should not take on the State where it is strongest. We should rather take on the state where it is weakest, and that is on the political front. That means, I believe, that we have to rethink the whole relation of internal and external opposition, and extra-parliamentary and parliamentary politics.[29]

Sanctions. The imposition of sanctions as a strategy to achieve political objectives is a highly involved and complex issue that has enjoyed considerable attention from scholars with a wide range of interests. The one thing that strikes one when reading their works on the subject, whether they are of radical or moderate persuasion, is the qualified caution with which they preface their predictions and generalizations on sanctions. This is in sharp contrast to the confident statements of those who argued for and against sanctions as a means of resolving or ending the conflict in South Africa. More hot air and nonsense have been spoken on sanctions than make sense. It is as ridiculous to claim that sanctions will not have an impact as it is to claim that they will certainly be successful in achieving the proclaimed objectives. However, people's attitudes on sanctions against the South African regime have been used to judge them on their "commitment to

[29] André Du Toit, "Beginning the Debate," *Die Suid-Afrikaan*, September 1987, p. 20.

the struggle" or their "opposition to apartheid." The simplistic argument is that if you're for sanctions, you're against apartheid and if you're against sanctions, you're for apartheid. If the issue of sanctions is not to continue to be a divisive factor in opposition or to continue to obscure more relevant problems, then at least the debate must be kept open to the extent that questioning accepted strategies in one movement or organization is not immediately a cause for excommunication from the general "struggle."

It is important to distinguish sanctions from disinvestment and divestment. The word "sanctions" refers to governmental action of a punitive kind directed at a target state with the purpose of realizing specific objectives, such as a regime change or destabilization. "Disinvestment" refers to the sale of foreign companies' assets to local interests. "Divestment" refers to the selling of stocks and shares in companies that trade with a target state. The imposition of sanctions is primarily a political action; disinvestment and divestment, an economic one. What is more, sanctions are imposed by *another* state against a target state; it is an external factor that presumably has to affect an internal situation. Different states can impose different sanctions on different aspects of the internal situation. The consequences of such sanctions may be direct or indirect, positive or negative, long term or short term. Furthermore, sanctions can have both economic and political consequences, and evidence is fairly conclusive that economic effects do not necessarily have the desired political effects.[30]

Two general observations concerning the South African economic and political situation should caution one on being too optimistic about the inevitable success of sanctions. The economy has a viable industrial base, some 60 percent of its export earnings are from low-volume, high-value, difficult-to-sanction items, such as strategic minerals. Accordingly, the economy has a capacity to generate a significant percentage of its annual capital needs internally.

[30] A summary of literature on sanctions is contained in "Background Briefing No. 38," South African Institute for International Affairs, 1987.

The political dynamics of the South African state and the way in which power and privilege are structured make for a well-insulated power elite. The Afrikaner group in particular is by far the best insulated with 40 percent employed in the state and its supporting structures. Therefore the paradox of sanctions will be (at least in the short to medium term) that certain blacks and English businesses (especially those that rely heavily on exports) will be hurt more than the power elite itself.[31]

The present British ambassador to South Africa was intimately involved with the British involvement in Rhodesia's transformation to Zimbabwe and made a first-hand analysis of the impact of his government's sanctions on that country.

> The purpose of sanctions was conceived initially as being either preventative or remedial. Their main effect, however, has invariably been punitive. There are international circumstances in which it may become necessary to take some punitive action, falling short of the use of force, either to weaken the regime to which sanctions are applied, or, by penalizing it for one undesirable action, to try to deter it from further action of that kind. . . . To abandon altogether the idea of recourse to sanctions in response to acts of aggression or other flagrant violations of international law or human rights, would be to reduce the choice of response to one between military action and acquiescence — an unattractive choice at best of times, and particularly so in the nuclear age. In cases where "real" sanctions are applied, provided (a) they affect a significant proportion of the target country's external trade (or external finance); and (b) there is sufficient international support, they can impose some penalty on the target country. They may have some deterrent effect, though they are not likely to do so if the regime believes its survival in any event to be at stake. Once applied they may, if sufficiently effective, weaken the target regime, but they will not necessarily change its behaviour.[32]

31 Ibid., p. 4.

32 Robin Renwick, *Economic Sanctions*, Harvard Studies in International Affairs, no. 45 (Cambridge, Mass.: Harvard University Press, 1981), p. 92.

To reduce such complex arguments to the empty tautology that if the outside world were to impose mandatory sanctions, this would bring those in control of the South African state either to their senses, or to their knees, is ridiculous. But to insist further that such a view be uncritically supported as a precondition to be part of the "democratic struggle" is simply counterproductive.

Participation versus Nonparticipation. This issue as a matter of strategy has been dealt with by implication in the discussion on opposition movements and groups. Suffice to say here that, to the extent that nonparticipation as a strategy becomes an end in itself, rather than a means to an end, it will be a divisive issue in the opposition to the state's policies. It has been shown that participation in some spheres is more effective than in others and that these circumstances can change. Rather than adopt an inflexible approach to participating on structures sanctioned by the state, each such opportunity should be evaluated as a basis for organizing resistance and working for a democratic alternative. At present it is more effective to do so in the areas of labor and education than in politics, but this too can change, as the state is forced to make concessions or relax its co-optive demands.

CONCLUSION

The three lectures have attempted to come to grips with the current dynamics of reform and revolt in South Africa. We started off by tracing the ideological shift from apartheid to separate development to the total onslaught. Each shift was necessitated to adjust and legitimize white minority domination, which remains the central issue of domestic and international conflict in South Africa. It was also shown how the shift to the total-onslaught ideology coincided with and facilitated the South African state's reform policy.

In the second lecture, I tried to trace the organizational background and changes for reform. The point was made that it was difficult to understand the problems relating to the state's reform policy without placing it within the overall context of the South African state's redefinition of its security interests. This is reflected in the deployment of a National Security Management System. This security system pervades the state bureaucracy and directly affects the nature of the reform process on the different constitutional, social, and economic levels. The distinctive feature of the state's constitutional reform is one of co-optive inclusion of the different racial groups without sacrificing white control. Just as revolt against apartheid and separate development was revolt against the minority domination, so the revolt against the South African state's reform policy as part of the total strategy to meet the total onslaught continues to be a revolt against white minority domination.

Thus reform and revolt are intimately linked to one another. The objective of reform is to establish a multiracial autocratic government. The broad objective of those caught up in revolt is to establish a nonracial democratic government. However, there is a fundamental disparity in access and control of resources between those who reform and those who revolt. Although the state is low on legitimacy, it is extremely powerful and, security-wise, well organized. Those in revolt enjoy high legitimacy, but because of repression and other circumstances are not as cohesive and well organized. One of the circumstances responsible for this is deep division on matters of strategy. Greater flexibility is needed to overcome this problem and to consolidate democratic opposition to the state on a broad front.

The struggle is essentially political. Just as the myths of apartheid and separate development had to be exposed as an ideological justification for white domination, so the total onslaught will have to be exposed as well. Until a strategically significant number of whites, and particularly Afrikaners, accept that their future can be ensured not by continued minority domination but by identifying with a genuine democratic alternative, the pattern of reform, revolt, and repression is likely to continue for quite a while. This still remains the enduring challenge of those who would wish to rid South Africa of racism and exploitation and who work for a nonracial and democratic alternative.

A Place as Good as Any

JOSEPH BRODSKY

THE TANNER LECTURES ON HUMAN VALUES

Delivered at
The University of Utah

November 16, 1987

JOSEPH BRODSKY, winner of the 1987 Nobel Prize for Literature, was born in 1940, in Leningrad, and began writing poetry at the age of eighteen. In March 1964 Mr. Brodsky was sentenced to five years in exile in the Arkhangelsk region of northern Russia, but his sentence was commuted two years later because of internal and international protests. On June 4, 1972, Joseph Brodsky became an involuntary exile from his native country. After brief stays in Vienna and London, he came to the United States.

Mr. Brodsky is currently Andrew Mellon Professor of Literature at Mount Holyoke. In 1978, he was awarded an honorary degree of Doctor of Letters at Yale University, and in the following year he was inducted as a member of the American Academy and Institute of Arts and Letters, a position from which he subsequently resigned. In 1981, Brodsky was a recipient of the John D. and Catherine T. MacArthur Foundation's award.

Joseph Brodsky is the author of *Selected Poems*, translated by George L. Kline and with a foreword by W. H. Auden. His equally acclaimed collection *A Part of Speech* was published in 1980, and *Less Than One*, a compilation of Mr. Brodsky's essays, won the National Book Critics Circle Award for Criticism in 1986.

In the spring of 1988, Farrar, Straus and Giroux will publish a new volume of poems, *To Urania*, as well as a collection of the work of nineteenth-century Russian poets, *An Age Ago*, selected and with a foreword by Joseph Brodsky. His play *Marbles* is slated for publication in 1989.

As anyone knows who has been reading the papers lately, Joseph Brodsky was born in Leningrad in 1940. In 1964 he was convicted by the Soviet authorities of "social parasitism" and sentenced to five years' hard labor in northern Russia, a place pleasantly called Archangel. He was released after twenty months. Then, in 1972, he was deported from the Soviet Union and came to the United States, where he has made his home ever since. He has taught at the University of Michigan, Columbia University, and Mount Holyoke College, where he still teaches. Two collections of his poems have appeared in English: Selected Poems *in 1973 and* A Part of Speech *in 1980. In 1986 a selection of essays,* Less Than One, *appeared and won the National Book Critics Circle award that year for nonfiction. In 1981 Joseph Brodsky won a MacArthur Award, and just last month won the 1987 Nobel Prize in literature. All this is by way of formal introduction.*

Let me say, however, one more thing about Joseph Brodsky that should have special significance for this audience. And that is, his formal education ended with the eighth grade. Those of you who are thinking of leaving school, take heart; it may not be too late to cultivate an independence of spirit that will, with your unappreciated genius, culminate in being awarded the Nobel Prize. But so far as I know, Joseph Brodsky's genius was never unappreciated by those who could read. Even before he came to this country, most of us had heard of him. Some of his poems had been translated and published in anthologies. I actually sent him a New Year's card a few years before he landed on our shores, without ever expecting to meet him. But that was a long time ago and not exactly central to his being here in Utah to participate in the Tanner Lectures.

That a poet should be asked to give a lecture that has to do with human values seems only appropriate, because at the heart

*of any poet's enterprise is the assertion of human values. The
better the poet, the more memorable the assertion, and the more
memorable the assertion, the more enduring the values. History
has made it clear that institutions like governments, churches,
schools, cannot be entrusted with the preservation of such values,
precisely because these institutions have not been nearly fastidious
enough about language. After all, a language that attempts to
reach as many people as possible is necessarily going to be very
general; and as a result it will lack both subtlety and accuracy
and will not be useful in the truthful description of anything.
Poets, on the other hand, are not in the habit of speaking to a
million people at once, so they can be as particular as they wish.
They do not speak through language, they speak language. It is
what they have to say. They do not wish to be right as, say,
moralists do; they wish rather that the language be right. They
know — as perhaps moralists do not — that the slovenly, in-
accurate use of language makes it easier for us to have foolish
thoughts. It is this concern for language that gives poets — in the
long run — greater authority than moralists and, I might add,
even institutions. It certainly accounts for Joseph Brodsky's
authority.*

*It is not this having been exiled from the Soviet Union that
has made him so compelling a figure but his decision to keep
writing despite all else. After all, exile was a decision made for
him, and one for which he cannot be held accountable. His writing, however, is that for which he will always be held accountable.
Brodsky is important because his poetry is important.*

*Now this brings me to the title of tonight's lecture, "A Place
as Good as Any." It is, as you might surmise, about travel. More
precisely, it is a vision of travel; a vision of our elsewheres and
what we have done to them by our inability to experience them as
anything but a composite. With the aid of the camera and the
credit card we have reduced the world to snapshots and souvenirs;
so our travel amounts to little more than show and tell — with*

*the emphasis on the show. And the only values in question tend
to be the sort that have the greatest impact on one's American
Express card. We're off on the wrong track, and Joseph Brodsky's
lecture tonight is a warning. If the cities we travel to are empty,
it is because our capacity for invention is limited—and the limited
cities we encounter are only the first stage of our journey into
nowhere. None of this diminishes, however, the pleasure I have
in introducing to you one of the greatest poets of the twentieth
century, Joseph Brodsky.*

Mark Strand

I

The more one travels, the more complex one's sense of nostalgia becomes. In a dream, depending on one's mania or supper or both, one is either pursued or pursues somebody through a crumpled maze of streets, lanes, and alleyways belonging to several places at once; one is in a city that does not exist on the map. A panicky flight originating as a rule in one's hometown is likely to land one helpless under the poorly lit archway in the town of one's last year's, or the year's before, sojourn. It is so much so that eventually your traveller finds himself unwittingly sizing up every locale he encounters for its potential value as a backdrop for his nightmare.

The best way to keep your subconscious from getting overburdened is to take pictures: your camera is, as it were, your lightning rod. Developed and printed, unfamiliar facades and perspectives lose their potent three-dimensionality and their air of an alternative to your life. Yet one can't click nonstop, one can't constantly put things in focus — what with clutching the luggage, the shopping bags, the spouse's elbow. And with particular vengeance the unfamiliar three-dimensional invades the senses of unsuspecting innocents at railroad stations, airports, bus stations, in a taxi, on a leisurely evening stroll to or from a restaurant.

Of these, railroad stations are the most insidious. Edifices of arrival for you and those of departure for the locals, they insinuate travellers, tense with excitement and apprehension, straight into the thick of things, into the heart of an alien existence, pretending to be precisely the opposite by flashing their gigantic CINZANO, MARTINI, COCA-COLA — the fiery writing that evokes familiar walls. Ah, those squares before railroad stations! With their fountains and statues of The Leader, with their feverish bustle of traffic and cinema billboards, with their whores, hypodermic youths, beggars, winos, migrant workers; with taxicabs and stocky cab drivers soliciting in loud snatches of unfathomable tongues! The deep-seated anxiety of every traveller makes him register the location of the taxi stand in this square with greater precision than the order of appearance of the great master's works in the local museum — because the latter won't constitute a way of retreat.

The more one travels, the richer one's memory gets with exact locations of taxi stands, ticket offices, shortcuts to platforms, phone booths, and urinals. If not often revisited, these stations and their immediate vicinities merge and superimpose on each other in one's mind, like everything that's stored for too long, resulting in a gigantic brick-cum-cast-iron, chlorine-smelling octopal ogre, submerged in one's memory, to which every new destination adds a tentacle.

There are apparent exceptions: the great mother, Victoria Station in London; Pier Luigi Nervi's masterpiece in Rome or the garish monumental monstrosity in Milan; Amsterdam's Central with one of its fronton dials showing the direction and speed of the wind; Paris's Gare du Nord or Gare de Lyon with the latter's mind-boggling restaurant room, where, consuming superb canard under frescoes à la Denis, you watch through the huge glass wall trains departing down below with a faint sense of metabolic connection; Frankfurt's Hauptbanhof thrust right in the heart of the red-light district; Moscow's Three-Railroad-Stations Square — the ideal place to ladle despair and indirection even for those whose native alphabet is Cyrillic. These exceptions, however, do not so much confirm the rule as form the core or kernel for subsequent accretions. Their Piranesean vaults and staircases echo, perhaps even enlarge, the seat of the subconscious; at any rate, they remain there — in the brain — for good, waiting for addition.

II

And the more legendary your destination, the more readily this gigantic octopus comes to the surface, feeding equally well on airports, bus terminals, harbors. Its real dainty, though, is the place itself. What constitutes the legend — artifice or edifice, a tower or a cathedral, a breathtaking ancient ruin or a unique library — goes first. Our monster salivates over these nuggets, and so do travel agencies' posters, jumbling Westminster Abbey, the Eiffel Tower, Saint Basil's, the Taj Mahal, the Acropolis, and some pagodas in an eye-catching, mind-skipping collage. We know these vertical things before we've seen them. What's more, after having seen them, we retain not their three-dimensional image but their printed version.

Strictly speaking, we remember not a place but our postcard of it. Say "London," and your mind most likely will flash the view of the National Gallery or the Tower Bridge with the Union Jack logo discreetly printed somehow in a corner or on the opposite side. Say "Paris" and ——. There is perhaps nothing wrong with this sort of reduction or swapping, for had a human mind indeed been able to cohere and retain the reality of this world, the life of its owner would become a nonstop nightmare of logic and justice. At least its laws imply as much. Unable or unwilling to be held accountable, man decides to move first and loses either count or track of what he experiences, especially for the umpteenth time. The result is not so much a hodge-podge or a jumble as a composite vision: of a green tree if you are a painter, of a mistress if you are a Don Giovanni, of a victim if you are a tyrant, of a city if you are a traveller.

Whatever one travels for — to modify one's territorial imperative, to get an eyeful of creation, to escape reality (awful tautology though this is), the net result, of course, is feeding that octopus constantly hungry for new details for its nightly show. The composite city of your subconscious sojourn — nay! return — will therefore permanently sport a golden cupola; several bell towers; an opera house à la La Fenice in Venice; a park with gloom-laden chestnuts and poplars, incomprehensible in their postromantic swaying grandeur, as in Graz; a wide, melancholy river spanned by a minimum of six well-wrought bridges; a skyscraper or two. After all, a city as such has only so many options. And, as though semiconscious of that, your memory will throw in a granite embankment with its vast colonnaides from Russia's former capital; Parisian pearl-gray facades with the black lace of their balconies' grillwork; a few boulevards petering out into the lilac sunset of one's adolescence; a gothic needle or that of an obelisk shooting its heroin into a cloudy muscle; and, in winter, a well-tanned Roman terracotta; a marble fountain; poorly lit, cavelike café life at street corners.

Your memory will accord this place with a history whose particulars you probably won't recall but whose main fruit will most likely be a democracy. The same source will endow it with a temperate climate adhering to the four-seasons principle and segregating palm trees to railroad stations' grillrooms. It will also give your city Reykjavik-on-Sunday-type traffic; people will be few if any; beggars and children, however, will speak the foreign tongue fluently. The currency will carry images of Renaissance scholiasts; the coins, feminine profiles of the republic; but the numbers will still be recognizable, and your main problem — not of paying, but of tipping — can, in the end, be solved. In other words, regardless of what it says on your ticket, of whether you'll be staying in the Savoy or the Danieli, the moment you open your shutters, you'll see at once Notre Dame, Saint James, San Giorgio, and Hagia Sophia.

For the aforesaid submerged monster digests legends as eagerly as reality. Add to that the latter's aspiration for the glory of the former (or the former's claim to enjoying, at least once upon a time, the status of the latter). Small wonder, then, that your city should, as though it's been painted by Claude or Corot, have some water: a harbor, a lake, a lagoon. Smaller wonder still that the medieval ramparts or molars of its Roman wall should look like an intended background for some steel-cum-glass-cum-concrete structures: a university, say, or more likely an insurance company headquarters. These are usually erected on the site of some monastery or ghetto bombed out of existence in the course of the last war. Small wonder, too, that a traveller reveres ancient ruins many times over the modern ones left in the center of your city by its fathers for didactic purposes: a traveller, by definition, is a product of hierarchic thinking.

In the final analysis, however, there is no hierarchy between the legendary and the real, in the context of your city at least, since the present engenders the past far more energetically than the other way around. Every car passing through an intersection makes its equestrian monument more obsolete, more ancient, telescoping its great local eighteenth-century military or civic genius into some skin-clad William Tell or other. With all four hooves firmly on the plinth (which, in the parlance of sculpture, means that the rider has died not on the battlefield, but in his own presumably four-poster bed), this monument's horse would stand in your city more as an homage to an extinct means of transportation than to anyone's particular valor. The birds' kaka on the bronze tricorn is all the more deserved, for history long since exited your city, yielding the stage to the more elementary forces of geography and commerce. Therefore, your city will have not only a cross between a bazaar in Istanbul and a Macy's; no, a traveller in this city, should he turn right, is bound to hit the silks, furs, and leather of via Condotti and, if he turns left, to find himself buying either fresh or canned pheasant at Fauchon (and the canned one is preferable).

For buy you must. As the philosopher would have put it, I purchase therefore I am. And who knows that better than a man in passage? In fact, every well-mapped trip is in the end a shopping expedition: indeed, one's whole passage through the world is. In fact, next to taking pictures, shopping comes in second at sparing one's subconscious an alien reality. In fact, that's what we call a bargain, and with a credit card you can go on infinitely. In fact, why don't you call your whole city — it surely ought to have a name — simply American Express? This will make it as legal as being included in the atlas: no one will dare to challenge your description. On the contrary, many would claim they've been there, too, a year or so ago. To prove this, they'll produce a bunch of snapshots or, if you are staying for a meal, even a slide show. Some of them have known Karl Malden, that city's dapper old mayor, personally for years and years.

III

It is an early evening in the town of your memory; you are sitting in a sidewalk café under drooping chestnuts. A streetlight idly flashes its red-yellow-green eye above the empty intersection; higher up, swallows crisscross a platinum, cloudless sky. The way your coffee or your white wine tastes tells you that you are neither in Italy nor in Germany; the bill tells you that you are not in Switzerland, either. All the same, you are in Common Market territory.

On the left, there is the Concert Hall, and on the right there is the Parliament. Or it is the other way around: with architecture like this, it's hard to tell the difference. Chopin was through this town, so was Liszt, and so was Paganini. As for Wagner, the book says he went through this place three times. So did, it seems, the Pied Piper. Or maybe it's just Sunday, vacation time, midsummer. "In summer," the poet said, "capitals grow empty." An ideal season for a coup d'etat, then, for introducing tanks into these narrow cobblestone streets — almost no traffic whatsoever. Of course, if this place is indeed a capital . . .

You have a couple of phone numbers here, but you've tried them already twice. As for the goal of your pilgrimage, the National Museum, justly famous for its Italian Masters, you went there straight from the train, and it closes at five. And anyhow, what's wrong with great art — with Italian Masters in particular — is that it makes you resent reality. If, of course, this is a reality. . . .

So you open the local Time-Out and consider theater. It's Ibsen and Chekhov all over the place, the usual continental fare. Luckily, you don't know the language. The National Ballet appears to be touring Japan, and you won't sit through *Madama Butterfly* for the sixth time even if the set was designed by Hockney. That leaves movies and pop groups, yet the small print of these pages, not to mention the bands' names, makes you briefly nauseous. On the horizon looms further expansion of your waistline in some Lutece or Golden Horseshoe. It is actually your widening diameter that narrows your options.

The more one travels, though, the better one knows that curling up with Flaubert in the hotel room won't do either. The sounder solution is a stroll in an amusement park, a half an hour in a shooting gallery, or a video game — something that boosts the ego and doesn't require knowledge of the local tongue. Or else take a taxi to the top of the hill that dominates the view and offers a terrific panorama of your composite city and its environs: the Taj Mahal, the Eiffel Tower, Westminster Abbey, Saint Basil's — the whole thing. This is yet another nonverbal experience; a "wow" will suffice. Of course, if there is a hill, or if there is a taxi . . .

Return to your hotel on foot: it's downhill all the way. Admire shrubs and hedges shielding the stylish mansions; admire the rustling acacias and somber monoliths of the business center. Linger by well-lit shop windows, especially those selling watches. Such a variety, almost like in Switzerland! It's not that you need a new watch; it's just a nice idea of killing time — looking at the watches. Admire toys and admire lingerie: these appeal to the family man in you. Admire the clean-swept pavement and perfect infinity of avenues: you always had a soft spot for geometry, which, as you know, means "no people."

So if you find somebody in the hotel bar, it's most likely a man like yourself, a fellow traveller. "Hey," he'll say, turning his face toward you. "Why is this place so empty? Neutron bomb or something?" "Sunday," you'll reply. "It's just Sunday, midsummer, vacation time. Everyone gone to the beaches." Yet you know you'll be lying. Because it is neither Sunday nor the Pied Piper nor a neutron bomb nor beaches that makes your composite city empty. It is empty because for an imagination it is easier to conjure architecture than human beings.

The Penalty of Imprisonment

LOUIS BLOM-COOPER

THE TANNER LECTURES ON HUMAN VALUES

Delivered at
Clare Hall, Cambridge University

November 30 and December 1 and 2, 1987

Louis Blom-Cooper QC is one of England's foremost constitutional lawyers and one of the most active proponents of penal reform.

Educated at King's College, London, and at the Universities of British Columbia, Amsterdam, and Cambridge, Blom-Cooper was called to the Bar in 1952 and was appointed a QC in 1970. From 1967 to 1982 he was Joint Director of the Legal Research Unit at Bedford College, London, and he has been a Visiting Fellow at Queen Mary College, London, since 1983.

Between 1966 and 1979 he served as a magistrate in London and was also a member of the Board of Visitors at Wandsworth Prison. During this time he was a prominent member of the Home Secretary's Advisory Council on Penal Reform, serving *inter alia* on the Wootton Committee (which resulted in the introduction of Community Service as a disciplined sentence for offenders as an alternative to imprisonment). For ten years, between 1973 and 1983, Blom-Cooper was Chairman of the Howard League for Penal Reform.

In addition to numerous articles, Blom-Cooper has published seven books, including *Law and Morality* (1976), *Progress in Penal Reform* (1975), and *The A6 Murder* 1963). He has made a study of the language used by lawyers and published *The Law as Literature* in 1962 and *Language and the Law* in 1965.

I. GAOLS AND GOALS: SETTING THE TRAP

Of such Ceremonies as be used in the Church, and have had their beginning by the institution of man, some at the first were of godly intent and purpose devised, and yet at length turned to vanity and superstition: some entered into the Church by undiscreet devotion, and such a zeal as was without knowledge; and for because they were winked at in the beginning, they grew daily to more and more abuses, which not only for their unprofitableness, but also because they have much blinded the people, and obscured the glory of God, are worthy to be cut away, and clean rejected.

> "Of Ceremonies, Why Some May Be Abolished,
> And Some Retained,"
> from the Preface to the Book of Common Prayer

INTRODUCTION

Imprisonment as an instrument of man's control over his fellow creatures has existed from time immemorial; but as the state's prime weapon of penal sanction for serious crime, it is of comparative modernity. Throughout the ages the uses and abuses of imprisonment have increasingly obscured the purposes of social control, to the point where prison as the core of the penal system in a democratic society is highly questionable. Penological thinking is full of confusion. The question, given extra urgency by the chronic overcrowding of our prisons, is whether imprisonment should be "cut away, and clean rejected."

Overcrowding is perhaps the most obvious prison problem, although others, such as the denial of human rights and dignity, are of more fundamental significance. The fact that it is the former that immediately attracts attention only goes to show how the English give priority to pragmatism over principle. Overcrowding, moreover, is not just a matter of numbers, although a daily average prison population of over 50,000, well in excess of the certified normal accommodation, tells its own tale. Overcrowding contributes to the problems of control and security. It presents the prison administration with practical problems which no amount of ingenuity will turn away. Victorian prison cells, which were designed for both sleeping and work, are ample for single sleeping accommodation, but shared by three for more than sixteen hours a day (sometimes twenty-three) they are not merely inhumane but squalid. The presence of three chamber pots makes the situation socially and hygienically indefensible. The provision of water closets in prisons is not ungenerous; the problem is allowing access to them for prisoners who are locked up. In new buildings there is an answer to this problem, as can be seen in prisons like Albany (with its system of electronic unlocking) and the new Holloway prison (where toilets are provided in every cell), but in older establishments a solution is barely in sight, mainly because of the prohibitive cost and the shortage of space for the prisoners during installation.

Overcrowding is also not just a problem of accommodation. It infects all the prison services — water supply, drainage, cooking facilities, workshop space, educational and recreational areas; in consequence both time and space for those necessary activities have become grossly inadequate. But "high cost squalor" (as one prison governor recently described it) is not the only dehumanizing and defeating aspect of imprisonment.

Human beings in prison face a loss of identity, the more so in the press of population. It is most marked among those who have to stay inside for long periods of time.

> Each day is like a year
> A year whose days are long

So wrote Oscar Wilde in *The Ballad of Reading Gaol*. To survive psychologically intact, long-term prisoners, above all, need to be relieved of the intolerable burdens of limited amenities and petty restrictions. The prospect of achieving this goal would be improved by lessening the time spent inside by minor and less serious offenders. Twenty-five years ago the number of life-sentence prisoners was only two hundred. Today there are more than two thousand. The painful process of adjustment to indeterminate sentences presents a constant threat to staff-inmate relationship; it is no accident that the most serious unrest has not been in the overcrowded local prisons but in the long-term establishments, where, despite better physical conditions, the psychological pressures are more intense.

The whole prison scene is bleak. Many prisoners actually prefer the shared cell; for those who lack inner resources, the companionship of others is to be preferred to the solitariness of the single cell. But for most, the enforced close and intimate relationship is barely a mitigation of the hardships endemic in prison. The real pains of imprisonment are, of course, the boredom of everyday prison life, only partially relieved in the most favorable conditions, and the absence of choice, of freedom to seek privacy or companionship. The Victorian prisons, with their lofty halls, with cells opening onto lines of galleries narrowing in distant perspective, succeeded admirably in their unconscious purpose of reducing their occupants to insignificance. While modern prison building attempts to counter all this, it cannot remove the inevitable effects of imprisonment in diminishing the self-esteem (if they retain any) of those who are admitted.

The monotony in the small-scale pattern of existence and the lack of opportunities for acceptable expressions of tenderness in a rough masculine society are damaging, once the initial effect of such a jolt to ordinary habits of living has passed. Separation from partner and children disrupts family relationships and makes resettlement on discharge difficult. The serious disadvantage is that to live in any community is to be affected by its standards and attitudes, and identification with a criminal community means a rejection of those of normal society. For the recidivist prisoner the continuing round of conviction, imprisonment, release, and reconviction, like a revolving door, is a process both familiar and perhaps inevitable. For society the essential task is to limit prison's defeating consequences, both in the prison setting and on release, but that is a task which prison staff find daunting, dispiriting, and indeed impossible unless the numbers in prison are severely cut and the support after release considerably improved. Any moral satisfaction society may feel in imprisoning the offender has to be set against its true cost in suffering to the offender and to his family and the not inconsiderable cost in maintaining him, estimated to be about £13,000 a year. It is not a question of whether the offender "deserved" the punishment but of its counterproductive consequences. These factors present the very strongest incentive to any society to limit, and as nearly as possible to abandon, the use of imprisonment. In a state of overcrowding the incentive should be overwhelming. How is it then that as a society we have become so ineluctably wedded to an institution that is so palpably ineffective and inhumane?

The history of social control is the history of the struggle to reduce the use of violence, both between individuals and inflicted by the ruler or the state upon citizens. From the blood feuds of the house of Agamemnon to the duels of relatively recent times, it has been recognized that private vengeance undermines society and wastes lives. William the Conqueror abolished the death penalty, and through the centuries mutilation, branding, ducking stools, and other punishments ranging from the barbarous to the degrading have been abandoned. Although capital punishment meanwhile was reintroduced, its deterrent effect was far from certain. Then, as now, the most professional offenders had a realistic assessment of their chances of not being caught at all; then, as now, the more severe the punishment, the more ruthless people were in trying to avoid it. Many juries and even law enforcers recoiled from applying it. Daniel Defoe, who had been imprisoned and pilloried (literally) in 1702–1703 by the Tory government for his satirical pamphleteering, captured the way in which punishment makes the malefactor think not of his (or her) victims but of himself: in *Moll Flanders* (1722) the heroine, in Newgate awaiting trial, says: "I seem'd not to Mourn that I had committed such Crimes, and for the Fact, as it was an Offence against God and my Neighbour; but I mourn'd that I was to be punish'd for it." The death penalty was progressively abolished, first for larceny from the person in 1808, and then for the other two hundred offenses for which it was then permissible, except murder, treason, piracy, and arson in Her Majesty's dockyards; these were the only capital crimes remaining in 1861. Several civilized countries abolished it in the nineteenth century, but it took until 1965 for the United Kingdom to rid itself of the death penalty for murder.

But (to revert to the eighteenth and early nineteenth centuries) a replacement for the death penalty had to be found. At first the solution was transportation — to the American colonies until the War of Independence; then, until 1867, to Australia. Until this period gaols were used primarily as a staging post — for prisoners held awaiting trial, execution at Tyburn, or transportation to the colonies. There were a few houses of correction and bridewells, mainly for vagrants and the unemployed rather than for felons; they were intended to aid the poor and destitute as well as to correct the idle and dissolute, which shows that the tradition of trying to do two incompatible things at once in custodial institutions has a long history. It was not until the Australian colonies began to refuse entry to any more convicts that once again a replacement had to be found. This time the solution was internal banishment: lacking a Siberia, the Victorians adapted their prisons to a new purpose. Thus imprisonment as the ultimate penal sanction became an accretion to the law enforcement system and not just a method of temporary containment pending death or transportation.

Often, indeed, criminal process and punishment were not even used, but held in reserve. In medieval times, when prosecution was in the hands of the victims, they often preferred to bring a civil action to obtain compensation, because if a felon was prosecuted and convicted his property was forfeited to the Crown. Similarly, in the eighteenth century, people of substance relied mainly on the *threat* of prosecution, which would be withdrawn in return for confession, restitution, and apology. Not infrequently, the victim was the master and the offender his servant, and the latter's dependency was reinforced by this apparent clemency. But as the prosecution was taken over by governmental authority (in practice the police), the victim was left with no part to play except reporting the offense and possibly giving evidence. In essence it was a bargain, whereby the state accepted responsibility for dealing with offenders in return for the victim forgoing any claim to self-help.

Already reformers and others had turned their attention to gaols. George Fox, a Quaker imprisoned for his religious beliefs, saw at first hand in the mid-seventeenth century that prisons were universities of crime. Toward the end of the eighteenth, John Howard (1792) found the same but concluded that the cure for communal squalor was the single cell. He recognized, however, that prisoners should be able to see the rules under which they were kept and that there is "a way of managing some of the most desperate, with ease to yourself, and advantage to them," a truth which has been glimpsed at intervals ever since. The system must be based on the values it upholds. The philosopher Jeremy Bentham, taking a wider sweep, recognized that all punishment is evil; unfortunately he thought that it was justifiable, and possible, to use the evil to induce people to be good. His ideas were enshrined in the Millbank Penitentiary; but they didn't work. Under the Rev. Daniel Nihil, as governor, "the most successful simulator of holiness became the most favoured prisoner, [so that] sanctified looks were . . . the order of the day, and the most desperate convicts in the prison found it advantageous to complete their criminal character by the addition of hypocrisy" (Mayhew and Binney 1862). Many of those who could not adapt to the rigid and artificial regime went mad; for this and other reasons Millbank became one of the few major prisons ever to be demolished. (The Tate Gallery, built with sugar slave money, now stands on the site.)

In 1817 the Quaker Elizabeth Fry began her work of educating women prisoners. For those destined to be executed, this provided only a more humane way of passing their last days; but for those who would return to society, there was conflict between her goal and methods and those of the courts. Sentences were intended to punish and coerce; Mrs. Fry had no power to punish, and she kept discipline by persuading the prisoners to agree to rules and by rewards. She was not able, in the prevailing climate of opinion, to make the consequential point that if what the offenders needed to persuade and enable them to live law-abidingly was education, prison was not the most suitable place to provide it. Alexander Maconochie was to encounter a similar conflict of aims; as governor of the remote penal colony of Norfolk Island in the 1840s, he devised a system of marks, by which prisoners could earn early release by good behavior, and he promoted patriotism by giving them a good dinner on the queen's birthday. The reconviction rate went down; but his political masters wanted their convicts punished regardless of consequences, and he was recalled. Two years later floggings, and riots, returned to Norfolk Island. Returning to England, he became governor of Birmingham prison and introduced the marks system, but after another clash with his violently punitive deputy governor and the local justices, he was forced to resign.

Rehabilitative efforts were not always so humane. Reformers were trying to come to grips with the fact that prisoners learned criminal ways from each other; the more optimistic even believed that by a regular regimen, removed from the corrupting influences of the real world, offenders could be reformed. In America in the 1820s and 1830s, this led to the Pennsylvania and Auburn penitentiaries. Both involved silence; under the Pennsylvania system isolation was almost total, while at the Auburn prison in New York State, it was modified to the extent of allowing prisoners to work together — but without conversing or even exchanging glances. Discipline was enforced with the whip in Auburn, the iron gag in Pennsylvania, cold showers or the ball and chain elsewhere. Not for them Maconochie's insight that to accustom offenders to yield to external pressures was the opposite of what was required when they returned to face the world. The Quakers who devised these methods had at least paused to ask what was the purpose of the prison; but they left out of account that few people are rehabilitated through silent penitence—except Quakers.

Such were the theories in fashion (and fashion often has more to do with penal policy than reason or experience, let alone humanity) when the end of transportation was in sight and the first of the new wave of Victorian prisons was built, at Pentonville in 1842. Solitary confinement was literally built into the design. Elizabeth Fry's last public protest was against these cells, which even had opaque ground-glass windows — though at first they did have sanitation. But in vain: more than fifty warehouses for the living dead were built by the end of the century. They have become, quite literally, monumental mistakes. A strict centralized regime was introduced in 1878; the Home Office began, as it meant to continue, by removing the independence of the previously outspoken inspectors, and the commissioners withheld reports from publication on the grounds that that would "seriously impair their dignity and prestige and weaken their administration." Although the rigors of the regime had to be moderated because so many prisoners became insane, as late as 1877 the incidence of insanity among prisoners apparently sane on admission was still admitted to be at least three times that in the general population; according to one estimate the proportion in local prisons doubled to 226 per 10,000 in the fifteen years after the introduction of a strict centralized regime in 1878. The suicide rate among prisoners in 1877 was as high as 17.6 per 1,000; the problem was still acute in 1890, with many prisoners leaping from the upper landings, and the authorities at last responded — not by altering the regime but by putting up safety netting.

The Victorians did not believe in idleness. Early in the century prisoners were often gainfully employed; but finding work was difficult for the authorities. Hence the invention of the crank and the treadwheel. The former could be installed in solitary cells; the prisoner was required to turn it several thousand times to obtain each meal. The uselessness of the toil enhanced the punishment. Some cranks lifted sand which was then dropped; others drove a fan above the prison: "grinding the wind." This method of punishment gave rise to an early example of penal policy by misleading metaphor: "grinding rogues straight." The policy assumed, first, that prisoners were in some way morally "warped," rather than responding to the poverty of the nineteenth century; even if that were accepted, grinding as a means of rectifying the problem would be about as much use as grinding a warped gramophone record; that is, it destroys what needs to be preserved: loyalty, respect, self-esteem, the desire to work, even the ability to work. To quote Wilde's *Ballad of Reading Gaol* again:

> Something was dead in each of us,
> And what was dead was Hope.

A more modern metaphor describes the nineteenth-century prison system as a social dustbin or a massive machine for the promotion of misery.

How Long to Languish in Gaol?

A perennial problem with time-based sanctions is determining how long they should last. An act of 1717 which gave statutory force to the practice of transportation fixed the term at seven or fourteen years in all cases, and this practice was followed in successive statutes. The only apparent basis for these terms was that seven is a number symbolizing completion or perfection, particularly in the Bible: there were seven sins in Talmudic law, and the Menorah (the candlestick representing Israel and used in Jewish worship) has seven branches. The Bible also calls for debts to be extinguished after seven years and for people to forgive "unto seventy times seven"; but forgiveness has never been accorded a prominent place in criminal justice.

Terms of transportation were, by piecemeal changes to the law, converted to penal servitude in the mid-nineteenth century, and new penalties were introduced; judges were given more discretion in statutes laying down maxima rather than fixed penalties. But the five acts of 1861, which formed the core of the modern criminal calendar, merely consolidated the confused existing position and did not attempt to grade the punishments in proportion to the seriousness of the crimes. Indeed property offenses tended to carry severer punishment than most offenses of violence. Sentences of penal servitude were almost all for five, seven, ten years, or life, and few, if any, for six, eight, or nine. Further legislation, such as the Security from Violence Act of 1863, passed after the panic reaction to garrotings in London, did not improve matters, and the inevitable inconsistencies between judges led to further confusion.

A further problem was that sentences were widely considered too long. Even the hard-line chairman of the Prison Commission, Sir Edmund du Cane, wrote that "every year, even every month and every week to which a prisoner is sentenced beyond the necessity of the case, entails an unjustifiable addition to the great mass of human sorrow" (ACPS 1978). He argued that it was possible to cut sentence lengths and thus reduce the amount of unnecessary hardship to prisoners and their families without any loss in the efficiency of the law. The home secretary, Sir William Harcourt, urged the lord chancellor in 1884 to convey to the judges the view that "the deterring and reformatory effect of imprison-

ment . . . would be as well and even more effectually accomplished
if the average length of sentences were materially shortened"
(ACPS 1978). One person who rebelled against unnecessary
severity was Charles Hopwood, QC, a Liberal member of Parliament, a barrister, and the recorder of Liverpool. Before his appointment in 1886 the average length of sentence was thirteen
months and six days; by 1892 he had reduced it to two months
and twenty-two days. He gives an example: "A poor woman
pleaded guilty before me, charged with stealing a duck. I looked
at her record. She had already endured, for stealing meat,
12 months'; again, for stealing butter, seven years' penal servitude; again, for stealing meat, seven years'; again, for stealing
meat, seven years'; or 22 years of sentences for stealing a few
shillings' worth of food! My sentence for the duck was one
month, and I regret it now as too much. I have never since seen
her" (ACPS 1978). His leniency did not unleash a crime wave,
although it received a lash of the tongue from the local magis-
tracy. He was able to quote the report of the head constable of
Liverpool to the Watch Committee in 1891, that never since the
first returns of crime were published in Liverpool in 1857 had the
statistics disclosed so small an amount of crime; compared with
the previous year the number of indictable offenses had decreased
by 21 percent, burglaries by 37 percent, and serious crimes of
violence by 42 percent. "Of course," he adds wryly, "I do not
claim the credit of the decrease, though doubtless I should have
had the discredit of the increase, had there been one" (ACPS
1978).

It was beginning to be recognized that imprisonment was not
the only choice. As long ago as 1841 John Augustus had begun
his voluntary work in the Boston Police Court, which developed
into probation. The Police Court Mission began similar work
in England in the last quarter of the century. William Tallack of
the Howard Association, in a pamphlet in 1881, saw its potential
and urged its introduction into the official system; the Probation

of First Offenders Act was passed in 1887 and the more comprehensive Probation of Offenders Act twenty years later. Tallack
was also among those who spoke at various international con-
gresses of the rightness of reparation by the offender to the victim,
but at that time the idea foundered on the problem that most
offenders had no money.

RE-THINK OR DOUBLE-THINK?
THE GLADSTONE COMMITTEE

By the 1890s, then, there was a fair amount of experience for
those willing and able to see it. Locking people away, whether
they are herded together or kept in inhuman isolation, is not very
effective at changing people's behavior on their return to freedom.
Long sentences work no better than short ones, and perhaps worse.
Punishments intended to deter are also not very effective. Even
if they are indeed terrifying, people do not necessarily react as
intended; they often do not think of the punishment until after
they have committed the crime and are then devious in trying to
avoid it. Brutal punishments brutalize (both the punisher and the
punished); people respond to fair treatment — which does not
exclude firmness.

But the central feature that was not appreciated was the conflict among the aims of the law enforcement system. If the main
method of inducing people to obey the law is to threaten grim
punishments, the effect on those individuals who are caught is
often either to destroy them or to make them antipathetic to
society. Probably the majority of hardened criminals is hardened
in prison. Conversely, to treat offenders in the way most likely to
persuade and enable them to be law-abiding will not terrify the
remainder. This problem also determines the day-to-day administration of penal regimes. A policy of harshness encourages those
members of staff who take pleasure in asserting power and inflicting pain; but an administration which aims to be fair and humane
brings out the natural tendency of the majority of staff to treat

those in their charge decently and help them as best they can —
which makes the prison less terrifying.

In the early 1890s the harsh tendency was in the ascendant.
The chairman of the Prison Commission, Sir Edmund du Cane,
was not an inhumane man, but his system embodied a rigid combination of punitive deterrence and efficiency. This policy was
publicly challenged by the chaplain of Wandsworth prison, the
Rev. W. D. Morrison. (The Official Secrets Act, which inhibits
today's prison staff from exposing abuses, was still in the future;
Morrison was, however, dismissed soon afterward for rashly
speaking out in public.) Morrison wrote in *The Nineteenth Century*, the *Fortnightly Review*, and the *Times* and is credited with
a series of articles in the *Daily Chronicle* in January 1894. The
silent and separate system, imposed on prisoners, was described
by Morrison as "torture," especially for less hardened prisoners;
prison inspectors reported to the chairman of the commission, not
to the home secretary; the staff were underpaid, overworked, and
badly selected; there was, he wrote, a "complete and utter break-
down of our local prison system." Yet "the great machine rolls
obscurely on, cumbrous, pitiless, obsolete, unchanged." The articles, and the paper's leader column, called for a Royal Commission; the following year H. H. Asquith, as home secretary in the
Liberal administration, appointed a departmental committee with
his under-secretary, Herbert Gladstone, as chairman.

The evidence presented to the Gladstone Committee, and its
report, reflected a widespread revulsion against the inhumanity
of the philosophy of deterrence, aggravated by the centralized control instituted by the Prison Act of 1877. It drew from the head
of the Home Office, Sir Godfrey Lushington, the statement that:

> I regard as unfavourable to reformation the status of a pris-
> oner throughout his whole career; the crushing of self-respect;
> the starving of all moral instinct he may possess; the absence
> of all opportunity to do or receive a kindness; the continual
> association with none but criminals . . . ; the forced labour and

the denial of all liberty. I believe the true mode of reforming a man, or restoring him to society, is in exactly the opposite direction to all of these. . . . But of course this is a mere idea. It is quite impracticable in a prison. In fact, the unfavourable features I have mentioned are inseparable from prison life. (Prisons Committee 1895, para. 25)

Even Sir Edmund du Cane described imprisonment as "an artificial state of existence absolutely opposed to that which nature points out as the condition of mental, moral and physical health."

The logical conclusion from such testimony would have been that it was not in the public interest to send people to prison, except for individual offenders who were a clear and serious danger to the public. The risk of exposure to less serious offenses may even be increased by imprisonment, after which there is a high rate of reoffending. A subsequent study found that of 2,568 men undergoing penal servitude on a given day, 1,124 (44 percent) had been sentenced to that penalty before; if local prisons were included, 1,546 men had been convicted six times or more. The committee published figures showing how the probability of a further prison sentence increased with each term of imprisonment from 30 percent after the first time to 79 percent after the fifth. So much for individual deterrence. But the committee's remit was to study prisons, not sentencing.

The report of the committee (in 1895) was, by common consent, a landmark. Condemning separate confinement, it recommended more association for work and instruction, relaxation of the silence rule (though talking was still regarded as a "privilege"), a distinct regime for juveniles in prison, and separate treatment for drunkards. But above all it introduced rehabilitation as a primary aim: "the system should be made more elastic, more capable of being adapted to the special cases of individual prisoners; that prison discipline should be more effectually designed to maintain, stimulate or awaken the higher susceptibilities of prisoners to develop their moral instincts, to train them in orderly and industrial habits and whenever possible to turn them out of prison better men and women, both physically and morally, than when they came in" (Prisons Committee 1895, para. 25). Sir Edmund du Cane retired and was succeeded by Sir Evelyn Ruggles-Brise. In 1898, with the passing of a new Prison Act, the crank and the treadwheel were abolished, remission (of one-sixth of the sentence) for good conduct was introduced, and the secretary of state was given power to amend the rules for the treatment of prisoners without seeking fresh legislation. It was found that greater humanity led to "quieter and more amenable" prisoners. The probation system was greatly strengthened in the Probation of Offenders Act of 1907, which also introduced in a small way the principle of compensation by offenders to victims; and the Borstal system, introduced in 1900, was confirmed in the Prevention of Crime Act of 1908.

At last a serious, but unavailing, attempt had been made to break out of the trap in which law enforcers had become imprisoned by the dead weight of tradition. A new principle had been officially introduced. But there was a snag: the old one had not been discarded. The new era following the Gladstone Committee was based on deterrence combined with rehabilitation; and the inherent contradiction, and indeed conflict, between the two has continued ever since.

The effects of the new climate took some time to show themselves. As regards those who passed sentence, the number of men and women they sent into local and convict prisons fluctuated above 150,000 a year from 1879 until 1913, with a peak of almost 200,000 in 1905. The daily average prison population declined somewhat after 1879, indicating some shortening of average sentence lengths. The number of offenses punished by imprisonment fell from 139,000 in 1913 to 57,000 in 1914 and decreased further as the war went on; by 1917 the prison population was below 10,000. This was not due entirely to the emptying of the prisons into the trenches: in 1914 the Criminal Justice Administration Act allowed time for fines to be paid (as the prison commissioners and the Howard Association had both urged), and this reduced admissions by some 50,000 according to one estimate, with a further 25,000 attributable to increased employment and wages, which enabled fines to be paid. A further factor was the restriction on the consumption of intoxicants: normally, it was said, higher wages and convictions for drunkenness go together, but during the war they did not. The reduced use of prison does not appear to have endangered the public: from 1905 to 1913 the number of indictable crimes recorded by the police only twice fell below 97,000; from 1913 to 1919 it never rose above 90,000.

The new emphasis on rehabilitation was adopted by the prison commissioners only with great caution. In their reports they stressed retribution and deterrence as well as "reformation." Whether or not one agrees with them, they deserve credit at least for spelling out their order of priorities. Retribution came first, and they were not impressed by "loose thinkers and loose writers" who thought otherwise.

A special place in the political history of law enforcement belongs to Winston Churchill, home secretary in the Liberal administration in 1910–11. He was impressed by, among other things, Galsworthy's play *Justice* (1910), which depicts the effects of imprisonment and especially of solitary confinement. Both he and Ruggles-Brise were present at its first night. (Whether or not this was a case of *post hoc ergo propter hoc*, is not certain.) He reduced the period of solitary confinement with which prison sentences then began (1911). On visiting Pentonville prison he was perturbed at the number of juveniles in prison for trifling offenses, and "with a view to drawing public attention in a sharp and effective manner" to this evil, he simply used his powers of executive release to free many of them early. The idea of a home secretary giving a "short, sharp shock" to public opinion, rather than to young offenders, is an appealing one. He obtained a grant from the Treasury to pay for lectures and concerts in convict prisons (1909–10) and appointed a committee on the supply of books to prisoners (1910). He extended prisoners' privileges (1910). He urged the greater use of probation; and in regard to prison sentences, a minute of his on a Home Office file in 1910 asks, "Has not the time come for new maxima?" He believed in the "treasure that is the heart of every man," and with characteristic regard for language he warned: "There is a great danger of using smooth words for ugly things. Preventive detention is penal servitude in all its aspects" (1910). Perhaps best known of all, he made a fine declaration of principles which should underlie the treatment of offenders, at the end of his speech on the Prison Vote (20 July 1910):

> The mood and temper of the public in regard to the treatment of crime and criminals is one of the most unfailing tests of the civilization of any country. A calm and dispassionate recognition of the rights of the accused against the State, and even of convicted criminals against the State, a constant heart-searching by all charged with the duty of punishment, a desire and willingness to rehabilitate in the world of industry all those who have paid their dues in the hard coinage of punishment, tireless efforts towards the discovery of curative and regenerating processes and an unfaltering faith that there is a treasure, if you can only find it, in the heart of every man — these are the symbols which in the treatment of crime and criminals mark and measure the stored-up strength of a nation, and are the sign and proof of the living virtue in it.

One significant effect of the war was the number of people imprisoned for offenses newly created under the Defence of the Realm Act of 1916 and for conscientious objection to military service. Together with the women imprisoned from about 1905 onward for their activities in the campaign for women's suffrage, they included an articulate and influential group who would otherwise have been unlikely to see the inside of a prison or to believe prisoners' accounts of the regime. A committee was formed to collate their experiences and to inquire into the prison system generally. This they did with remarkable thoroughness, despite the refusal of the Prison Commission to provide information, to allow its staff to do so, or to supply a copy of Standing Orders. Fortunately, considerable evidence had already been collected from 50 prison officials; 290 ex-prisoners also gave testimony, as well as after-care workers and others. Published sources, such as the prison commissioners' annual reports, were fully used. The result, *English Prisons To-day*, was published in 1922, edited by Stephen Hobhouse and Fenner Brockway (now Lord Brockway).

This 700-page report is a detailed account of the prison system, scrupulously fair and free of rhetoric. It recorded some creditable aspects of the system and described some of the inhumanities which have now been abolished, such as leg irons, the convict crop (a convicted person's shaved head), and the broad arrow uniform. But it also gave details of the absence of industrial training, the lack of exercise, the practice of throwing excreta out of the window to avoid being locked up with it in the cell, the censorship of letters and the restrictions on visits, complaints of unsympathetic doctors obsessed with the prevention of malingering; there are harrowing accounts of prisoners lapsing into insanity and the use of "observation cells" (in effect, solitary confinement) aggravating the mental condition of the suicidal. The unfair system for grievances is described, with a recommendation that the disciplinary function of boards of visitors should be separated from their role as a safeguard for prisoners against unfair treatment. Only two years ago the Prior Committee had to repeat this proposal for reform — but once again the home secretary has rejected it. Thus despite improvements in the last sixty years, most of these failings are still on the agenda for reformers today.

THE AGE OF OPTIMISM

Suddenly a new climate prevailed. The year 1922 saw not only the publication of *English Prisons To-day* and the Webbs's masterly analysis, *English Prisons under Local Government* but also the appointment of Maurice Waller as chairman of the Prison Commission — an appointment urged on the home secretary by Margery Fry. Alexander Paterson became a commissioner at the same time. Margery Fry also negotiated the merger of the two existing reform groups into the Howard League for Penal Reform and became its first secretary. At that time it operated rather as a think-tank for a sympathetic administration; a later chairman of the Prison Commission, Sir Lionel Fox, was to describe it as "Her Majesty's loyal Opposition" to the commission. The commission quickly started to make reforms, improving the visiting facilities, informing the prisoners of some of the rules, abolishing the silence rule, improving education: in short, reversing the priority from retribution to rehabilitation.

The new spirit was most marked in the Borstals, under the inspiring leadership of Alexander Paterson. Discipline was based less on any particular system or on punishment, more on education and personal influence. Many of the governors were "characters." At Huntercombe, Sir Almeric Rich would punish boys by making them pick up flints from the field — and did it himself alongside them to show that he shared responsibility for their misbehavior. If he put a boy in a punishment cell overnight he would stay in the next cell, to give moral support if needed. Another Borstal governor, John Vidler, didn't exactly punish a boy for not working: he said that work was a privilege, and the boy wouldn't be allowed to work until he changed his attitude. After three days in a cell, with as many books as he wanted, the boy decided he'd rather work. The institutions were supposed to be based on public schools; their "housemasters" were expected to be bachelors, and worked until 9 P.M., with a day off a week and a weekend a month. As preparation for their work they were likely to be sent by Paterson to work in an East End settlement to learn at first hand, as he had done, the conditions from which many Borstal boys came.

A basic insight of the leadership of this time was that people respond to being trusted. The contrast is highlighted by two details of Borstal history. When the first institution was opened at the village of Borstal, near Rochester, in 1901, its original inmates were transferred there in chains. Thirty years later, led by another remarkable governor, W. W. Llewellin, a party of lads went from Feltham, near London, to Lowdham Grange, near Nottingham, to start the first open Borstal; they marched, camping en route, and not one absconded. Later he took another party from Stafford to North Sea Camp, near Boston in Lincolnshire. After the war even the young IRA volunteer Brendan Behan refused a chance to run away from Hollesley Bay Borstal because he didn't want to let the governor down. Between the wars, the proportion of ex-Borstal trainees who did not reoffend within two years was over 60 percent; of those who have undergone youth custody (the present-day equivalent of Borstal), over 60 percent *are* reconvicted, and over 80 percent of fifteen-to-sixteen-year-olds.

In the face of these success stories it must be remembered that there was another side. First, Borstals could, until 1961, choose their customers, and so they received the most promising young people; many were first offenders and not the rejects of approved schools and detention centers in, respectively, the prewar and postwar years. Second, because of the glowing picture of Borstals at their best, painted by the reformers and the prison authorities, Parliament set a long period (originally three years, later reduced to two) for Borstal training; and it is virtually certain that courts often sent young people there who did not deserve incarceration, for the sake of the training. Unfortunately, they did not know that the training was very limited. There were allegations of brutality at some Borstals, one of which was later closed as a result.

For adults also there were some relaxations in the regime, a spill-over from Borstal techniques. Educational facilities were improved, and in 1929 an earnings scheme for prisoners was started, at the suggestion of the Howard League and with the help of one of the Cadbury charitable trusts. The earnings of eight to ten pence per week were worth more, allowing for inflation, than prisoners receive today.

The improvements were far from universal. The grievance and disciplinary system criticized by Hobhouse and Brockway remained unaltered until the 1970s. Educational and other reforms were still regarded as something of a privilege. There were disturbances in Parkhurst in 1926 after cuts in the educational facilities, to which 85 percent of prisoners had no access during the year — and in the 1980s cutbacks in education were again contributing to the tension in the prisons. In 1927 it was "not thought necessary" to appoint prison visitors to Dartmoor and Parkhurst. In Dartmoor things were, if anything, worse. In 1928 there was no educational adviser and no definite intention of appointing one; there were only nineteen lectures and ninety-five classes for young convicts in a whole year. The financial crisis forced a reduction of staff in prisons generally, with a cut in the working day to about five hours. In January 1932, after attacks on officers, there was a serious riot at the prison: the administrative block was set on fire, and police had to be called in to restore order. An official inquiry under Herbert du Parcq, KC (later to become a judge and a law lord) found, not for the first or the last time, that Dartmoor was unsuitable for use as a prison. Significantly, no government has set up an independent public inquiry into any modern prison disturbance. The home secretary, Herbert Samuel, stood firm against those who said that courts and prisons were becoming too soft; as the *New Statesman* remarked, the trouble at Dartmoor could hardly be blamed on "modern methods of prison treatment," since Dartmoor had remained almost untouched by them. Cicely Craven, the secretary of the Howard League, similarly, wrote to the home secretary: "The main criticism to be levelled against modern prison administration is not that there is an excess of leniency; but that there is stagnation."

The situation was not helped by the sentence of "preventive detention," introduced in 1908 with the intention of containing the "professional" criminal; in practice it netted mainly habitual petty offenders and incapacitated them still further for life outside. The prison commissioners, while still holding to the belief that prison could serve the double purpose of prevention and cure, did not think that lengthy periods of imprisonment would be long supported by public opinion, and they recognized that a man might be worse for prison experience and could leave with ideas of revenge upon the society that had deprived him of freedom. They concluded, however, that prisons should be improved, not that they should be abolished. A Departmental Committee on Persistent Offenders recommended the reform of preventive detention, the provision of adequate work in prisons, with payment of a proper rate for the job, and employment for ex-prisoners. Proposals were made to improve the effectiveness of the voluntary after-care societies. As usual, part of the problem lay in employment conditions in the world outside prisons; and part was caused by the fact of imprisonment itself, which then required a great deal of further effort to mitigate its damaging effects.

The interwar period is nevertheless generally seen as one of progress; the prison population remained stable at about 11,000 for two decades, and in 1938 a criminal justice bill was introduced, proposing the abolition of corporal punishment (which was already little used because courts recognized its ineffectiveness) and a reduction in the incarceration of young offenders through the establishment of hostels, to be known as Howard Houses. If a spectator of the penal scene at the outbreak of war could feel that further progress was simply being postponed, he would not have predicted anything radical. The penal system remained in essence what it had been since the abandonment of transportation. But although much of the harshness had been removed and the idea of rehabilitation had been introduced, the twin philosophies in all their confusion persisted. There was no discernible escape from the penalty of imprisonment; the trap had been set.

II. CONFLICTS IN CRIMINAL JUSTICE: CAUGHT IN THE TRAP

By the time war broke out in 1939 it seemed as if progress was being made toward a more humane system of criminal justice and penal practice. The old barbarities had been largely swept away, and the institutions which replaced them were intended, in part at least, to be reformative. The prison population had been more or less constant for two decades, at about 11,000, largely owing to the increased use of probation. A criminal justice bill had been introduced, intended to reduce further the use of imprisonment for young offenders, replacing it by residence in Howard Houses (something like strict, but not necessarily punitive, probation hostels) followed by supervision. The bill would also abolish corporal punishment except in prisons. But it had not completed its passage when war was declared.

The preservation of freedom and justice was high among the aims of those who fought in the Second World War, but from 1939 to 1945 it had to wait for its application on the domestic front: the conduct of the war itself had to take priority. The criminal justice bill of 1938 was shelved, and little happened on the criminal justice front, apart from an increase in prisoners' remission for good conduct from a quarter to a third of the sentence as an expedient to reduce the prison population. A bill similar in most respects to the prewar bill, notably in abolishing corporal punishment, was introduced in Parliament in 1947. But the climate of opinion had changed somewhat, and the Howard Houses proposed in 1938 were replaced in the 1948 act by detention centers, which were explicitly punitive — the "short, sharp shock" was the rallying cry of those intent on curbing juvenile delinquency, perceived as a growing evil. One reason for the change may have been the continuing rise in recorded crime figures: in the decade from 1928 to 1938 the number of indictable offenses recorded annually increased by about 150,000; in the next decade it went up by about 240,000. There was much talk of the "glasshouses" used by the army, and no doubt a number of members of Parliament had had occasion to send misbehaving soldiers there; probably rather fewer legislators had been on the receiving end. Be that as it may, detention centers were introduced either to combat crime or to satisfy those who believed them to be necessary to make up for the abolition of corporal punishment, despite the evidence. Home Office research showed that flogging made men more likely to reoffend, so that simply to abolish it would make the public safer. As for "glasshouses," little is known about their effectiveness, but the belief that men "never came back for a second dose of the punishment" may be due to special factors, such as the accepted disciplinary ethos shared by those in the armed forces, and to the fact that many offenders were discharged from the army, so that any future offending would not come to the notice of their former superior officers.

Optimism nevertheless prevailed. The proportion of offenders sent to prison continued to go down; in some years the numbers convicted of indictable offenses, and even the prison population, actually decreased. In 1958 the First Offenders Act was passed; it had been promoted by the Howard League to try to discourage courts from sending an offender to prison for the first time. The Criminal Justice Act of 1961 required all young adults to be sent to Borstal if the court decided on custody for an intermediate term, and it actually gave the home secretary power to abolish the use of short sentences of imprisonment (six months or less for offenders under twenty-one years old) as soon as there were enough detention centers to replace the prison space otherwise used. But the power was never exercised: the Advisory Council on the Penal System report in the 1970s was to herald its demise. It was also in a spirit of optimism that the league pressed for research: the 1948 act gave the Home Office power to spend money on research, and in 1959 R. A. Butler, as home secretary, was persuaded to establish the Cambridge Institute of Criminology. This coincided with the publication of *Penal Practice in a Changing Society*, a government publication that was redolent of hope for the future in prescribing means of reducing the reliance on imprisonment. It also, unhelpfully, heralded the burgeoning prison building program. Blundeston, opened in 1963, was the first prison built since Camp Hill (1912), whose construction was authorized by Winston Churchill. There was still a feeling that with more knowledge of the causes of delinquency it would be possible to find solutions. The idea of a scientifically based penal policy received a severe setback in the 1960s, however. A Royal Commission on the Penal System had been appointed; but a request from one of its members, Professor Leon Radzinowicz, the director of the recently established Cambridge (England) Institute of Criminology, for substantial research backing along the lines of the American President's Commission was turned down. Two years into the commission's work there developed a schism over penal philosophy. Unprecedentedly for a Royal Commission, it was dissolved and was replaced in 1966 by the Advisory Council on the Penal System with a remit to study specific topics. Meanwhile the government, urgently concerned to reverse the growth of the prison population, turned to fresh legislation. The Advisory Council, over the next twelve years, produced a series of reports, largely designed to shift the emphasis from custody to noncustody. Despite this, or because of it, the council was included among the 'quangos' discarded by an incoming Conservative Administration of 1979 that did not want independent advice on penal matters. The competing philosophies of contemporary penology remain unresolved, awaiting, perhaps, resolution by a revived Royal Commission. Even if it were to suffer the same fate of breaking up in disarray, we could hardly be worse off.

MIXED MOTIVES: DETENTION CENTERS

It has often been pointed out that sentencing practice might be very different if the courts were responsible for the budget from which their sentences have to be paid for. They are probably the only official agency which, subject only to trying to observe some degree of consistency, can pursue whatever policy its members like; they must observe maxima set by Parliament, but Parliament in doing so does not have financial considerations in mind and does not even have to provide an estimate of the cost of setting the penalty for any particular offense. There is another built-in conflict, however, identified by Timothy Raison, MP, in a Note of Dissent to the report of the Advisory Council on the Penal System (ACPS), *Young Adult Offenders* (1974). This is that the *goals* of the sentencers are different from those of the institutions to which they commit people. "We send someone to school or hospital so that he may be educated or treated, and that is what schools and hospitals set out to do. But we send an offender to prison largely to deter him from further offences or to register society's disapproval of his action. But once he is there, we try to treat him. Only keeping the offender out of circulation is clearly common to both sets of objectives." The contradiction is even more fundamental than Raison says: a further major reason for sending a person to prison is to deter *other* people from offending.

An example of the contradictions inherent in a law enforcement policy that is part punitive, part rehabilitative is found in the story of detention centers. The catch-phrase used to describe them, the "short, sharp shock," was another example of the misleading metaphor in penology: as Baroness (Barbara) Wootton pointed out, the Gilbertian phrase referred to decapitation. Some people in any case found three months a long, blunt shock. The motives for introducing detention centers (in the Criminal Justice Act of 1948) and augmenting them (in 1961) were, as usual, mixed. For some, they were a sop to buy off the opposition to the abolition of corporal punishment, and therefore had to be as much of a "short, sharp shock" as possible; to others, they were a way of persuading courts not to send young offenders to prison — indeed, it was anticipated at least that they would replace imprisonment. At first, the greater problem was not that the staffs' aims differed from those of the courts but that they were too enthusiastic in achieving the punitive goal. From the establishment of the first centers in the 1950s, there were repeated complaints of pointless and degrading work and even of brutality. The prison crop, abolished in the 1920s, was reintroduced. The reception procedure was often a chilling, impersonal, and humiliating experience. Visits were restricted and letters censored, as in prison. Solitary confinement and dietary restriction were used as punishments. Much of the work was deliberately hard and boring, such as separating old electric cables into their component materials — a modern version of oakum-picking, of which Hobhouse and Brockway (1922) remarked that "the effect of attempting to make prison labour 'deterrent' with a view to inculcating a distaste for prison is to make labour itself distasteful." The same might be said of cleanliness, tidiness, and routine. For girls, the regime was so obviously unsuitable that it was abolished, following a visit to the one center by the Advisory Council on the Penal System and an immediate interim report to which the home secretary responded favorably.

Against this background an attempt was made, in the Criminal Justice Act of 1961, to make the sentence more constructive by grafting on compulsory after-care; but there was still unease, and the home secretary asked the Advisory Council to report on detention centers. Without dwelling on the allegations of brutality, they made it clear in their report (1970) that the bishop of Exeter (Dr. Robert Mortimer) and his colleagues on the subcommittee believed in a more educative regime, including remedial education for the one in four of the intake whose reading age was ten or below. The teaching of illiterate boys to read was a marked feature of the program for those under school-leaving age. The Advisory Council tried, optimistically, to square the circle by proposing that discipline should remain firm and the regime brisk and exacting but constructive; the punitive aspect of the detention center should be limited to the deprivation of liberty. Within a year or two several centers were enthusiastically expanding their remedial education programs; some used electric typewriters, then a new and expensive gadget, as a teaching aid. The militaristic approach had all but disappeared by the time the ACPS had reported; the centers had become little more than mini-Borstals, with the same constructive training, only shorter in duration. In 1974 the ACPS recommended a generic sentence of youth custody. It has taken fourteen years, via an absurd revival in 1980 of the "short, sharp shock" philosophy, to reach that sensible objective.

In 1980 Lord (then Mr. William) Whitelaw reinvented the wheel by introducing at two centers (and later two more) a "brisker tempo," hard physical work and physical education, less association, an earlier time for lights out, and more parades and inspections. This was called an experiment, as if the period of the 1960s had not been an experiment that had palpably failed. Mr. Whitelaw had earlier admitted that he had no idea whether it would work. The "experiment" was set up in a way that made clear evaluation impossible; nevertheless the research report, whose publication was delayed until 1984, was able to conclude that there was no improvement in reconviction rates. Over half were reconvicted within a year, both in the experimental centers and in the rest. Worse than that, the "trainees" disliked the work but enjoyed the drill and tough physical education — the opposite of the desired result.

The home secretary by now was Mr. Leon Brittan, who had been the junior minister responsible for implementing the "experiment." He responded by extending tougher regimes to all detention centers — another setback for a research-based policy of criminal justice. The only lesson the politicians chose to draw from the research was that the drill should be stopped; they had missed the point that what mattered was not that it was strenuous but that to do it correctly was an achievement. The boys are now back to tasks like polishing floors by hand: also an achievement of sorts, but since it could be achieved more appropriately by machine, their real achievement is keeping their tempers when they are made to do such unnecessary tasks. Some centers and individual prison officers subverted the punitive intentions of the politicians, as they had done in the 1960s, by introducing social skills courses and other educative activities. At other centers allegations of brutality began to surface once again. In one, prison officers even behaved in a humiliating way toward youths in the presence of prison inspectors. The chief inspector noted in his report for 1985 that for many of the staff "there was an inherent tension between the demands, on the one hand, of the brisk physical regime and, on the other, of the need to care for inmates." There has been a drop in the numbers of fourteen- to sixteen-year-olds sent to junior detention centers; but courts are apparently sending at least some of the fifteen- to sixteen-year-olds to youth custody centers instead. Whether this is because youth custody sentences are longer (over four months) or because, to a limited extent, they include some form of training, is not clear. But detention centers are all of a piece with a mischievous social policy that should now be consigned to the penal history museum, along with the rack and the thumbscrew.

THE DECLINE OF REHABILITATION

The Advisory Council saw from the outset that detention centers could not be thoroughly reviewed without rethinking the principles on which the treatment of young adult offenders was based, in the wake of the Children and Young Persons Act of 1969, which had done the same for the younger children in trouble. The 1969 act was the last major attempt to enact the rehabilitative ideal; it was based on the philosophy that many young people who offend have had a deprived upbringing and that society's response should be to allow social workers to help them overcome their disadvantages. The vagueness of this concept was reflected in its name, "Intermediate Treatment." Courts complained that after making a care order, they were likely to meet the offender in the street a week later: another example of anecdotal penology. Without necessarily being punitive, they wanted to make sure that "something" happened to the offender; this probably accounts for some of the increase in the use of detention centers at this period.

In 1974 the Advisory Council produced a thorough, sensible, but not very radical report, *Young Adult Offenders*; but it came too late to avoid the first financial retrenchment following the economic crisis. It recommended the abolition of detention centers and Borstals in favor of a single, educative Custody and Control Order, with supervision after release; to encourage the use of noncustodial sanctions, a stricter one would be introduced, called a Supervision and Control Order. The orders favored considerable use of discretion: in releasing inmates from custody, and in detaining those on supervision for up to seventy-two hours on suspicion that the offender was contemplating another offense. This idea was imported from America and provoked fierce opposition, particularly from probation officers: unlike their American counterparts, some — particularly the younger members of the service — see themselves primarily as social workers, rather than law enforcement officers, and they did not want to become, as the catchphrase of the time had it, "screws on wheels." But by taking on after-care, prison welfare, parole, and community service orders, the probation service had become an important segment of penal practice. There was another problem with the proposals: the catch-phrase for this was "widening the net of social control." This means that whenever a new measure is introduced intermediate in severity between imprisonment and probation, with the intention of persuading the courts to use it in place of prison, the courts will also tend to use it where probation would have been adequate, as a sort of novel penal toy to which the judiciary are magnetically attracted. Not only is this excessive in itself, but if the offender breaches the order, he is likely to be given a more severe sanction than for not complying with a probation order. Thus he is doubly worse off, and may even end up in prison for an offense which did not deserve it.

This effect was strikingly demonstrated in relation to adults, in the introduction of suspended sentences in the Criminal Justice Act of 1967, to be buttressed a decade later by the partially suspended sentence introduced in 1976. In theory fully suspended sentences were prison sentences, but only their symbolic value would be enforced; provided the offender was not reconvicted, he suffered only the stigma of the prison sentence, not its reality. But the courts frequently used the new power in place of lesser penalties; moreover they did not think that stigma alone was enough, so they made up for it by lengthening the sentences that they suspended. Thus offenders who reoffended went to prison, and for longer than if suspended sentences had not been invented. After a temporary drop, the prison population rose at least as fast as before.

A second innovation in the 1967 act was parole, and here again confused motives ultimately led to a system that has become widely discredited in the eyes of penal reformers, prison administrators and staff, and prisoners, alike. It was partly an expedient to try to limit the prison population; partly an example of anecdotal penology. The white paper *The Adult Offender* (1965) referred to tales told by prison governors, who said that they often recognized, in long-term prisoners, a "peak of response" after which they (the prisoners) began to deteriorate. Parole is supposed to allow prisoners to be released at this peak. But the system is enmeshed in a tangle of contradictions. A governor may recognize the "peak" in some prisoners, but the chances are against a local review committee, let alone a remote parole board, being able to identify it in thousands of cases a year. Prisoners have to serve at least one-third of the sentence and, in the original scheme, a minimum of twelve months from the date of sentence before being eligible, so it was idle to reach one's peak before then. Also, there are extra criteria: parole depends not only on "responding," but on the seriousness of the offense and on conduct while in prison; failure on any one of these criteria jeopardizes early release. A fortunate offender with a home and job to return to is probably a "better risk" than one without these advantages and therefore stands an unfair chance of being released sooner. The offender who is a "worse risk" is less likely to get parole and therefore is released at the end of his sentence without a period of supervision in the community. To meet this point some offenders are given parole early, to ensure that they do have some supervision; the others naturally regard this as unfair. In November 1983 Mr. Leon Brittan, as home secretary, added to the sense of unfairness by restricting parole for certain long-term prisoners; for short-termers, however, the minimum qualifying period was reduced. Unforgivably, Mr. Brittan also withdrew two life-sentence prisoners from open prison to closed conditions so that the new policy would be applied to them. He received judicial upbraiding from the Master of the Rolls, Sir John Donaldson (now Lord Donaldson of Lymington), when the policy was subjected, unsuccessfully, to judicial review. It is generally believed, though the courts deny it, that sentences have been lengthened to take account of parole.

The catalog of contradictions is a long one; what it adds up to is that a fair system of parole is impossible, at least as long as there are several conflicting criteria, and members of the Parole Board, striving to be both fair and humane, have been attempting the impossible. (Attempting the impossible, however, is contemplated illogically by the criminal law. If, for example, I hand over a packet of tea leaves, thinking that it is cannabis, I am guilty of attempting to traffic in proscribed drugs.)

Above all, the system was designedly based on executive action, with no element of judicial review. The European Commission on Human Rights, however, has decided that on recall a prisoner is entitled to due process of law. That case provided the impetus for the setting up of a Departmental Committee to Review Parole under the chairmanship of Lord (Mark) Carlisle (himself a former member of the Advisory Council and a junior minister at the Home Office in the Heath administration). The unraveling of that penological knot will call for some ingenuity.

THE GREAT DEPRESSION

By the end of the 1960s the earlier optimism was turning perceptibly to depression. Rising affluence and welfare benefits had not brought a reduction in recorded crime figures. Rehabilitative sanctions, including noncustodial ones, fell out of favor, although for different reasons. Courts felt that they did not work because they were too "soft," besides having a tendency to transfer decisions about offenders from courts to social workers. Reformers began to take exception to the parole system by which a person could be deprived of liberty for "treatment" purposes for a long time for a minor offense if he did not "respond" — which could mean that he was not given any treatment to respond to or that he refused to submit meekly to prison regimentation. Even research, which liberal reformers had hoped would show how to reduce crime, fell from grace: surveys of research on rehabilitative projects which had appeared to show promising results served only to demonstrate that in many cases their design was flawed, so that their findings were inconclusive. A widely quoted American article by Robert Martinson, entitled "What Works" (1974), concluded, "With few and isolated exceptions, the rehabilitative efforts that have been reported so far have had no appreciable effect on recidivism." "Nothing works" became a slogan which made a generation of prison staff and probation officers wonder if their jobs were worthwhile. Predictably morale was low, never more so than in Borstals, where devoted staff became thoroughly disillusioned.

There were answers to these strictures, but somehow they did not attract attention. If research did not prove that a project had succeeded, that did not necessarily prove that it had failed. Projects which spelled out clear and specific goals, such as teaching literacy or social skills, stood a fair chance of success. Martinson's own findings did not justify his conclusions; indeed a few years later he himself revised them: "Contrary to my previous position," he wrote in 1979, "some treatment programs do have appreciable effect on recidivism. . . . New evidence from our current study leads me to reject my original conclusion. . . . I have hesitated up to now, but the evidence in our survey is simply too overwhelming to ignore." The word "treatment" was itself ambiguous: formerly it had implied the "medical model," in which the offender was seen as "maladjusted" and needed to be diagnosed and "cured"; now it was becoming more like a contract, in which the offender is encouraged to identify his own problems and agrees to accept help in overcoming them.

But the damage was done. Especially in prisons, people drew the wrong conclusions. The rehabilitative ideology was no longer fashionable, and it fell into desuetude. The Home Office brown book, *Prisons and the Prisoner* (1977), supported the dispiriting approach of "humane containment," to be endorsed by the May Committee on Prisons in 1979. They might have said, "The treatment offered in prisons is inadequate and is counteracted by the harmful effects of imprisonment itself, therefore we must improve the treatment and offer it outside prison whenever possible." Instead they said, "Nothing works anyway, so we may as well give up trying and restrict ourselves to 'humane containment' as an end in itself." Rule number one of the Prison Rules, 1964, though a pious hope, was at least idealistic: "The purpose of the training and treatment of convicted prisoners shall be to encourage and assist them to lead a good and useful life." In practice, this was superseded by a more negative approach known as "positive custody" — "The purpose of the detention of convicted prisoners shall be to keep them in custody" — with preparation for discharge last on the list of objectives (Committee of Inquiry 1979, para. 4.26).

This uninspired, even nihilist, approach was not helped by an administrative change in the mid-1960s. For nearly a century — from 1878 onward — the prisons had been managed by the Prison Commission, and for forty years it, and especially its successive chairmen, had a tradition of adopting liberal principles and defending them against the outcry when anything went wrong. In 1963, however, the commission was absorbed into the Home Office. The motive was good; the effect, bad. It was considered necessary to bring the custodial and noncustodial parts of the system under one roof — probation had from its inception been handled within the Home Office. The sensible move would have been to redefine the Prison Commission's role so as to include the noncustodial side. In the Home Office a different tradition prevails: the minister must be protected from embarrassment. Formerly, it was said, a prison governor could do anything that was not forbidden; now he can do nothing unless he has permission. To make matters worse, in 1966 George Blake escaped from Wormwood Scrubs. The laxity in preventing escapes from custody caught up with the prison service; so lax was it indeed that the prison administration had no photograph of Blake on file so as to alert police forces, the media, and the public. The response was predictable. In his report on the matter, Lord (Louis) Mountbatten recommended stricter security measures, most of which were brought in, and humane ones to reduce the pressures to escape, most of which were not. He also recommended a single fortress prison for those whose escape would present a major danger to the public or embarrassment to the government; but concentration of such prisoners in one prison was rejected in favor of dispersal, which has not been a resounding success. The official reaction to Mountbatten was retrogressive. The emphasis on security put the prospect of penal progress back twenty years.

SENTENCING: CHASING THE CHIMERA

As the new subject of criminology was developed during the 1960s, after the establishment of the Institute of Criminology at Cambridge, criminologists began to look at a new aspect of the law enforcement process: sentencing. In 1969 Dr. Nigel Walker, of Nuffield College, Oxford (later professor of criminology and director of the Institute of Criminology at Cambridge), published *Sentencing in a Rational Society*; a year later Dr. David Thomas, at Cambridge, produced *Principles of Sentencing*. They sought to elucidate the principles followed by courts when passing judgment. First, Nigel Walker identified several aims present in the process of deciding a sentence. Some were practical, such as to reduce crime by deterrence or rehabilitation; others symbolic, such as retribution against the offender and denunciation of the offense. Then David Thomas examined the decisions of the Court of Appeal (Criminal Division), focusing more specifically on the types and lengths of sentences and the reasons given. Unfortunately he undertook his study at a time when a practice of imposing long sentences had already grown up. He identified two main types of sentence, the "individualized," or "rehabilitative," and the "tariff," or "deterrent." The courts, like M. Jourdain speaking prose, discovered that they had method and principles all along. The judges avidly imbibed Dr. Thomas's work as standardizing their erratic sentencing policy and practices. As one man commented, after being sentenced to seven years' imprisonment for a not very serious indecent assault, "Some people are mighty careless about other people's time." The trouble was that the appeal court judges saw only the alleged excesses of the sentencing courts and set about correcting them (if at all) on the basis of a biased sample.

But even then the picture was not as clear as that. Courts were not always sure which principle they were applying: Borstal, for example, might be "deterrent" because it was custodial, or "rehabilitative" because it provided training. (In fact, in the period of gross overcrowding in the late 1960s, the average period in Borstals had fallen from about eighteen months to eight — and training was available only for part of that time.) The punitive purposes, such as deterrence and retribution, were assumed to be more or less the same, but in fact they are based on different principles. A retributive sentence reflects the seriousness of the offense, regardless of its effect on the offender; a deterrent one is exactly the opposite — a murderer might need no deterrent other than the conviction itself to prevent him from repeating his offense, while, as we have seen, the prospect of many years of penal servitude can be insufficient to deter a hungry woman from stealing food.

The edifice of sentencing is erected on at least two fondly held judicial shibboleths: *(a)* that sentences have a significant and positive impact on the volume of crime, as courts, politicians, and the media profess to believe; and *(b)* that the sentencing structure combining all these purposes is consistent and produces an equal distribution of fairness among offenders.

It is worth looking briefly at the ostensible purposes of sentencing, as identified by these scholars. The main one is a utilitarian one: crime reduction. It is supposed to be achieved by four main methods — individual deterrence, general deterrence, rehabilitation, and containment. Let us consider these in turn.

The first method is intended to deter the individual offender from reoffending. Apart from the fact that people protest vehemently that they will not be caught next time, the problem here is that it is hard to impose methods that are sufficiently frightening, without also being barbaric. If we were to countenance cutting off the hands of thieves, it might possibly prevent the handless and helpless from thieving again. Even socially tolerable sanctions serve only to incapacitate a person for law-abiding life and often make him more inclined to avenge himself on society than to conform to its wishes. Punishment makes people think of themselves, not of their victims.

Second, deterrent sentencing is supposed to deter other potential offenders. This was the principle on which Admiral George Byng was shot, according to Voltaire's sardonic remark: "Dans ce pays-ci il est bon de tuer de temps en temps un amiral pour encourager les autres" (In this country it is thought desirable to kill an admiral from time to time to encourage the others [*Candide*, chap. 23]). Here more than anywhere there is an ethical problem which is usually skirted round. There are strong arguments for saying that to inflict harm on anyone with the intention of influencing other people cannot be ethically or socially justified. As Lord Justice Herbert Asquith said, all exemplary punishments are unjust, and they are unjust to precisely the extent that they are exemplary. Even if the principle were accepted as a necessary evil, it could be acceptable only if it could be shown to work. But there is no conclusive evidence, except for some further examples of anecdotal penology, or at least impressionistic evidence so fondly exhibited by judges. Thirty years ago, for example, after an outbreak of attacks on black people in Notting Hill, nine youths were sentenced to four years' imprisonment (at least double the normal sentence). The judge, Mr. Justice (later Lord) Cyril Salmon, made a firm condemnation of racial harassment — which was fine, but piling on the agony of extended incarceration was wholly unnecessary. The attacks stopped, and the sentences were given the credit. But investigation by researchers has shown that other factors, such as increased police activity, are just as likely to have been responsible. If anything, it is the probability of being caught that makes the best deterrent: an old truism, but supported by modern research. The trouble is that the detection rate for most crimes is depressingly low — hence the lack of deterrent effect.

Deterrents can indeed have side effects that are counterproductive. Once a crime has been committed, the more severe the penalty, the more a person is under pressure to threaten witnesses, including the victim, in order to escape conviction. Conversely, in cases such as child abuse, the prospect of seeing a father (for example) sent to prison for a long time may make the victim feel not only more afraid but also more guilty at the prospect of reporting him. The burden of proof should be on the courts to show that punishment, especially imprisonment, is in the public interest. It might help if probation officers, too, presented their recommendations in terms of the public interest. This would still, in the great majority of cases, lead them to recommend noncustodial sanctions — but with a better chance that these would be acceptable to the courts. The basic problem about deterrence is that it proceeds upon the assumption that offenders calculate cause and effect before engaging in the criminal act. The fact is that most offenders — at least those who land up in prison — have a sense of their own immunity, or even, like gamblers, enjoy the risk, and pay little regard to the consequences of their acts.

The subject is in any event very complex, but perhaps these few points will be enough to persuade our legislators and our popular press that increasing penalties is not necessarily the best way to counter crimes, however unpleasant; indeed if we put our faith in quack remedies, it may divert us from the search for more effective ones — to say nothing of better preventive policies.

The third practical objective of sentencing is to rehabilitate the offender. The efficacy of "rehabilitative" sentences is at least open to question, as we have seen, even if some critics have been unduly dismissive. Often the educative measures have not been given the resources they need, or have been conducted in prison, which outweighs their beneficial effects; or the research itself has been inadequately designed, but that does not necessarily mean that the claims of the project itself are invalid. Some "rehabilitative" sentences, particularly those based on indeterminate duration or compulsory treatment, can be more restrictive than punitive ones. A further problem with the rehabilitative sentence is that it does not appear to hold the offender responsible for his actions; by appearing to see the causes of his offense in his psychological makeup or his social surroundings, it fails to symbolize the fact that he did wrong and, in many cases, a victim suffered.

Fourth, it is often argued, even if offenders are neither deterred nor rehabilitated, at least they can be contained. There are some offenders for whom this is inevitable, if they pose an intolerable danger to others. But at the other end of the scale there are many whose offenses do not justify a severe sentence; imprisoning them is as likely as not to increase the chances that they will reoffend, and given the low rate of detection, particularly of petty crimes, imprisoning for a few weeks or months the small number who are caught is not going to have a significant effect on the total volume of crime.

The argument here is not that no one is ever deterred by the prospect of punishment, nor that prisons do not contain some people who would otherwise be outside committing crimes; it is that, except in the most serious cases, any such effects are liable to be heavily outweighed by the damaging effects of imprisonment; worse than that, if society puts its trust in a method of crime control which is ineffective or even counterproductive, it is actually endangering its citizens through complacency. For those with long memories, one might say that prisons are to crime as the Maginot Line was to the invasion of France: the fortifications were impregnable, but the German army in 1940 bypassed them with consummate ease, to the discomfiture of the Allied commanders.

But even if imprisonment, and punishments generally, achieve no tangible results at all, there is still another possible justification: retribution. The first thing to say about this is that current practice is unjust: imprisonment is the most serious punishment in the land, yet many people are in prison for what are by any standards minor offenses. But leaving that aside, various justifications are offered for retributive sentencing. It can be seen as canceling out the advantage gained by the offender through the crime. But most important, it symbolizes the fact that the offender's behavior is not tolerated. Professor Walker has called this function "denunciation." When there is an outcry against a particular sentence because it is too "lenient," what it means is that it is considered to be less than sentences imposed on other offenders who have committed crimes of comparable gravity. Alternatively, people compare the harm done to the victim with the impact of the sentence on the offender: a young woman may have been crippled or even killed, for example, by a drunken driver, who is only fined, or is only disqualified from driving, or only receives a short prison sentence, which may even be suspended. Part of the trouble here is that the law and its penalties are based on the state of mind of the offender, rather than on the harm inflicted on the victim: to drive while drunk is only reckless or negligent, and there was no deliberate intent to kill or injure that person. This was the basis for Barbara Wootton's (1963) compelling assault on the lawyers' adherence to *mens rea*: society's interest is in the harm inflicted on the victim, and the offender's motive or intention is relevant only to the disposal on conviction. This could be overcome if the scales of justice were balanced using a different system of weighting: rather than attempt the impossible calculation involved in making the offender endure an amount of suffering proportionate to his guilty intentions, he would be required to cancel out his crime, even if only symbolically, by reparative acts, or payments, proportionate to the harm caused to the victim or the community.

With such disparate aims in sentencing policy and practice, it is not surprising that there is inconsistency. The common mistake is to assume that this is due to the human fallibility of judges and magistrates; that if only they had better training, or detailed guidelines, or stricter legislative constraints, something like a fair and effective sentencing policy could be devised. Here we should acquit the judges. The reason why it is not achieved is that it is unachievable. It is almost inevitable that a sentence, adequate on retributive grounds, will be too light or too heavy on deterrent grounds, too short or too long for purposes of rehabilitation, and so on. To attempt to balance the aims against each other is to ensure that none of them is attained. It is essential to decide which of the objectives is to take precedence, if there is a clash. This has in effect been done in those states of America which have adopted sentencing guidelines. Reacting against both the indeterminate sentence and the inconsistency of courts, these states have decreed that sentencing should be based on a tabulation: a certain category of offense must lead to a certain penalty. One of the best-known schemes of this kind is in Minnesota. A sentencing commission has been established; this insulates policy from the legislature, which does, however, have the last word. The commission has drawn up a table, in which the columns represent the number of the offender's previous convictions and the horizontal rows indicate the category of offense. Each box in the table contains a main number, which represents the length of the sentence in months, with a lower and a higher number, indicating the differences to be allowed for mitigating or aggravating circumstances. This does not, however, completely tie down the judges; judges may depart from the guidelines if they give reasons. If there is a public demand for a change in the sentence for a particular offense, referral to the commission provides a pause to ensure that this will not introduce inconsistencies in relation to other sentences. The entire scale of sentences, more or less consistent in relation to each other, is adjusted downward if the prisons become full: not exactly a principled basis for sentencing but a practical and economical one.

What this amounts to is that the adoption of sentencing guidelines cuts through the ambiguities and puts one principle of sentencing in first place: punishment. The question can then be posed to legislators and electors: do you recognize that what you are doing, at great financial and human cost, is simply to inflict further pain on the offender and his family (in addition to what he has already caused to the victim) because you have admitted the reality that any attempt to rehabilitate offenders has been subordinated to retribution? If what is most important is to symbolize society's condemnation of wrongdoing, is there not a constructive method of doing so? There is a good case for saying that the principle with the fewest objections is the reparative goal: this does not prevent the others being present as desirable side effects. There is, however, a danger: if reparation were *added* to the list of aims, without being adopted as the *primary* goal, this would add to the confusion.

CHANGING PRACTICE IN A PENAL SOCIETY

The 1960s ended with two very problematic innovations in the criminal justice system of this country: parole and suspended sentences; the 1970s began with some developments of great potential significance. They had their origins in the introduction, in 1964, of *ex gratia* state compensation for victims of violent crime (shortly to be put on a statutory footing), and in two reports by the Advisory Council on the Penal System, in 1970: *Non-custodial and Semi-custodial Penalties* (chaired by Baroness Wootton) and *Reparation by the Offender* (chaired by Lord Justice, later Lord Chief Justice, John Widgery).

One suggestion, put forward at a Howard League conference in 1970, was for a requirement to attend a day training center (the more general term is now "day center"), in the context of a probation order. Although the Wootton report did not give as much prominence to this idea as to the community service order, the centers were introduced in the act of 1972, which was amended in 1982. This may not seem a major innovation, but it is significant for two reasons. One is that day centers have provided a focus for a change in the definition of "rehabilitation"; this was regarded less and less as a form of diagnosis and treatment for "maladjusted" or otherwise deviant offender-patients and more as offering offender-clients themselves an opportunity to define the difficulties they face and helping them to devise programs toward overcoming them. Second, a day center can provide continuity for probation initiatives, such as literacy programs, social skills training, groups for sexual offenders, and so on, which otherwise tend to fade out when the individual probation officers who started them leave the area. Day centers now exist in almost all probation areas, though not in all districts; they can provide courts with a useful sanction when probation officers recognize that imprisonment would be worse than useless but feel that something more specific than a standard probation order and supervision is required.

The main recommendation of the Wootton Committee was the community service order, included in the same act. This is probably the most significant innovation in the theory and practice of criminal justice for at least half a century. In essence it is a way of giving effect to the basic principle that a person harms the community by his offense and should therefore make amends by doing something beneficial for the community. But there is more to it than that. The intention is that the offender should use any skills or qualities he possesses for the common good, rather than merely endure the mind-crippling boredom which is a dominant feature of present-day prison life. Those who complain that community service is not unpleasant enough are wide of the mark, because the objective is reparation *by* the offender, not punishment *of* the offender. There is a possibility of enabling him to build himself up into a good citizen, rather than portraying him as an outcast. As far as possible his task in the community will be related to his abilities rather than to his offense. To encourage this approach, the courts have been given the power only to order community service, not to specify the type; that is done by the probation service, usually after discussion with the offender. This prevents the courts from imposing tasks that are ill-suited to the individual offender or fanciful or punitive. The Advisory Council recommended that, wherever possible, offenders should work either with beneficiaries in person or alongside volunteers; this avoids a basic criticism of prisons — that they herd together those who have nothing in common except their criminality — and offers the hope that the offender may pick up different attitudes from those of his usual associates. To avoid the charge that this would be a form of forced labor, which is forbidden under international conventions, the imposition of a community service order depends on the consent of the offender — not an entirely free consent, it is true, because in many cases the alternative would be a custodial sentence; but it does mean that community service can be avoided by anyone who is very reluctant to undertake it.

There have been problems with community service, practical and theoretical. The practical ones have been mainly associated with finding enough tasks of the right kind. This can be time-consuming, and some probation areas have had to limit the number of community service orders they can recommend to the courts — an injustice to the offender, if imprisonment was not necessary, and a false economy if ever there was one, given the much higher cost of imprisonment. Community service orders are for a maximum of 240 hours, taking up to a year to complete; this means that they are not considered suitable for very serious offenses. The work must be of a kind which would not otherwise be done by employees earning their livelihood. To ensure this, representatives of trade unions have been closely associated with community service from the start, although in fact a number of tasks such as decorating the homes of old people have been allowed. Voluntary organizations do not always find it easy to provide or supervise tasks, especially if the person is available only at weekends. Travel can be a problem particularly in rural areas. As a result, some community service organizers have resorted to what is deprecatingly called a "chain-gang" approach. The offenders are put into groups and given manual work with no contact with beneficiaries or other members of the public. On paper this makes supervision more economical, but in practice it is difficult for the supervisor to exercise control in those circumstances. Some tasks are not of benefit to sections of the public most in need; some people might regard clearing canals as conservation, for example, but to the offenders it may seem like working for "bloody boat owners."

Nevertheless a large number of imaginative tasks have been found, and a high proportion have been completed satisfactorily. A few examples include work for homeless people, one-to-one placements helping handicapped children to read or to swim, working with police cadets on a conservation project, running a coffee bar in a courthouse, providing transport for old people, taking disabled people shopping. Some of these, such as the last-mentioned, combine group placements with direct contact with beneficiaries.

A more fundamental problem with community service orders, however, has been the confusion of aims which appears to be endemic in criminal justice. In the effort to make the new measure acceptable to all shades of opinion, the Advisory Council wrote:

> The proposition that some offenders should be required to undertake community service should appeal to different varieties of penal philosophy. To some, it would be simply a more constructive and cheaper alternative to imprisonment; by others it would be seen as introducing into the penal system a new dimension with an emphasis on reparation to the community; others again would regard it as giving effect to the old adage that the punishment should fit the crime; while still others would stress the value of bringing offenders into close touch with those members of the community who are most in need of help and support.

It might change the offenders' outlook and be seen by them as "not wholly negative and punitive," and they might gain from "the wholesome influence of those who choose voluntarily to engage in these tasks" (ACPS 1970b). Thus the advantages claimed included punishment, rehabilitation, avoidance of imprisonment, and reparation. Inevitably, these goals proved incompatible; predictably, different courts, probation officers, and supervisors put them in different orders of priority. This causes not only inconsistency but injustice. In one court an offender who in no way deserves imprisonment may be given a community service order because it is thought to be beneficial to him; but if he reoffends and appears before another court, which regards community service as the "last chance" before imprisonment, it will regard him as having had that last chance (although that was not the intention of the previous court) and send him to prison.

There is evidence that a majority of the public, including victims of crime, favor the idea of community service by offenders, and that offenders themselves generally feel that it is a fair sanction, which is important in terms of promoting respect for the law. It seems, therefore, that community service is worth retaining. But if we accept that one aim of any sanction should have priority, for the sake of consistency and justice, which should it be? It is no surprise to find that the utilitarian goal of reducing crime is probably not achieved better by community service orders than by any other sanction. About half of offenders are reconvicted within two years of the imposition of the order, which is comparable to the proportion reconvicted within two years of release from custody. It is clearly not a punishment, since it can succeed even when offenders enjoy it — some even continue their tasks voluntarily afterward. It does not seem to have helped the system by reducing the prison population: not only the number but the *proportion* of convicted offenders has risen since community service came into effect in 1973, whereas the decrease has been in the proportion of offenders fined. The other aim is reparation, and here community service orders have been among the most successful sanctions: about three-quarters of offenders complete the required number of hours of reparation, and most of the remainder complete at least some hours. Reparation to the community, then, is a largely achievable goal and is largely accepted by the community.

A third development at the beginning of the 1970s was the return of reparation as a sanction, recommended by the Widgery Sub-Committee of the ACPS. It considered the desirability of leaving the victim to pursue a remedy in the civil court, but this would seldom be worthwhile, even if "nil contribution legal aid" were available to the victim as plaintiff, or if the state undertook the proceedings on the victim's behalf. The subcommittee suggested that the whole matter should be dealt with at one hearing, in the criminal court, and that the victim should not be required to apply to the court, as had been the case since the Probation of Offenders Act of 1907. The result was a considerable increase in the number of compensation orders made, particularly for property offenses, although in cases of violence, compensation orders are much less common, partly because the offenders are more likely to be sent to prison, where they have almost no opportunity to make reparation. Reparation can be regarded as an improvement in principle: the victim receives some compensation, the offender is required to pay it. In practice it has not worked quite so well. Some victims did not really want compensation, especially if it was to arrive in irregular driblets for several months, reminding them of an experience they would rather forget; but they were not asked. There was no procedure for agreeing on the amount of the compensation; the Court of Appeal decided that if this raised complicated or contentious questions, the criminal court was not the place to resolve them. Little attention is paid to the *presentation*, to the symbolic effect of compensation. The victim receives a check from the court, with a form giving bare details; the offender, similarly, has to pay compensation to the court in exactly the same way as he pays a fine, and there is no procedure for reminding him that compensation is not merely a different form of penalty paid to the state but a repayment to the person whom he wronged by his act.

Ten years later the Criminal Justice Act of 1982 took the process further. It provided that where the offender is not in a position to pay both a fine and compensation, the latter takes precedence, and that a compensation order can be made in its own right, unaccompanied by a penalty. This is potentially of great significance, implying as it does that society's response to a crime can take the form of compensation to the victim rather than punishment by the state; but it has not had as great an impact as it might, because courts have tended to look on compensation as a form of punishment, rather than as an alternative to punishment. Thus they are denying to both victims and offenders the feeling that amends have been made. Nevertheless the restorative principle is now firmly on the statute book, and it may be predicted that it will have a place in future sentencing textbooks. The current criminal justice bill proposes to reinforce it by requiring courts to state a reason if they do not make a compensation order. It is to be hoped that the procedure will be revised so as to place more emphasis on the reparative purpose, rather than the retributive.

An even more significant step toward reparation stemmed from the report of a Howard League Working Party, *Profits of Crime*, following the law's failure to secure forfeiture of the ill-gotten gains of the drug smugglers caught by "Operation Julie." This report outlined a method of seizing the ill-gotten gains of crime and freezing them in bank accounts before, or at the time of, the offender's arrest. The court of conviction would then have assets readily available for confiscation by the state. The principle was adopted in relationship to drug offenders in the Drug Trafficking Offenses Act of 1986 and will be extended to all serious fraud cases in the new criminal justice bill now before Parliament.

Other developments were taking place in the 1970s which had not yet come to prominence. One was the Victims Support Scheme, originated in Bristol in 1974. The principle is very simple: volunteers contact people who have been victims of crime to see whether they can offer support or practical help. But, as with reparation, the implication are considerable: the criminal justice system cannot be regarded as complete unless it takes account of the victim. At about the same time, in North America, this was being recognized in another way: where victim and offender knew each other, they were invited to try to resolve their differences before mediators, rather than through the criminal courts. Later the principle was extended to crimes by strangers. There is considerable interest in these ideas in this country; experimental projects have been funded by the Home Office, and a Forum for Initiatives in Reparation and Mediation (FIRM) has been established to spread the idea and promote good standards.

SENTENCING: ANOTHER TRY

Later in the 1970s a new attempt to reform sentencing was made by the Advisory Council on the Penal System. It was prompted, once again, by the desire to reduce the excessive use of imprisonment (for the sake of the prison system as well as of offenders); but the council took the opportunity to try to introduce some consistency. This was not a re-think of the underlying principles, such as has been considered in the foregoing discussion; it started from the undeniable premise that maximum penalties have been fixed by Parliament during the past hundred years without any coherent basis to them. The arbitrary starting point, as we have seen, was the biblical number seven, which had been used in the days of transportation. Over the years the judges had been conscious of the inconsistencies and had done their best to iron them out through the notional construction of the informal tariff. For that reason the Advisory Council took as its starting point, in proposing a revision of statutory maxima, the sentences actually imposed by the courts; there was another, more pragmatic, reason — namely, that if the principles were based on the judges' own practice, it would not be possible for critics to say that an extraneous body of people was claiming to know better than the courts.

The pressure on prison accommodation was becoming so great that the Advisory Council had issued an interim report in 1976 urging a reduction in the use of imprisonment; it had a marginal impact, but only for a year or two, when sentence lengths reverted to form. In its final report, *Sentences of Imprisonment: A Review of Maximum Penalties*, published in 1978, it attempted to combine consistency with a gentle downward thrust, by setting the "normal maxima" at the level below which 90 percent of current sentences fell. Courts would not lose their discretion to impose longer sentences if they felt it necessary to protect the public: the "normal maxima" could be exceeded under certain stringent conditions and with appropriate safeguards. Unlike previous proposals of the Advisory Council, however, these were not to be adopted. They were never even debated in Parliament and have received no ministerial approbation. From one side they were attacked as giving courts too much power, because it was suggested that if the "normal maximum" was exceeded, according to strict rules defining dangerousness, no further maximum would be prescribed. It was also attacked by academic criminologists for introducing a system of "bifurcation" of sentences, separating out the ordinary offender from the exceptional, dangerous one on predictive grounds.

But from the other flank, the popular press succeeded in making the proposals politically unacceptable; ignoring the word "normal," they presented the scheme as meaning that, for example, the maximum penalty for rape would be seven years. The headline writers called it a "Rapists' charter." Sensible public debate was rendered impotent, and there could be no rational discussion, except in academic circles. With hindsight it may be that the fundamental flaw was for the Advisory Council to suppose that imprisonment could, or should, be a yardstick by which society's response to criminal conduct would be meted out. It had proceeded upon the retention of the sentencing structure as reflected in practice. That may be a clue to the search for a sounder principle for upholding the law.

CONCLUSION

The efforts during the last four decades have brought little for society's comfort. There has been an unceasing silting up of the prisons and thus an increasing reliance on a scarce and costly resource. The prison system lurches from crisis to crisis, unrelieved by the imposition of a sound penal policy. Much, but not all that much, has been achieved to mitigate the worst effects of more and longer terms of imprisonment. Whatever may be said against parole, without it the crisis in the prison population would have been even more chronic. Noncustodial penalties have undoubtedly been on the whole beneficial. But they have only nibbled at the edges of a system at heart socially unhealthy and unproductive, without resolving the contradictions in its philosophy. The prison system needs at the very least to be turned inside out. To that challenging assertion I shall turn in the final lecture.

III. DEPOPULATING THE PRISONS: ESCAPING THE TRAP

Prisons exist because societies have found it expedient from time to time to provide places in which to segregate some of their citizenry from social intercourse. Originally they were not designed to be punitive; not unknown before the rapid growth in population in the nineteenth century, but intensified by it, imprisonment has over the years been variously used more or less to satisfy fluctuating purposes — punishment (retribution, the socalled "justice model"), deterrence (general and individual), rehabilitation (reform), humane containment, or social defense. These several purposes have vied with one another for preeminence; none of them has attained such a status; instead they have intermingled profitlessly and even harmfully. A simple, uncon-

fused, minimalist use of imprisonment, in order to justify the interference in human liberty by a modern industrialized society in
response to certain kinds of social problems, has barely been
argued for, although there has been a growing movement for a
reduction in the prison population and a moratorium on new
prison building. Reductionism has an appeal to the moderate
mind. Minimalism attracts the radical thinker.

Given this state of flux, the proper function (whatever it be)
of imprisonment as a major response to crime cannot be regarded
as either static or immutable. Whereas in the nineteenth century
imprisonment was regarded as the ordinary consequence of a conviction for a range of serious or repeated offenses — and often for
trivial ones too — this century has seen society's repertoire of sanctions enlarged, to soften the iron equation between crime and punishment. Prison remains, however, the core of the contemporary
penal system. The proposal for change must be to make noncustodial sanctions the normal response to all crimes, with prison
as a resort where dangerousness positively dictates containment,
or where a period of temporary removal from society is necessary,
and not merely justifiable, to sustain or support a program of social
reeducation in the community. This fundamental change must be
judged in the context of the criminal process, which itself faces
a crisis.

Criminal justice as operated today presents a twofold problem.
First, it is failing to be fair, humane, and effective. It is not fair
because sentences are inconsistent, many people are in prison for
minor offenses, others are sent to prison for too long, and the
prison disciplinary system is in need of major reform — to name
but a few injustices. To say that our prisons are inhumane is a
cliché — not only in the notoriously overcrowded local prisons,
with their degrading squalor and enforced idleness, but in the
longer-term, high-security prisons, with their restrictions on cor-
respondence and visits and their isolated locations, which could
hardly be better designed to break any family ties which the

offender may have had before his sentence. The operation of the parole system and repressive security procedures are an extra burden for long-term prisoners. The ineffectiveness of the machinery of justice is also clear, both from the number of crimes committed and the numbers who reoffend after being dealt with by the system. So much is generally acknowledged.

But there is a second, largely unacknowledged problem. This lies in the fact that the criminal justice system, as at present constructed, is not even *capable* of being fair, humane, and effective. The criminal process cannot be fair so long as there are differing objectives with no agreement as to which of them is given priority. To punish some while attempting to rehabilitate others is bound to lead to anomalies. Only a minority of offenders are caught; to add to their punishment in the uncertain hope of frightening others over whom they have no control and whom, for the most part, they do not know, would be unfair even if it worked and is indefensible when it doesn't. In the last century, the prison administrator du Cane saw that there was no logical basis for matching an amount of culpability with a period of time in prison; there still isn't.

Humanity and punishment are at loggerheads. The more punitive, the less humane, and vice versa. Any punishment that is at all severe, moreover, is bound to inflict hardship on the offender's family, if he or she has one.

In a similar way, fairness and effectiveness also conflict. Even if it were possible to prescribe how long the punishment or compulsory treatment of a particular individual would need to be in order to be effective, this would bear no relation to the seriousness of his offense. Experience shows, too, that insofar as punishment is effective in changing behavior, it does so only under specific conditions: it must be certain, inflicted soon after the prohibited behavior, reinforced at intervals, and combined with a proper opportunity and incentive to behave in a different way. The criminal justice system is deficient in all these respects. Conversely, it has been shown that the effects of rewards on behavior are much more long-lasting, even if the rewards are intermittent; they need not be tangible but include the opportunity to gain self-respect and the respect of others and a reasonably satisfying life. This is not a panacea to abolish selfish behavior: many people who apparently have every advantage still turn to crime, as recent events in the City have shown. But the majority of offenders who are caught by the criminal justice agencies, and who cause the most fear, are the have-nots who have little inclination to conform and have experienced educational failure and social rejection. For them the incentives to conform are weak. In our society we are all bombarded by propaganda which constantly hammers home the philosophy that status and happiness depend upon the possession of money and goods, but many young men and women have poor prospects of acquiring much of either through socially acceptable means. Any process of law which makes them feel further rejected can only exacerbate the problems it seeks to solve. This is not a plea for softness but for insight and realism. The starting point for reducing crime, therefore, should be the rewards of doing right rather than the fear of the consequences of wrongdoing: not *criminal* justice but *social* justice, and that means applying rewards as well as dis-rewards.

DEFINING THE GOALS

Attitudes to criminal justice, as well as to imprisonment, are trapped under the accumulated weight of tradition. This is compounded by an element of conviction penology, a reluctance either to question assumptions or to base policy on research. In looking forward to the twenty-first century, we shall be well advised to start with a clean slate — and nowadays if you stand outside a prison, you will not have to wait long before a prisoner climbs on the roof and throws one down at you.

The first requirement of the framers of any rational penal policy is to try to define the aims of society in regard to antisocial behavior. As a starting point, four in descending order of priority could be suggested:

1. To try to reduce the level of crime and other ways in which people harm each other (crime reduction)

2. To show a prime concern for the victims of crime, and as far as possible restore them to their previous condition (victims' support)

3. To show offenders and others that lawbreaking is not tolerated (denunciation)

4. To contain the few from whom society can be protected in no other way (residual imprisonment)

REDUCTION OF CRIME

Crime prevention policy has to be both specific and general. At a specific level, ordinary precautions are still needed: the increasing anonymity and mobility of modern society, particularly in large cities, means that locks, streetlights, and other security measures will continue to be necessary for the foreseeable future. But it is important not to rely on them entirely, nor to become preoccupied with them. In that case people would be fearful to walk in the streets, which in turn would become deserted and dangerous. The Englishman's home would not be an accessible castle but an impregnable citadel; that would be intolerable.

Crime prevention should also involve the community. Neighborhood Watch, so long as it does not become a forum for vigilantes, may be part of the solution; schemes of this kind not only use the local community but also help, with police assistance, to build it up when it is withering away. Often, something more active is needed; it may require the help of a catalyst from outside. Numerous schemes have been promoted, by NACRO among others, (which, although its name is the National Association for the Care and Resettlement of Offenders, devotes considerable energy to crime prevention as well as to penal policy). An ex-

ample among many is the Bushbury Triangle project in Wolver-
hampton. In 1981 the area had many empty houses, a high level
of transfer requests, high crime rates, no on-site community facilities, and much damage, litter, and disrepair. Local agencies were
brought together in a steering committee, considerable trouble
was taken to consult residents, and an action plan was developed.
In addition to home security improvements, there was a modern-
ization program and a fencing scheme (of the garden variety, not
as a receptacle for stolen goods); a residents' association was
established and a community center set up in two empty houses,
which residents agreed to manage. In 1985 a careful evaluation
was made: it found that burglaries and vandalism of both shops
and dwellings had been substantially reduced. Thus the project
reduced crime and helped to recreate a sense of community.

It has to be remembered that there is no such thing as "crime,"
only crime*s*. Each type of criminal event has to be approached
with a different preventive policy. The prevention of offenses
against the Inland Revenue and the Health and Safety legislation
requires measures quite different from those designed to combat
sexual assaults and football hooliganism. They may have in
common that some individuals are pursuing their own gratifica-
tion at the expense of others; but the means of educating them
to understand this, and to make it more difficult for them to offend
without being detected, vary according to the nature of the specific
criminal event, let alone the offense with which the lawyers label it.

A crime control strategy needs to operate at many different
levels. Criminal justice is only one level, and a costly and cumber-
some one at that. It has been shown, for example, that young
people are more likely to engage in delinquency if parental discipline is too authoritarian, neglectful or inconsistent, and if it uses
physical punishment; if children feel unwanted; or if there is
violence in the family. Family problems can be tackled not by lectures from politicians but, for example, by television programs
designed to help parents understand discipline and "positive par-

enting"; by providing respite services with baby-sitting or holidays for families under stress; and by crisis interveners or mediators, professionals, or volunteers brought in after the police have been called to a case of domestic violence, to offer help with problems in the hope of avoiding a recurrence. Schools can go some way toward making up for the deficiencies in the upbringing provided by children's own parents, but only if they are given the resources for the task. Challenging recreational programs for young people are also needed; and for a society to fail to provide work for many thousands of young people is both dangerous and disgraceful. A prospect for a life of unemployment, and even unemployability, is more than any person should be asked to face.

The essential point about a policy for persuading people not to behave badly toward one another is that it does not belong primarily in the department of criminal justice. It is a social problem and calls for a social solution. A person's behavior is noted by the police occasionally, by other people much of the time, and by him or herself all the time. The effectiveness of social control varies proportionately; the trouble is, so does the difficulty of persuading people to exercise it. The Fraud Squad of Scotland Yard can, for example, police a small proportion of the activities of the Stock Exchange; the City's own watchdog, the Securities and Investments Board, somewhat more; but if every member is committed to the principle "My word is my bond," standards will be upheld. This is not to suggest, of course, that the morality of the City begins and ends with paying its bills; the increasing interest in ethical investment, avoiding companies whose stock-in-trade is damaging to life and health, suggests one way in which the morality of the finance houses could be taken further.

It is not easy to change attitudes and behavior, but neither is it impossible; in recent years we have seen how public education can make an impact on, for example, dropping litter, environmental conservation, drinking and driving, and sexual promiscuity — although needless to say there is still a long distance to go. The power of example is also important; although it is hard to show that when prominent people behave well others are inspired to follow their example, there can be little doubt that when those at the top fall short of high standards, they give everyone else an excuse to do likewise. Crime control cannot, of course, depend entirely on such lofty ideals, but without them it will be more difficult. We will devote our attention to such matters at least the more readily if we do not delude ourselves into believing the criminal process to be effective, or allow ourselves to be distracted from sensible measures by the inutility (not to say futility) of imprisonment.

This is not the place to draw up a detailed blueprint for an entire system of law enforcement, but an outline and some examples may suggest the direction in which we might hope to move in the twenty-first century. Let us consider first a case involving assault and malicious damage. Those are, under our present system, legal categories carrying specific maximum penalties. But in many cases the background is one of neighbors or workmates having a dispute in which they end by coming to blows. No purpose is served by invoking the full weight of the criminal law; often it is difficult to determine who the aggrieved party was, and it is likely that both have put themselves in the wrong. The way to resolve such incidents is through the underlying dispute, not through reaction to a particular act which is classified as a particular criminal event. For cases of this kind a more appropriate forum would be a neighborhood mediation center, where both parties could meet, with trained volunteers acting as mediators. There would be no need to decide exactly what took place, nor to allocate blame; the process would be future-oriented, and the mediators would help the disputants to agree on future behavior which both could accept.

In more serious cases, perhaps involving a theft committed by a stranger, the same procedure would be available, but if either of the parties did not wish to take part in mediation the case would have to go to court. There would also have to be a hearing, of course, if the accused did not admit guilt. The court would make a compensation order if the victim wished it; if he or she did not, or if there was no individual victim, a community service order could be imposed, or the compensation would be paid to the state. The latter would be the equivalent of a fine but would be regarded as compensating the community for the harm caused by the offense. In cases where the offender's behavior appeared to be linked to specific problems, such as drug or alcohol addiction, illiteracy, lack of skills, or inability to control aggression, reparation could take the form of attendance at a day center to try to overcome them. There would be no question of imprisonment, unless there were aggravating factors which took the case into the most serious category.

If an offense does not merit imprisonment, neither does failure to comply with the noncustodial sanction imposed. Failure to abide by this principle, which might be thought self-evident, leads to the imprisonment of more than 20,000 fine defaulters annually in England and Wales. The first essential is to make sure that the fine is within the offender's ability to pay, by linking the amount to his income, using the day-fine principle. A fine is inappropriate where the offender's financial difficulties led to the offense, although that would not preclude at least partial restitution. Enforcement measures should be noncustodial; they could include distraint, provided that does not cause hardship to innocent members of a family. Further sanctions, some of which are available already, could include loss of civil rights, such as the right to drive a car, to be a company director, to vote, or to possess a passport. The ultimate sanction could be "civil death" — the withdrawal of all of these rights and privileges, which would be appropriate for serious property offenders and large-scale fraudsters and other "white-collar" criminals, in addition to swingeing financial penalties after payment of compensation (but the restrictions should not impede their ability to earn legitimately the amount necessary to pay the compensation).

In more serious cases, the compensation or community service would extend over considerably longer periods than are usual now, in order to make up for the harm done at least symbolically, even if the loss itself could never be made good. The court would make a separate decision to authorize the use of custody if required for public protection. The effect of this would be similar to being on parole: the person would live in the community but be required to notify the authorities of his address and to report regularly, and be subject to recall if these or other conditions were breached. The safeguards for placing a person in custody should be more stringent than at present. Where there appeared to be an immediate public danger, the court would order custody immediately. Just as we put a dangerous psychopath into a special hospital, so a violent sociopath should be imprisoned for so long as there is a real risk of serious repeated violence. The sole criterion for this would be public protection. Likewise, the protection of the public would determine release. Deciding when a person may safely be released can never be easy or certain; but with only one criterion, rather than three or more as in the present parole scheme, there would be an improved chance of decisions approaching fairness and consistency. The purpose of custody would be to work toward release at the earliest possible time; the number of cases in which eventual release was not possible would be extremely small.

It may be interesting to consider the effects of this approach on one type of crime which excites strong feelings: child abuse within the family (whether cruelty, neglect, or sexual or emotional abuse). The primary approach would be to provide help with whatever problems were leading to the abuse: ignorance of parenting, intolerable housing, psychosexual disorders, or other conditions. Such a response would make it easier for the victim to report the offense, without the guilt and fear associated with being responsible for a parent's imprisonment. There is evidence that abused children remain intensely loyal to their parents and are reluctant to expose them to the criminal process. Some offenders would also be less reluctant to admit the offense. Thus in some cases, perhaps many, it would be possible to work out a plan with the offender, with supervision, treatment, the offender's removal from home, or other appropriate measures to protect the child. Only if the offender refused to comply would it be necessary to use the criminal law at all, and even then the family would not be broken up by imprisonment, except where no other course was possible in the interests of protection of the child or other children. This would do much more for children than the proposal in the criminal justice bill to increase the maximum penalty for child cruelty and neglect from two to ten years' imprisonment — a typical knee-jerk reaction, without sensible thought as to its effect.

CONCERN FOR VICTIMS

A poster shows a lawyer, a social worker, and a policeman and his dog chasing after an offender, while in the middle stands a bemused victim, completely ignored. This represents, without too much exaggeration, the way victims were treated in criminal justice until very recently. In the last twenty-five years, however, a change has begun which may indicate the direction for the future. There is a growing concern and care for the victim; this is offered by members of the local community through Victims Support Schemes, by whom that poster is issued. There is also, in more and more cases, compensation by the offender or the state. Such visible concern would become, not merely a humane addition to soften the edges of the victim's burden, but an essential part of society's balanced response to crime.

Consider for a moment what happens when there is a serious accident, like the fire at King's Cross. The first response is to look after the victims; only then is effort devoted to inquiring into how it was caused, how future accidents can be avoided, and — at the end of the list — whether anyone was culpable. Concern for the victims is shown in practical ways, through first aid and hospital treatment, if required, and symbolically, by a message of sympathy or a visit from someone of suitably high status. There is an obvious difference between accidents and crimes, in that crimes are for the most part caused by someone's deliberate act (though the border-line is not sharp: some crimes result from negligence, are not culpable because of mental illness, and so on). The focusing on the action and intention of the wrongdoer appears to have dis-tracted our attention from the needs of the victim. Perhaps it is partly because of our desire to find someone to blame — as, for example, the public indignation directed at the Meteorological Office following the recent hurricane. We are too fond of looking for scapegoats.

The future response to crime, then, would do well to give priority to caring for the needs of victims. Victims Support Schemes now serve about three-quarters of the population of this country, and increasing numbers of them are offering help to victims of the most serious crimes. This expression of concern is made to victims regardless of whether the offender is known. The same is true of compensation by the state to victims of crimes of violence. A further step could be to extend this concern and compensation to victims of crimes against property, at least those living in areas of high crime rates who cannot afford insurance or cannot obtain it at all. The existence of insurance favors the better-off, again disclosing an unequal distribution of social justice.

Concern should also be shown in the way victims are treated in the criminal justice process. At present the victim is, in law, no different from any other witness; he or she is often kept waiting, called to give evidence at very short notice, subjected to an ordeal in the witness box, and kept in ignorance of the progress of the case. Now that Victims Support Schemes are drawing attention to these practices, there are moves toward a more victim-centered procedure. This is to be welcomed — provided of course that it does not erode the rights of the accused.

There is one more way in which concern can be shown to the victim: by requiring the offender to pay compensation (if the victim wishes it, of course). When there is no individual victim, community service could be seen as reparation to the community, rather than as punishment or rehabilitation. This has the advantage that it holds the offender accountable, not allowing him to escape from his problems into prison, but it does not stigmatize him more than he has already done by his own actions, and it offers him an opportunity to work toward reacceptance in the community. Often what the victim wants most is not financial reparation but action to make it less likely that others will become victims in a similar way; in such cases the offender can make amends by undergoing a course of training, counseling, or therapy relevant to his problems. This can usually be done while on probation or in a day center.

DENUNCIATION OF THE OFFENSE

In a country which still has a monarchy and a State Opening of Parliament, to say nothing of religious observances, it is scarcely necessary to remind people of the importance of symbolism. In the administration of justice, it is as important as anywhere. The formalities of the courtroom are redolent of symbolism and need to be retained. Formal dress, the trappings of the law, and due deference (but not obsequiousness) to the court are all helpful symbols of the majesty of justice — although the dock is an anachronism which we could well do without. But we must accordingly take care to express the right meaning and to use appropriate symbols to do so. The trouble with the rehabilitative ideal was not only that it did not work as well as some of its advocates claimed but also that its message appeared to be: "You are not to be held fully accountable for what you have done; it is largely because you are maladjusted or come from a deprived environment. We will try to treat your condition." The message of punishment, in effect, is: "Behave well, because otherwise *you* will be made to suffer (if you are caught)." Is it not more appropriate to admonish the offender and everyone else: "Behave well, because otherwise you will hurt *other people*, whether you are caught or not; and if you are caught, you will be required to pay back"? The symbol shifts from pain inflicted *on* the offender by the impersonality of the state, to reparation made *by* the offender to his victim, and enforceable by the state. The offender becomes involved in his own penal treatment, rather than have penalties thrust upon him. Hence probation and deferment of sentence were sound sanctions, as are community service orders and compensation.

With this restorative, rather than retributive, principle of justice, the symbolism of the criminal justice system can become a more potent and fair-minded one. Not only that, but an extra step can be inserted into the process of law enforcement, so as to reduce both the burden on the system and the extent of its intervention into people's lives. Many of the less serious offenders could be dealt with in the same way as the tax fraudsters, with the administrative imposition of monetary penalties and restitution. Instead of saying: "You have offended, therefore you must go to court and be punished," the law enforcement agencies would say: "You have offended, therefore *if you do not make proper reparation* you will go to court." Instead of being devalued by overuse and consequent shortcomings in the quality of justice, the courts would be held in reserve: the likelihood of a court appearance itself would be the main deterrent. If the legal process were more selectively applied, it would carry proportionately a higher degree of social obloquy on those few who were brought there. This would also have the effect of removing the present monstrous discrimination, in which a major institution of the state introduces a gross form of inequality between certain white-collar offenders (some of whom have damaged the life or health of their employees or their customers) and other lawbreakers.

PUBLIC OPINION

It is a common misconception that measures of this kind would not be acceptable to a punitive public. The evidence has repeatedly shown otherwise. People want an adequate response, but not necessarily a punitive one — and this is as true of victims as of the public at large. In a National Opinion Poll for the *Observer* newspaper in March 1983, 85 percent thought that it was "a good idea" to make some offenders do community service instead of being sent to prison, and 66 percent wanted them to pay compensation to their victims; 56 percent did not even want burglars sent to prison. Marplan, in a survey for the BBC Broadcasting Research Department, found that 93 percent thought offenders should have to "made good the consequences of their crime wherever possible," and 63 percent thought that the money from fines should go to victims. Several other surveys, both here and in other countries, have pointed in a similar direction. An interesting Canadian study found that, when asked to comment on a case where a person charged with second-degree murder was found guilty of manslaughter and sentenced to eighteen months' imprisonment, 80 percent of a sample said that the sentence was too lenient; but in a second sample, given a 500-word summary of the background of the case instead of an inadequate news report, only 15 percent thought it was too lenient, and 44 percent thought it too harsh.

RESIDUAL IMPRISONMENT

Locking people up for its own sake, or for the sake of inflicting pain, would be excluded. (Let us remember that words like "penalty" mean the infliction of pain, or at the very least unpleasantness, as Professor Nils Christie of the University of Oslo, Norway, has pointed out.) But penal reformers, contrary to their caricature, accept that some people have to be deprived of their liberty for the protection of others. The loss of liberty need not be total. If a person has shown him or herself unfit to drive a motor vehicle, or to be a director of a company, but abides by the law in other respects, permission to engage in that specific activity is withdrawn. Law enforcement is a problem, but that should not lead us to reach for an unacceptable alternative. At present this is commonly done for a fixed period; perhaps it should be done until the offender has shown that he can be trusted. Total deprivation of liberty would be held in reserve for those who have shown themselves liable to commit serious acts of violence.

Every sentence is an intervention in the offender's life and a restriction upon his leisure, if not his liberty. In almost all cases the restriction does not need to be primarily custodial. To some extent this is already recognized, since the majority of sentences consist of probation, fines, and other noncustodial measures. But the fact that these are commonly called "alternatives to imprisonment" — in strict usage there can only be one alternative — implies that prison is somehow the norm, and anything else is not quite the real thing, or at least is an act of mercy or leniency. Many people, from penal reformers to home secretaries and directors-general of prisons, struggling to accommodate all those sent to prison by the courts, have urged that the dividing line should be pushed further toward noncustodial sentences. But as long as this concept persists, there is little hope of progress. It is not a push or a shove in the direction of noncustody that is required. It is a complete reversal of roles — the official response to crime would be primarily (if not exclusively) noncustodial. Custody is a device, rarely needed, to either shut away the violent, much as we do in the mental health system, or to buttress the program of sound reeducation in the community. In effect, we should turn the penal system inside-out.

The basic principle would be reparative; by way of enforcement, society, through its courts, would impose only one sanction, restriction on leisure time or even choice of action, and this would normally be noncustodial. Custody could be used in support of the noncustodial measure, primarily in cases of major violence, but only until it was judged that the offender could be released without unacceptable risk to the public. Thus a noncustodial sentence for a serious offense could include an element of custody, but that would be invoked only if necessary, and with due safeguards. The reason for the custody would be to protect the public, not to inflict punishment for its own sake; this limitation, and the major reduction in numbers, would overcome many of the evils endemic in a retributive prison system.

Imprisonment itself would become wholly exceptional, because prisons would contain only those who needed to be there for the protection of the public. This means that they would be composed largely of highly disturbed and difficult inmates. The few prisons that remained in use would be differently designed to express their new function. They would be small and located in centers of population, in order to facilitate visits by the prisoners' families and to provide access to community resources.

CONCLUSION

The starting point for this critique has been the crisis in our prisons. The shameful fact that the United Kingdom uses imprisonment more than any of our partners in the European Community is now well known. Descriptions of the squalor, inhumanity, and lack of sanitation in our prisons have been repeated, literally ad nauseam. It is essential to grasp, and to persuade our elected representatives to admit, that the solution for prison overcrowding is not to build more prisons, unless it can be shown that every week or month of every prison sentence is necessary for the protection of society. This is manifestly not the case. Prisons do protect society only to the extent that they temporarily restrain the minority of offenders who are prone to commit acts of serious violence; but for other purposes, notably deterrence, they are at best ineffective and at worst counterproductive. It does not make sense to subject people to inhumane (or even humane) conditions or harsh sentences, especially when it is difficult for them to find accommodation and work after release; the result is to make them reluctant or even unable to obey the rules of a society which treated them so.

The cost of imprisonment is not the strongest argument against its use. If it were effective, it would be money well spent. But the prison population includes people who resort to crime because they are homeless or live in subhuman housing conditions; to provide adequate low-cost housing would cost less than the average of £65,000 which the Home Office is spending on the construction of each new prison cell. That would buy a flat in London or a row of houses in the north of England. Others become criminal when they are unemployed; it would have cost much less to employ them than to imprison them at an average cost of £13,000 a year. Twenty new prisons, at 1987/88 prices, cost £690 million, plus another £230 million annually for their upkeep, and experience since 1945 has been that building new prisons has not relieved overcrowding but merely increased the prison population, until we now find ourselves with one person in every thousand in prison.

It is hard to find any informed observer of criminal justice who believes that this level of imprisonment is either necessary or desirable. The Home Affairs Committee of the House of Commons, the Expenditure Committe, the May Committee on the Prison Service, and the chief inspector of prisons, to say nothing of the 1985 United Nations Congress on Crime Prevention and the Treatment of Offenders, are all among those who have recommended reducing the prison population. Yet the official response is at best resoundingly muted, and at worst obdurate in its deafness.

Home Office ministers have a habit of stating that they are obliged to follow the wishes of the courts and that it would be wrong to "interfere." But this applies only to individual cases and not to the generality of offenders; the range of sanctions available, and the maximum intervention for specific offenses, are rightly decided by Parliament. But every time ministers commit themselves to building more prisons, while restricting the amount of money spent on constructive sanctions in the community, they are influencing policy by their allocation of resources. It is in a way unfortunate that probation hostels, day centers, and community service programs do not allow overcrowding; when their places are full, courts have to find an alternative, and often it is a custodial one. It should therefore be a requirement that no prison should be built or enlarged until there are enough places available in noncustodial projects to meet all needs.

In the blueprint of a rational penal policy we should reverse the trend of expansionism in prison building, start to disgorge large numbers of prisoners, and begin to dismantle most of our prisons, beginning with the most remote. For too long we have drifted along, entrapped in a system that simply perpetuated the use of imprisonment as the primary, appropriate response to serious (and some less than serious) unacceptable social behavior. Imprisonment has persistently imposed a penalty (whether deserved or not) upon the many offenders sent inside by a flawed criminal justice system. But as a society we have inflicted an even greater penalty on ourselves. A rational and compassionate society incarcerates only those of its citizenry who literally cannot be safely and conveniently accommodated by, and within, the communities which spawned and nurtured their own delinquents. For any other purpose, prisons are, to quote from my text, taken from the Book of Common Prayer, "worthy to be cut away, and clean rejected."

REFERENCES

Advisory Council on the Penal System (ACPS). 1970a. *Detention Centres*. London: HMSO.

———. 1970b. *Non-custodial and Semi-custodial Penalties*. London: HMSO.

———. 1974. *Young Adult Offenders*. London: HMSO.

———. 1978. *Sentences of Imprisonment: A Review of Maximum Penalties*. London: HMSO.

Ashworth, Andrew. 1983. *Sentencing and Penal Policy*. London: Weidenfeld.

Committee of Inquiry into the United Kingdom Prison Services. 1979. *Report*. (Chairman: Mr. Justice May.) Cmnd. 7673. London: HMSO.

Crow, Iain. 1979. *The Detention Centre Experiment*. London: NACRO.

Fox, Lionel W. 1934. *The Modern English Prison*. London: Routledge and Kegan Paul.

Fry, Margery. 1951. *Arms of the Law*. London: Gollancz, for Howard League.

Galaway, Burt, and Joe Hudson, eds. 1981. *Perspectives on Crime Victims*. St. Louis, Mo.

Hobhouse, Stephen, and A. Fenner Brockway, eds. 1922. *English Prisons To-day: Being the Report of the Prison System Enquiry Committee*. Privately printed.

Howard, John. 1792. *Prisons and Lazarettos*. Vol. 1: *The State of the Prisons in England and Wales*. 4th ed. Repr. Montclair, N.J.: Patterson Smith, 1973.

Howard League for Penal Reform. 1970. *Making Amends: Criminals, Victims, and Society*. Chichester: Barry Rose.

————. 1976. *No Brief for the Dock: Report of the Howard League Working Party on Custody during Trial*. Chichester: Barry Rose.

Ireland: Committee of Inquiry into the Penal System. 1985. *Report*. PL. 3391. Dublin: Stationery Office.

Marshall, Tony, and Martin Walpole. 1985. *Bringing People Together: Mediation and Reparation Projects in Great Britain*. Research and Planning Unit Paper 33. London: Home Office.

Martinson, R. 1974. "What Works: Questions and Answers about Prison Reform." *Public Interest*, no. 35, Spring.

————. 1979. "New Findings — New Views." *Hofstra Law Review*, 7, no. 2, pp. 243ff.

Mayhew, Henry, and John Binney. 1862. *The Criminal Prisons of London and Scenes of Prison Life*. New impression; London: Cass, 1968.

Playfair, Giles. 1971. *The Punitive Obsession: An Unvarnished History of the English Prison System*. London: Gollancz.

Prisons Committee. 1895. *Report*. (Chairman: H. J. Gladstone.) C. 7702. London: HMSO.

Radzinowicz, Sir Leon. 1966. *Ideology and Crime*. London: Heinemann.

Radzinowicz, Sir Leon, and Roger Hood. 1986. *A History of the English Criminal Law and Its Administration from 1750*. Vol. 5: *The Emergence of the Penal Policy*. London: Stevens.

Rose, Gordon. 1961. *The Struggle for Penal Reform: The Howard League and Its Predecessors*. London: Stevens.

Ryan, Mick. 1983. *The Politics of Penal Reform*. London: Longmans.

Shaw, A. G. L. 1966. *Convicts and the Colonies: A Study of Penal Transportation from Great Britain and Ireland to Australia and Other Parts of the British Empire*. London: Faber and Faber.

Stern, Vivien. 1987. *Bricks of Shame: Britain's Prisons*. Harmondsworth: Peguin, 1987.

Windlesham, Lord. 1981. *Responses to Crime.* Oxford: Clarendon Press, 1987.

Wootton, Barbara. 1963. *Crime and the Criminal Law.* Hamlyn Lectures. London: Stevens.

Wright, Martin. 1981. "Crime and Reparation: Breaking the Penal Logjam." *New Society*, December 10.

————. 1982. *Making Good: Prisons, Punishment, and Beyond.* London: Hutchinsons/Burnett Books.

————. 1987. "What the Public Wants: Surveys of the General Public, Including Victims." *Justice of the Peace*, February 14.

THE TANNER LECTURERS

1976–77

OXFORD   Bernard Williams, Cambridge University

MICHIGAN   Joel Feinberg, University of Arizona
"Voluntary Euthanasia and the Inalienable Right to Life"

STANFORD   Joel Feinberg, University of Arizona
"Voluntary Euthanasia and the Inalienable Right to Life"

1977–78

OXFORD   John Rawls, Harvard University

MICHIGAN   Sir Karl Popper, University of London
"Three Worlds"

STANFORD   Thomas Nagel, Princeton University

1978–79

OXFORD   Thomas Nagel, Princeton University
"The Limits of Objectivity"

CAMBRIDGE   C. C. O'Brien, London

MICHIGAN   Edward O. Wilson, Harvard University
"Comparative Social Theory"

STANFORD   Amartya Sen, Oxford University
"Equality of What?"

UTAH   Lord Ashby, Cambridge University
"The Search for an Environmental Ethic"

UTAH STATE   R. M. Hare, Oxford University
"Moral Conflicts"

1979–80

OXFORD   Jonathan Bennett, Univ. of British Columbia
"Morality and Consequences"

CAMBRIDGE   Raymond Aron, Collège de France
"Arms Control and Peace Research"

HARVARD   George Stigler, University of Chicago
"Economics or Ethics?"

MICHIGAN   Robert Coles, Harvard University
                "Children as Moral Observers"

STANFORD   Michel Foucault, Collège de France
                "Omnes et Singulatim: Towards a Criticism
                of 'Political Reason' "

UTAH   Wallace Stegner, Los Altos Hills, California
                "The Twilight of Self-Reliance: Frontier Values
                and Contemporary America"

1980–81

OXFORD   Saul Bellow, University of Chicago
                "A Writer from Chicago"

CAMBRIDGE   John A. Passmore, Australian National University
                "The Representative Arts as a Source of Truth"

HARVARD   Brian M. Barry, University of Chicago
                "Do Countries Have Moral Obligations? The Case
                of World Poverty"

MICHIGAN   John Rawls, Harvard University
                "The Basic Liberties and Their Priority"

STANFORD   Charles Fried, Harvard University
                "Is Liberty Possible?"

UTAH   Joan Robinson, Cambridge University
                "The Arms Race"

HEBREW UNIV.   Solomon H. Snyder, Johns Hopkins University
                "Drugs and the Brain and Society"

1981–82

OXFORD   Freeman Dyson, Princeton University
                "Bombs and Poetry"

CAMBRIDGE   Kingman Brewster, President Emeritus, Yale University
                "The Voluntary Society"

HARVARD   Murray Gell-Mann, California Institute of Technology
                "The Head and the Heart in Policy Studies"

MICHIGAN   Thomas C. Schelling, Harvard University
                "Ethics, Law, and the Exercise of Self-Command"

STANFORD   Alan A. Stone, Harvard University
                "Psychiatry and Morality"

UTAH   R. C. Lewontin, Harvard University
"Biological Determinism"

AUSTRALIAN
NATL. UNIV.   Leszek Kolakowski, Oxford University
"The Death of Utopia Reconsidered"

1982–83

OXFORD   Kenneth J. Arrow, Stanford University
"The Welfare-Relevant Boundaries of the Individual"

CAMBRIDGE   H. C. Robbins Landon, University College, Cardiff
*"Haydn and Eighteenth-Century Patronage
in Austria and Hungary"*

HARVARD   Bernard Williams, Cambridge University
"Morality and Social Justice"

STANFORD   David Gauthier, University of Pittsburgh
"The Incompleat Egoist"

UTAH   Carlos Fuentes, Princeton University
"A Writer from Mexico"

JAWAHARLAL
NEHRU UNIV.   Ilya Prigogine, University of Brussels
"Only an Illusion"

1983–84

OXFORD   Donald D. Brown, Carnegie Institution of Washington,
Baltimore
"The Impact of Modern Genetics"

CAMBRIDGE   Stephen J. Gould, Harvard University
"Evolutionary Hopes and Realities"

MICHIGAN   Herbert A. Simon, Carnegie-Mellon University
*"Scientific Literacy as a Goal in a High-Technology
Society"*

STANFORD   Leonard B. Meyer, University of Pennsylvania
"Ideology and Music in the Nineteenth Century"

UTAH   Helmut Schmidt, former Chancellor, West Germany
"The Future of the Atlantic Alliance"

HELSINKI   Georg Henrik von Wright, Helsinki
"Of Human Freedom"

1984–85

OXFORD   Barrington Moore, Jr., Harvard University
                *"Authority and Inequality under Capitalism
                and Socialism"*

CAMBRIDGE   Amartya K. Sen, Oxford University
                "The Standard of Living"

HARVARD   Quentin Skinner, Cambridge University
                "The Paradoxes of Political Liberty"
                Kenneth J. Arrow, Stanford University
                "The Unknown Other"

MICHIGAN   Nadine Gordimer, South Africa
                "The Essential Gesture: Writers and Responsibility"

STANFORD   Michael Slote, University of Maryland
                "Moderation, Rationality, and Virtue"

1985–86

OXFORD   Thomas M. Scanlon, Harvard University
                "The Significance of Choice"

CAMBRIDGE   Aldo Van Eyck, The Netherlands
                "Architecture and Human Values"

HARVARD   Michael Walzer, Institute for Advanced Study
                "Interpretation and Social Criticism"

MICHIGAN   Clifford Geertz, Institute for Advanced Study
                "The Uses of Diversity"

STANFORD   Stanley Cavell, Harvard University
                "The Uncanniness of the Ordinary"

UTAH   Arnold S. Relman, Editor, *New England Journal
                of Medicine*
                "Medicine as a Profession and a Business"

1986–87

OXFORD   Jon Elster, Oslo University and the University of Chicago
                *"Taming Chance: Randomization in Individual and
                Social Decisions"*

CAMBRIDGE Roger Bulger, University of Texas Health Sciences Center, Houston
"On Hippocrates, Thomas Jefferson and Max Weber: the Bureaucratic, Technologic Imperatives and the Future of the Healing Tradition in a Voluntary Society"

HARVARD Jürgen Habermas, University of Frankfurt
"Law and Morality"

MICHIGAN Daniel Dennett, Tufts University
"The Moral First Aid Manual"

STANFORD Gisela Striker, Columbia University
"Greek Ethics and Moral Theory"

UTAH Laurence H. Tribe, Harvard University
"On Reading the Constitution"

1987–88

OXFORD F. Van Zyl Slabbert, South Africa

CAMBRIDGE Louis Blom-Cooper, Q.C.

HARVARD Robert Dahl, Yale University

MICHIGAN Albert Hirschman, Institute for Advanced Study

STANFORD Ronald Dworkin, Oxford University

UTAH Joseph Brodsky, Russian poet

MADRID Javier Muguerza, Institute of Philosophy of the Superior Council of Scientific Investigations, Madrid

1988–89

OXFORD Michael Walzer, Institute for Advanced Study

CAMBRIDGE Fazlur Rahman, University of Chicago

MICHIGAN Toni Morrison, State University of New York at Albany

STANFORD Stephen J. Gould, Harvard University

UTAH Judith N. Shklar, Harvard University

CHINESE
UNIVERSITY OF
HONG KONG Fei Xiatong, Peking University

INDEX TO VOLUME IX, 1988

THE TANNER LECTURES ON HUMAN VALUES